P9-DMF-795

You ... have delivered us into the hand of our iniquity.

ISAIAH 64:7

Not the Way
It's Supposed to Be

A Breviary of Sin

Cornelius Plantinga, Jr.

WILLIAM B. EERDMANS PUBLISHING COMPANY
GRAND RAPIDS, MICHIGAN / CAMBRIDGE, U.K.

© 1995 Wm. B. Eerdmans Publishing Co.
All rights reserved

Wm. B. Eerdmans Publishing Co.
2140 Oak Industrial Drive N.E., Grand Rapids, Michigan 49505
P.O. Box 163, Cambridge CB2 9PU U.K.
www.eerdmans.com

Printed in the United States of America

20 19 18 17 16 15 14   24 23 22 21 20 19 18

Library of Congress Cataloging-in-Publication Data

Plantinga, Cornelius, 1946-
Not the way it's supposed to be: a breviary of sin / Cornelius Plantinga, Jr.
p.   cm.
Includes bibliographical references and index.
ISBN 978-0-8028-4218-3
1. Sin. 2. Christian life — Reformed (Reformed Church) authors.
I. Title.
BT715.P58   1994
241'.3 — dc20   94-23308
                                             CIP

Unless otherwise noted, the Scripture quotations in this publication are from the New Revised Standard Version of the Bible, copyright © 1989 by the Division of Christian Education of the National Council of Churches of Christ in the U.S.A., and used by permission.

Chapter 1 of this volume appeared in a different form in the pages of *Theology Today*. The author and publisher wish to thank the editors of that publication for permission to make use of this material.

Not the Way
It's Supposed to Be

A Breviary of Sin

Cornelius Plantinga, Jr.

WILLIAM B. EERDMANS PUBLISHING COMPANY
GRAND RAPIDS, MICHIGAN / CAMBRIDGE, U.K.

© 1995 Wm. B. Eerdmans Publishing Co.
All rights reserved

Wm. B. Eerdmans Publishing Co.
2140 Oak Industrial Drive N.E., Grand Rapids, Michigan 49505
P.O. Box 163, Cambridge CB2 9PU U.K.
www.eerdmans.com

Printed in the United States of America

20 19 18 17 16 15 14   24 23 22 21 20 19 18

Library of Congress Cataloging-in-Publication Data

Plantinga, Cornelius, 1946-
Not the way it's supposed to be: a breviary of sin / Cornelius Plantinga, Jr.
p.   cm.
Includes bibliographical references and index.
ISBN 978-0-8028-4218-3
1. Sin. 2. Christian life — Reformed (Reformed Church) authors.
I. Title.
BT715.P58   1994
241'.3 — dc20   94-23308
                                                    CIP

Unless otherwise noted, the Scripture quotations in this publication are from the New Revised
Standard Version of the Bible, copyright © 1989 by the Division of Christian Education of
the National Council of Churches of Christ in the U.S.A., and used by permission.

Chapter 1 of this volume appeared in a different form in the pages of *Theology Today*. The
author and publisher wish to thank the editors of that publication for permission to make
use of this material.

Not the Way It's Supposed to Be

A Breviary of Sin

Cornelius Plantinga, Jr.

WILLIAM B. EERDMANS PUBLISHING COMPANY
GRAND RAPIDS, MICHIGAN / CAMBRIDGE, U.K.

© 1995 Wm. B. Eerdmans Publishing Co.
All rights reserved

Wm. B. Eerdmans Publishing Co.
2140 Oak Industrial Drive N.E., Grand Rapids, Michigan 49505
P.O. Box 163, Cambridge CB2 9PU U.K.
www.eerdmans.com

Printed in the United States of America

20 19 18 17 16 15 14   24 23 22 21 20 19 18

Library of Congress Cataloging-in-Publication Data

Plantinga, Cornelius, 1946-
Not the way it's supposed to be: a breviary of sin / Cornelius Plantinga, Jr.
p.   cm.
Includes bibliographical references and index.
ISBN 978-0-8028-4218-3
1. Sin. 2. Christian life — Reformed (Reformed Church) authors.
I. Title.
BT715.P58   1994
241'.3 — dc20   94-23308
                                                         CIP

Unless otherwise noted, the Scripture quotations in this publication are from the New Revised Standard Version of the Bible, copyright © 1989 by the Division of Christian Education of the National Council of Churches of Christ in the U.S.A., and used by permission.

Chapter 1 of this volume appeared in a different form in the pages of *Theology Today*. The author and publisher wish to thank the editors of that publication for permission to make use of this material.

To Peter J. Kok —
reader, raconteur, family man, gamester, attorney,
Christian, amigo from youth — who has taught me
more about the topic of this book
than I can properly express.

Contents

Preface   ix

Acknowledgments   xiv

Introduction   1

1. Vandalism of Shalom   7

2. Spiritual Hygiene and Corruption   28

3. Perversion, Pollution, and Disintegration   39

4. The Progress of Corruption   52

5. Parasite   78

6. Masquerade   96

7. Sin and Folly   113

8. The Tragedy of Addiction   129

9. Attack   150

10. Flight   173

Epilogue   198

Index   200

Preface

In this book I am trying to retrieve an old awareness that has slipped and changed in recent decades. The awareness of sin used to be our shadow. Christians hated sin, feared it, fled from it, grieved over it. Some of our grandparents agonized over their sins. A man who lost his temper might wonder whether he could still go to Holy Communion. A woman who for years envied her more attractive and intelligent sister might worry that this sin threatened her very salvation.

But the shadow has dimmed. Nowadays, the accusation *you have sinned* is often said with a grin, and with a tone that signals an inside joke. At one time, this accusation still had the power to jolt people. Catholics lined up to confess their sins; Protestant preachers rose up to confess *our* sins. And they did it regularly. As a child growing up in the fifties among Western Michigan Calvinists, I think I heard as many sermons about sin as I did about grace. The assumption in those days seemed to be that you couldn't understand either without understanding both.

Many American Christians recall sermons in which preachers got visibly angry over a congregation's sin. When these preachers were in full cry, they would make red-faced, finger-pointing, second-person-plural accusations: "*You* are sinners — filthy, guilty, miserable sinners!" Occasionally, these homiletical indictments veered awfully close to the second-person singular.

Of course, the old preachers sometimes appeared to forget that their audience included sincere and mature believers. (You wondered what language they would have saved for Himmler or Stalin!) Such preachers were also capable of sounding self-righteous: their own hearts were pure, they wanted you to believe, and even when they were adolescent they yearned much less for sex than for Sunday school.

Still, you were never in doubt what these preachers were talking about. They were talking about sin. In today's group confessionals it is harder to tell. The newer language of Zion fudges: "Let us confess our problem with human relational adjustment dynamics, and especially our feebleness in networking." Or, "I'd just like to share that we just need to target holiness as a growth area." Where sin is concerned, people mumble now.

Why should we speak up? Why retrieve the awareness of sin? Why restate the Christian *doctrine* of sin? The reason is that although traditional Christianity is true, its truth saws against the grain of much in contemporary culture and therefore needs constant sharpening. Christianity's major doctrines need regular restatement so that people may believe them, or believe them anew. Its classic awarenesses need to be evoked so that people may have them, or have them again. Recalling and confessing our sin is like taking out the garbage: once is not enough.

But anyone who tries to recover the knowledge of sin these days must overcome long odds. To put it mildly, modern consciousness does not encourage moral reproach; in particular, it does not encourage self-reproach. Preachers mumble about sin. The other traditional custodians of moral awareness often ignore, trivialize, or evade it. Some of these evasions take time and training. As sociologist James Davison Hunter has observed, school teachers no longer say anything as pointed as "Stop it, please! You're disturbing the class!" For these are judgmental words. Instead, to a strong-armed youth who is rattling classroom windows with his tennis ball, educationally correct teachers put a sequence of caring questions: "What are you doing? Why are you doing it? How does doing this make you feel?"

The word *sin*, Hunter adds, now finds its home mostly on dessert menus. "Peanut Butter Binge" and "Chocolate Challenge" are sinful; lying is not. The new measure for sin is caloric.

But back around 1990 a few of the older breezes began to blow again. A mainline syndicated columnist wondered "Why Nothing Is 'Wrong' Anymore." In 1992 the vice president of the United States drew guffaws from talk show hosts when he complained that TV's Murphy Brown made voluntary single parenthood look like merely another lifestyle option — and a glamorous one at that — but he also drew widespread support from people (including *Newsweek* and *The Atlantic Monthly* cover story writers) who were otherwise barely tolerant of his quixoticisms.

In the summer of 1993, *The New York Times Book Review* ran a series on the seven deadly sins, authored by the likes of John Updike, Gore Vidal, and Mary Gordon, and MTV produced a special video on the same topic. Though, as John Leo commented in *U.S. News and World Report*, the *Times* pieces were often artsy and arcane, and the MTV production so fragmented and trivial as to suggest that its spokespersons really lacked a vocabulary and frame of reference sturdy enough for the topic, the fact that these sources addressed the topic at all was surprising and newsworthy.

That same summer, *Theology Today* devoted a whole issue to a serious discussion of sin, including essays on contrition, civil sin, and preaching on sin. Mindful of decades of trivializing where sin is concerned, Thomas G. Long titled his editorial introduction "God Be Merciful to Me, a Miscalculator."

In one of the best known and most widely reproduced editorials on morality in the nineties ("The Joy of What?" 12 December 1991), the *Wall Street Journal* recounted a number of public sex scandals — Anita Hill's abuse charges against Supreme Court nominee Clarence Thomas, Magic Johnson's confession that his HIV infection was a by-product of promiscuous sexual athleticism, William Kennedy Smith's grimy testimony in his Palm Beach rape trial. The *Journal* then said, "The United States has a drug problem and a high school sex problem and a welfare problem and an AIDS problem and a rape problem. None of this will go away until more people in positions of responsibility are willing to come forward and explain, in frankly moral terms, that some of the things people do nowadays are wrong." Remarkably, the *Journal* strongly implied that it was high time we got the word *sin* out of mothballs and began to use it again and to mean it.

Samuel Johnson said that we need to be reminded much more often than instructed. Sin is no exception. Indeed, for most of us a healthy reminder of our sin and guilt is clarifying and even assuring. For, unlike some other identifications of human trouble, a diagnosis of sin and guilt allows hope. Something can be done for this malady. Something *has* been done for it.

But reminders must be timely. Books on sin today must meet concerns and untie knots that did not worry Augustine and Calvin. They were not worried about the flattening of human majesty in modern naturalism or of human corruption in Enlightenment humanism. They did not wonder at the Californian tendency to conflate salvation and self-esteem. Nor did they meet a widespread cultural assumption that the proper place to inquire about the root causes of human evil is a department of psychology or sociology.

How must the doctrine of sin be taught in settings where pride is no longer viewed with alarm — where, in fact, it is sometimes praised and cultivated? Or where St. Paul's intimidatingly detailed lists of virtues and vices have shrunk to tolerance and intolerance, respectively? Or where democratic impulses have heightened our sensitivity to sins against inequality but have also invaded spaces formerly reserved for the transcendently holy? What can the Christian church say about sin in settings where it has itself contributed much to such tendencies, including the tendency to democratize God?

Modernity has shaped the human, and even the Christian, understanding of sin in important ways, some of them welcome and some not, and any restatement of the Christian understanding of sin must pay attention to these shapings.

In attending to them, I am deliberately writing for nontheologians and not just for the Christians among them. Adherents of other religions sin, too. So do secularists. Even if secularists do not think of their wrongdoing as an affront to the living God and would be unlikely to call it sin, they, like everybody else, do note, resent, and augment injustice, lawlessness, envy, meanness, and other indignities. Much of what follows will therefore be entirely comprehensible to them, even if they reject its context and presuppositions.

As for Christians, we are less likely than were our grandparents to learn the doctrine of sin in church, and few of us will compensate by reading the big twentieth-century theological treatments, such as those by Karl Barth, Reinhold Niebuhr, and Paul Ricoeur. What we do read about sin, including the adroit treatments of it by psychiatrists (particularly Karl Menninger and M. Scott Peck), is likely to focus dramatically on just a few aspects of sin — the loss of our consciousness of sin, for example, especially by means of self-deception. These books and the fine treatments of the seven deadly sins by such sociologists, psychologists, and journalists as Stanford Lyman, Solomon Schimmel, and Henry Fairlie do not offer a more general conceptual map of the area of sin.

What we need periodically are presentations of main themes that arise within the traditional Christian understanding of sin, presentations that bring these old themes forward through some of the currents of modernity in order to present them afresh in a common idiom, illustrated from a wide variety of literary, journalistic, and general sources. Hence this book — a brief theology of sin (a "breviary" of sin), with contemporary illustrations.

My goal, then, is to renew the knowledge of a persistent reality that used to evoke in us fear, hatred, and grief. Many of us have lost this knowledge, and we ought to regret the loss. For slippage in our consciousness of sin, like most fashionable follies, may be pleasant, but it is also devastating. Self-deception about our sin is a narcotic, a tranquilizing and disorienting suppression of our spiritual central nervous system. What's devastating about it is that when we lack an ear for wrong notes in our lives, we cannot play right ones or even recognize them in the performances of others. Eventually we make ourselves religiously so unmusical that we miss both the exposition and the recapitulation of the main themes God plays in human life. The music of creation and the still greater music of grace whistle right through our skulls, causing no catch of breath and leaving no residue. Moral beauty begins to bore us. The idea that the human race needs a Savior sounds quaint.

So the broader goal of this study is to renew our memory of the integrity of creation and to sharpen our eye for the beauty of grace.

Acknowledgments

I owe particular thanks to Ronald Feenstra and Mark Noll, who steered me toward this project; to Kenneth W. Kuiper, my teacher and friend, who read the whole manuscript and corrected it repeatedly; and to the members of the theological division at Calvin Theological Seminary — colleagues than whom none better can be conceived — who did the same. Thanks also to Melvin Hugen and Arie Leder, cross-divisional colleagues, who answered my queries in the areas of pastoral care and biblical theology, respectively.

I am grateful as well to members of the Rockport and Winter Park Colloquia, and to Daniel Migliore, Gabriel Fackre, Richard Mouw, Lewis Smedes, and Robert Roberts, all of whom commented on the prospectus for this book; to my student assistants across the past four years — John Zevalking, Jim Van Tholen, David Rylaarsdam, and David Den Haan; and especially to the Pew Charitable Trusts, whose generous grant gave me leave to work on this project.

And now to Kathleen, who has borne with my heightened interest in sin, and who has had to suppress ominous evidence that once I had gotten deeply into sin I might not be able to get out of it again — to you, Kathleen, I express my gratitude for your patience, irony, faith, and good humor. These qualities have reminded me again and again that beauty and strength have the last word.

Introduction

We all deal daily with annoyances. The first motorist in a green arrow left-turn lane is often some dreamer who lurches forward like a startled hippo just *after* the arrow has come and gone. Dental hygienists address older and wiser patients by their first names. We toss sixteen socks into a dryer but get only fifteen back. Such incidents are mere nuisances, and healthy people absorb them like small bursts of extra chlorine in their drinking water.

Deeper than annoyance lies an array of regrets. People regret early educational decisions that locked them into particular careers. They rue youthful follies and indiscretions. Usually when it is too late, they regret long neglect of friends and family members. In fact, memories of the past sometimes hurt us just because the roads we missed back there are now barricaded.

Perhaps most poignantly, thoughtful human beings suffer pangs from aging. They gain an acute sense of the one-way flow of time that carries with it treasures and opportunities and youthful agilities that seemingly will not come again. Worse, they know perfectly well how human life ends. In pondering the twenty-third psalm, Joseph Sittler once observed that though we walk through the valley of death just once, we spend our whole lives in the valley of the *shadow* of death. Middle-aged people notice that shadow more often than they used to.

But even further toward the alarm end of the trouble spectrum lie certain distresses that theologians call miseries. People feel walled in by loneliness, for example. Whether homesick or obsessively nostalgic or exiled or romantically forlorn or self-alienated so that they are not at home even in their own skin, lonely persons ache because they are separated.

People also suffer boredom, what Walker Percy called "the self being stuffed with itself."[1] People suffer fear. They fear cancer and job loss and the death of love. They fear war and God and the IRS. Some must deal with anxiety, a persistent and free-floating fear. Moreover, especially at those times that naturally provoke reflection on the shape of one's life — around the time of the twenty-fifth high school reunion, say — people sometimes suffer from a sense of futility, particularly in their work. Around that time, an advertising executive, for example, might pause and wonder what good it is, finally, to have spent an excellent mind and half a life's energies on the task of arousing human hunger for electric card shufflers.

The whole range of human miseries, from restlessness and estrangement through shame and guilt to the agonies of daytime television — all of them tell us that things in human life are not as they ought to be.

We are finite beings, as transient as the flowers of nature and just as vulnerable to its forces. Every season in every land, nature itself takes a terrible harvest of human beings by way of fire, wind, water, or sudden burial under snow or earth. Birth disorders, disease, and mechanical accidents take still more. Even strangers to these events, if they are compassionate, are sobered by them. Sometimes they are dismayed, even if only politely.

Annoyances, regrets, and miseries trouble us in all the old familiar ways. But none of these troubles matters as much as sin. The reason is that sin distorts our character, a central feature of our very humanity. Sin corrupts powerful human capacities — thought, emotion, speech, and act — so that they become centers of attack on others or of defection or neglect. Bad enough if we offend others involuntarily — by boorish insensitivity to their feelings, for ex-

---

1. Percy, *Lost in the Cosmos: The Last Self-Help Book* (New York: Farrar, Straus & Giroux, 1983), p. 71.

ample, or by an alienating form of complacency. We may not want these character flaws; in fact, we may not even know that we have them. But if our victims know that we have hurt them consciously, deliberately, even serenely, their attitude toward us is not merely rueful, as it would normally be if we had harmed them by accident. Their attitude is not just sorrowful, as it normally is when nature catches people in its great machinery. Instead, our victims face us indignantly. For they know we have violated them with something powerfully and peculiarly personal. We have *willingly* hurt them. We have done it on purpose.

Sin outstrips other human troubles by perverting special human excellences. When people devise and defend high-minded political fraud, when a musician feels a spasm of happy satisfaction over the sour review of a colleague's recital, when a drug dealer wants and plans the hooking of a fresh customer, when a teenager reviles his confused grandmother, when we put other people on a tight moral budget while making plenty of allowances for ourselves — when we human beings do these things, we exhibit a corruption of thought, emotion, intention, speech, and disposition. By such abuse of our highest powers, we who are fearfully and wonderfully made, we creatures of special dignity and responsibility, evoke not only grief and consternation but also blame.

Sin, moreover, lies at the root of such big miseries as loneliness, restlessness, estrangement, shame, and meaninglessness. This is a second reason why sin is the main human trouble. In fact, sin typically both causes and results from misery. A father who sexually abuses his daughter corrupts her: he breaks all the little bones of self-respect that hold her character together. Filled with shame and anger at her treacherous father and conniving mother, grieving for her lost and innocent self, the corrupted child is extremely likely to abuse *her* children or to assault her central nervous system with large quantities of alcohol or to make and break one rickety marriage after another.

Moreover, the veins of sin interlace through most of the rest of what is wrong in our lives — through birth disorders, disease, accident, and nuisance. Thousands of Third World children die daily from largely preventable diseases: out of laziness or complacency, certain grownups fail to prevent them. Thousands of First World children are born drug addicts: their mothers have hooked them in the womb. Some people with sexually transmitted diseases knowingly put new partners at terrible risk. It happens every day. Many accidents are, in retrospect, both accidental and predictable: somebody who needed to concentrate on his job in order to protect others (a pilot, for example, or a lifeguard, or a ship's captain) got drunk instead, or careless, or wholly preoccupied. Often, a number of such factors combine in some lethal and intricate way to bring havoc to human well-being.

Even ordinary traffic irritants (a certain breed of driver first cuts you off and then, to show that the move was intentional, offers you a gesture of international familiarity) may arise out of some routine kind of mismanaged life. The offending driver may simply be a person who has never bothered to curb his wrath and who might be both puzzled and wrathful at the suggestion that he should begin to do so.

But what about tornadoes, earthquakes, floods, forest fires, shark attacks? Surely here we have cases of purely natural as opposed to moral evil, and surely here it is pointless to refer disparagingly to human agency?

Yes and no. Many of these events do have natural causes. But we must distinguish the natural events themselves from the human suffering that afflicts those who happen to be in their way. Having one's home washed off its foundation is ordinarily an evil, but is a flood, all by itself, necessarily an evil event? Can we say that floods would play no role in a wholly good creation? And is all suffering from natural forces wholly outside human control?

The fact is that some "acts of God" need not become human disasters. These events might have been anticipated and then skirted so as to minimize suffering. People might have prepared for some of these events. Shoddy bridge and building construction, bribery of inspectors, greedy condominium development in known hurricane alleys or flood plains, ignorant disdain for the sudden power of mountain storms at twelve thousand feet — these and other human failures sometimes cause or at least exacerbate the suffering produced in a natural disaster. Sin usually plays at least some role in the kind and amount of evil we absorb from what we are used to thinking of as nonmoral events.

At the center of the Christian Bible, four Gospels describe the pains God has taken to defeat sin and its wages. The very shape of these Gospels tells us how much the pains matter: the Gospels are shaped, as Martin Kähler famously put it, as passion narratives with long introductions. Accordingly, Christians have always measured sin, in part, by the suffering needed to atone for it. The ripping and writhing of a body on a cross, the bizarre metaphysical maneuver of using death to defeat death, the urgency of the summons to human beings to ally themselves with the events of Christ and with the person of these events, and then to make that person and those events the center of their lives — these things tell us that the main human trouble is desperately difficult to fix, even for God, and that sin is the longest-running of human emergencies.

The Bible presents sin by way of major concepts, principally lawlessness and faithlessness, expressed in an array of images: sin is the missing of a target, a wandering from the path, a straying from the fold. Sin is a hard heart and a stiff neck. Sin is blindness and deafness. It is both the overstepping of a line and the failure to reach it — both transgression and shortcoming. Sin is a beast crouching at the door. In sin, people attack or evade or neglect their divine calling. These and other images suggest deviance: even when it is familiar, sin is never normal. Sin is disruption of created harmony and then resistance to divine restoration of that harmony. Above all, sin disrupts and resists the vital human relation to God, and it does all this disrupting and resisting in a number of intertwined ways. Sinful life, as Geoffrey Bromiley observes, is a partly depressing, partly ludicrous caricature of genuine human life.[2]

My project in this book is to show these things, to discuss them, to look at them from several angles, and to sharpen the profile of sin by comparing it with a couple of its conceptual neighbors. In short, the project is to present the nature and dynamics of sin.

To carry it out, I shall define sin, describe how sin corrupts

---

2. Bromiley, "Sin," in *The International Standard Bible Encyclopedia*, vol. 4, ed. Geoffrey W. Bromiley (Grand Rapids: William B. Eerdmans, 1988), p. 519.

what is good and how such corruption spreads, discuss the parasitic quality of sin and the ironies and pretenses generated by this quality, compare sin with folly and addiction, and conclude by describing a couple of the classic "postures" or movements of sin (attack and flight). A brief epilogue reminds us that whatever we say about sin will qualify whatever we say about grace.

The plan may look pretty academic, but the treatment will be only partly so. Or let me put it a little differently: this study has a traditional theological table setting, but the food comes not only from the Bible and St. Augustine but also from books on crime and addictions, from books by Garry Wills and William Manchester and Daniel Akst, from *Newsweek*, the movies, and NBC's *Today* show. The book is about sin, but a lot of the paragraphs are about sins.

Of course, in a book this size I could not begin to list and fully describe scores of individual sins from the gaudy to the petty. Instead, I will discuss several of the seven deadly sins, familiar habits of sinners, and some patterns of corruption as current as today's newspaper.

At the beginning and end, and here and there in between, I try to show what sin is *against*. In the Christian view, sin is not an independent entity or topic, and the only right way to frame it is with presentations of creation and redemption. Accordingly, this book begins and ends with sketches of shalom.

CHAPTER 1

Vandalism of Shalom

"Everything's supposed to be different than what it is here."

Mac in Grand Canyon

In the film *Grand Canyon,* an immigration attorney breaks out of a traffic jam and attempts to bypass it. His route takes him along streets that seem progressively darker and more deserted. Then the predictable *Bonfire of the Vanities* nightmare: his expensive car stalls on one of those alarming streets whose teenage guardians favor expensive guns and sneakers. The attorney does manage to phone for a tow truck, but before it arrives, five young street toughs surround his disabled car and threaten him with considerable bodily harm. Then, just in time, the tow truck shows up and its driver — an earnest, genial man — begins to hook up to the disabled car. The toughs protest: the truck driver is interrupting their meal. So the driver takes the leader of the group aside and attempts a five-sentence introduction to metaphysics: "Man," he says, "the world ain't supposed to work like this. Maybe you don't know that, but this ain't the way it's supposed to be. I'm supposed to be able to do my job without askin' you if I can. And that dude is supposed to be able to wait with his car without you rippin' him off. Everything's supposed to be different than what it is here."

The tow truck driver is an heir of St. Augustine, and his summary of the human predicament belongs in every book of theology.[1] For central in the classic Christian understanding of the world is a concept of the way things are supposed to be. They ought to be as designed and intended by God, both in creation and in graceful restoration of creation. They are supposed to include peace that adorns and completes justice, mutual respect, and deliberate and widespread attention to the public good.

Of course, things are not that way at all. Human wrongdoing, or the threat of it, mars every adult's workday, every child's school day, every vacationer's holiday. A moment's reflection yields a whole catalogue of wrongdoing, some of it so familiar we scarcely think of it any longer as wrong: a criminal in a forties *film noir* hangs up a pay telephone receiver and then, before exiting the booth, rips from the telephone book the page he had consulted and pockets it. At school, a third grader in a class of twenty-five distributes fifteen party invitations in a manner calculated to let the omitted classmates clearly see their exclusion. Her teacher notes but never ponders the social dynamics of this distribution scheme. Two old flames meet again for the first time since graduation and begin to muse with nostalgia and boozy self-pity over what might have been. Though each feels happily married to someone else, somehow the evening climaxes for the two grads in a room at the Marriott.

Perhaps we think most often of sin as a spoiler of creation: people adulterate a marriage or befoul a stream or use their excellent minds to devise an ingenious tax fraud. But resistance to redemption counts as sin, too, and often displays a special perversity.

In the summer of 1973, a British journalist named Jonathan Dimbleby filmed a dispiriting report of hunger in Ethiopia. To show some of the setting of this misery, the journalist juxtaposed shots of famished Ethiopians with shots of Emperor Haile Selassie's feasts. Newspeople from across the world soon showed up in Addis Ababa to cover the yoked stories of popular starvation and official comfort. The next wave of foreigners escorted substantial food gifts from

---

1. And Philip Yancey, who reminded me of this scene and of its redolence, belongs on every writer's list of fruitful and imaginative friends.

various countries. In the arrival of these gifts, Ethiopia's finance minister spied an opportunity. To the great emergency stores of food donated by compassionate peoples of the world, the minister applied a substantial customs duty. Of course, the donating nations were dumbfounded and said so. Their protest, in turn, dumbfounded the imperial court:

> "You want to help?" the minister asked. "Please do, but you must pay." And [the benefactors] said: "What do you mean, pay? We give help! And we're supposed to pay?" "Yes," says the minister, "those are the regulations. Do you want to help in such a way that our Empire gains nothing by it?"[2]

Shalom

As the great writing prophets of the Bible knew, sin has a thousand faces. The prophets knew how many ways human life can go wrong because they knew how many ways human life can go right. (You need the concept of a wall on plumb to tell when one is off.) These prophets kept dreaming of a time when God would put things right again.[3]

They dreamed of a new age in which human crookedness would be straightened out, rough places made plain. The foolish would be made wise, and the wise, humble. They dreamed of a time when the deserts would flower, the mountains would run with wine, weeping would cease, and people could go to sleep without weapons on their laps. People would work in peace and work to fruitful effect. Lambs could lie down with lions. All nature would be fruitful, benign, and filled with wonder upon wonder;[4] all humans would be knit together

2. Ryszard Kapuscinski, *The Emperor: Downfall of an Autocrat,* trans. William R. Brand and Katarzyna Mroczkowska-Brand (New York: Vintage Books, 1984), p. 118.

3. See, e.g., Isa. 2:2-4; 11:1-9; 32:14-20; 42:1-12; 60; 65:17-25; Joel 2:24-29; 3:17-18.

4. Cf. Irenaeus, *Against Heresies,* 5.33.3: "The days will come, in which vines shall grow, each having ten thousand branches, and in each branch ten thousand twigs, and in each true twig ten thousand shoots, and in each one of the shoots ten

in brotherhood and sisterhood; and all nature and all humans would look to God, walk with God, lean toward God, and delight in God. Shouts of joy and recognition would well up from valleys and seas, from women in streets and from men on ships.

The webbing together of God, humans, and all creation in justice, fulfillment, and delight is what the Hebrew prophets call *shalom.* We call it peace, but it means far more than mere peace of mind or a cease-fire between enemies. In the Bible, shalom means *universal flourishing, wholeness, and delight* — a rich state of affairs in which natural needs are satisfied and natural gifts fruitfully employed, a state of affairs that inspires joyful wonder as its Creator and Savior opens doors and welcomes the creatures in whom he delights.[5] Shalom, in other words, is the way things ought to be.

"The way things ought to be" in its Christian understanding includes the constitution and internal relations of a very large number of entities — the Holy Trinity, the physical world in all its fullness, the human race, particular communities within this race (such as the ancient people of Israel, the New Testament church, the American Federation of Musicians), families, married couples, groups of friends, individual human beings. In a shalomic state each entity would have its own integrity or structured wholeness, and each would also possess many edifying relations to other entities. The All Terrain Vehicle Sports Club, for example, might relate to forest streams by placing them off limits to its members in an effort to preserve their ecological health. "The way things ought to be" would also include in individual persons a whole range of intelligent responses to other creatures (and even to their relationships with still other creatures) — a spread of appropriate thoughts, desires, emotions, words, deeds, and dispositions. Gratitude, for example, is as fitting an emotional

---

thousand clusters, and on every one of the clusters ten thousand grapes, and every grape when pressed will give five and twenty metretes of wine. And when any of the saints shall lay hold of a cluster, another shall cry out, 'I am a better cluster, take me; bless the Lord through me'" (in *The Ante-Nicene Fathers,* vol. 1, ed. Alexander Roberts and James Donaldson [Buffalo: Christian Literature, 1885], p. 563).

5. See Nicholas Wolterstorff, *Until Justice and Peace Embrace* (Grand Rapids: William B. Eerdmans, 1983), pp. 69-72.

response to undeserved kindness as delight is to such created excellences as the velvety coat of a puppy or the honking of geese in a November fly-by or the hitchhiking home of young beetles on the backs of bees.

Of course, the shalomic dreams of the Hebrew prophets are visionary: the literal coursing of Chardonnay through mountain streambeds is not an essential feature of everybody's picture of an ideal world. Nor would all agree with Milton's portrait of Eden as a "happy rural seat of various view" or More's vision of Utopia as communist uniformitarianism. Still, every one of us does possess the *notion* of a world in which things are as they ought to be. Moreover, though we would stock this world and arrange its workings differently according to our varying ideas of what the Bible calls "good" (Would heavy metal music play any part in a perfect world? Would it, at least, be audible only to its own fans?), we would nonetheless agree on many of the broad outlines and main ingredients of a transformed world.

It would include, for instance, strong marriages and secure children. Nations and races in this brave new world would treasure differences in other nations and races as attractive, important, complementary. In the process of making decisions, men would defer to women and women to men until a crisis arose. Then, with good humor all around, the person more naturally competent in the area of the crisis would resolve it to the satisfaction and pleasure of both.

Government officials would still take office (somebody has to decide which streets are cleaned on Tuesday and which on Wednesday), but to nobody's surprise they would tell the truth and freely praise the virtues of other public officials. Public telephone books would be left intact. Highway overpasses would be free of graffiti. Tow truck drivers and erring motorists would be serene on inner-city streets.

Business associates would rejoice in one another's promotions. Middling Harvard students would respect the Phi Beta Kappas from the University of Southern North Dakota at Hoople and would seek to learn from them. Intercontinental ballistic missile silos would be converted into training tanks for scuba divers.[6] All around the world,

6. See Richard J. Mouw, *When the Kings Come Marching In: Isaiah and the New Jerusalem* (Grand Rapids: William B. Eerdmans, 1983), pp. 19-20.

people would stimulate and encourage one another's virtues. Newspapers would be filled with well-written accounts of acts of great moral beauty, and, at the end of the day, people on their porches would read these and savor them and call to each other about them.

Above all, in the visions of Christians and other theists, God would preside in the unspeakable beauty for which human beings long and in the mystery of holiness that draws human worship like a magnet. In turn, each human being would reflect and color the light of God's presence out of the inimitable resources of his or her own character and essence. Human communities would present their ethnic and regional specialties to other communities in the name of God, in glad recognition that God, too, is a radiant and hospitable community, of three persons. In their own accents, communities would express praise, courtesies, and deferences that, when massed together, would keep building like waves of a passion that is never spent.

Sin: A Definition

In biblical thinking, we can understand neither shalom nor sin apart from reference to God. Sin is a religious concept, not just a moral one. For example, when we are thinking religiously, we view a shopkeeper's defrauding of a customer not merely as an instance of lawlessness but also of faithlessness, and we think of the fraud as faithless not only to the customer but also to God. Criminal and moral misadventures qualify as sin because they offend and betray God. Sin is not only the breaking of law but also the breaking of covenant with one's savior. Sin is the smearing of a relationship, the grieving of one's divine parent and benefactor, a betrayal of the partner to whom one is joined by a holy bond.[7]

Hence in the most famous of the penitential psalms, traditionally ascribed to David after his adultery with Bathsheba, the author views his sin primarily, perhaps exclusively, as a sin against God:

---

7. The golden calf idolatry of Exod. 32, e.g., counts as treachery because it violates the covenant vows of Exod. 24:1-8.

Have mercy on me, O God,
   according to your unfailing love;
according to your great compassion
   blot out my transgressions.
Wash away all my iniquity
   and cleanse me from my sin.

For I know my transgressions,
   and my sin is always before me.
Against you, you only, have I sinned
   and done what is evil in your sight. (51:1-4, NIV)[8]

All sin has first and finally a Godward force. Let us say that *a* sin is any act — any thought, desire, emotion, word, or deed — or its particular absence, that displeases God and deserves blame.[9] Let us add that the disposition to commit sins also displeases God and deserves blame, and let us therefore use the word *sin* to refer to such instances of both act and disposition.[10] Sin is a culpable and personal affront to a personal God.

But once we possess the concept of shalom, we are in position to

8. The Jerusalem Bible translates vv. 3 and 4 in a way that, perhaps deliberately, leaves ambiguous the object of the confessed offense: "I have my sin constantly in mind, having sinned against none other than you." Does the psalmist think he has sinned against God preeminently or exclusively?

9. In my usage, *acts* include thinking, speaking, desiring, etc., as well as "deeds" when they are distinguished from thoughts and words, as in the General Confession from the Book of Common Prayer: "I have sinned in my thoughts, in my words, and in my deeds."

10. The offered definition is criteriological as opposed to ontological; i.e., it tells us how we know that something counts as sin rather than what sin itself actually is. In other words, the definition tells us what is sinful but not what is sin. The same would be true if we were to describe sin as the violation of God's law — a more typical and more immediate test for the presence of sin — or if we were to describe it as culpable shalom-breaking. To solve this problem, if it is a problem, we could describe sin as, say, the *power* in human beings that has the effect (including the criteriologically revealing effect) of corrupting human thought, word, and deed so that they displease God and make their authors guilty. We would then stipulate that this power lies paradoxically behind our neglects and inattentions as well as behind our assaults and trespasses.

enlarge and specify this understanding of sin. God is, after all, not arbitrarily offended. God hates sin not just because it violates his law but, more substantively, because it violates shalom, because it breaks the peace, because it interferes with the way things are supposed to be. (Indeed, that is why God has laws against a good deal of sin.) God is for shalom and *therefore* against sin.[11] In fact, we may safely describe evil as any spoiling of shalom, whether physically (e.g., by disease), morally, spiritually, or otherwise.[12] Moral and spiritual evil are agential evil — that is, evil that, roughly speaking, only persons can do or have. Agential evil thus comprises evil acts and dispositions. Sin, then, is any agential evil for which some person (or group of persons) is to blame. In short, sin is culpable shalom-breaking.

This definition may strike some as disappointingly formal: it tells us how an act qualifies as sin, but it doesn't tell us which acts qualify in this way. And, of course, questions about whether particular acts count as sin are old and numerous. Take a very homely incident. Suppose you are a dinner guest of a beaming but shaky hostess. As the evening progresses, you discover that her tastes and achievements in cookery lie at a discouragingly low level. At some point she asks you in front of six other guests how you like her Velveeta, Spam, and lima bean casserole.[13] The table falls silent, faces turn to you, and your hostess waits expectantly. Now what? On the spot, you have to make a decision, so you do. You do not tell the brutal truth. Nor do you evade ("I didn't know a casserole like this was even possible!"). You lie. Indeed, you lie winningly.

Have you disturbed shalom or preserved it?

Questions of this kind often arise when more than one moral rule applies to a given act and when to obey one rule is apparently

---

11. I am not denying that there may be other reasons as well why God hates and rejects sin.

12. I assume, of course, that the sorts of intellectual and physical limitations that fall within normal ranges for kinds and ages of creatures (no human being, for instance, is as fast as a computer or a thoroughbred) do not spoil shalom and do not count as evil.

13. For decades, Henry Stob tested the ethical wits of Calvin College and Seminary students with, among other tests, dinner scenarios of this kind. Across the years, only the casseroles changed, generally for the worse.

to disobey the other. In the case of the hostess, "Tell the truth" appears to lead one way and "Be kind" another.

But maybe this is overdramatizing the scene. Maybe we have a setting here in which shalom is better served by following custom than by agonizing over the applicability of moral rules. Maybe in some social settings a murmur of approval over a doubtful casserole is only a formality, only a customary nicety. Maybe it possesses no more moral or declaratory force than "Dear" at the start of a letter to the IRS.

Obviously, many moral dilemmas rise to a far more serious, and sometimes even agonizing, level. Bad enough to know the will of God and to flout it. But what if you simply do not know how to please God and build shalom? We Christians derive our vision of shalom from Scripture, from general revelation, from centuries of reflection on them, and from whatever wisdom God grants us. Often the yield from these sources is pretty plain: generally speaking, robbery, assault, malicious gossip, fraud, blasphemy, envy, idolatry, and perjury break the peace, while almsgiving, embracing, praising, harvesting, thanksgiving, complimenting, truthtelling, and worshiping God build it.

But how about killing another human being? Everybody agrees that *unjust* killing is evil and a disturbance of shalom; but which killings count as unjust? Slaying your parents to speed up the inheritance process surely qualifies, but how about slaying the marauder who cuts your phone line, forces your side door, enters your family home at 3 A.M., and threatens your nine-year-old with rape? Is it, so to speak, all right with God if you use force to defend your household and repel the invader? How much force? May you, for instance, blast away with a shotgun? Only after an initial warning? What if there isn't time? If you do shoot, must you aim someplace other than the torso or head? Does it matter whether the invader is drunk or crazy? Suppose there are three invaders and you are terrified: do these facts bear on your blameworthiness in the eyes of God if you shoot? As a householder, are you morally obliged to prepare nonlethal defenses in advance and to practice them?

Other than household defense, what about the famous hard cases that crop up in the abortion, euthanasia, and just-war debates *no matter what position you take in these debates?*

Questions of this kind, and attempts to clarify and answer them, can be found in books on ethics and on law, and readers who want to pursue such questions should turn to them. To think theologically about sin is a somewhat different project. Though in the chapters ahead we shall have occasion again and again to discuss particular sins, the first and main task is to locate and inspect the general phenomenon, to *place* sin and describe it.

This is where the definition comes in. "Culpable disturbance of shalom" suggests that sin is unoriginal, that it disrupts something good and harmonious, that (like a housebreaker) it is an intruder, and that those who sin deserve reproach. To get our bearings, we need to see first that sin is one form of evil (an agential and culpable form) and that evil, in turn, is the disruption or disturbance of what God has designed.

This design naturally includes not only the proper relation of people to people and of people to nature and of nature to God but also the proper relation of people to God. Human beings ought to love and obey God as children properly love and obey their parents. Human beings ought to be in awe of God at least as much as, say, a first-year violin student is in awe of Itzhak Perlman. They ought to marvel at God's greatness and praise God's goodness. Failure to do these things — let alone indulgence in outright scorn of God — is sin because it runs counter to the way things are supposed to go. Godlessness is anti-shalom. Godlessness spoils the proper relation between human beings and their maker and savior.

Sin offends God not only because it bereaves or assaults God directly, as in impiety or blasphemy, but also because it bereaves and assaults what God has made. Sexism and racism, for example, show contempt both for various human persons and also for the mind of God. God savors and wants not only humankind but also human kinds. In the cramped precincts of their little worlds, sexists and racists disdain such differences in kind.

In sum, shalom is God's design for creation and redemption; sin is blamable human vandalism of these great realities and therefore an affront to their architect and builder.

Of course such ideas annoy certain people. The concept of a design to which all of us must conform ourselves, whether we like it or not, appears absurd or even offensive to many. People who believe in naturalistic evolution, for example, think that human concepts, values, desires, and religious beliefs are, like human life itself, metaphysically untethered to any transcendent purpose. Our lives and values are rather the product of such blind mechanisms as random genetic mutation and natural selection.[14] In the view of such naturalist believers, there isn't any "way it's supposed to be" or anyone like God to sponsor and affirm this state of affairs. Thus, there isn't anything like a *violation* of the way it's supposed to be or anything like an affront to God — and hence there isn't anything that fits the definition of sin. In particular, the concept of sin makes no sense if human life, taken as a whole, is purposeless — only "the outcome of accidental collocations of atoms," as Bertrand Russell once put it[15] — for, at its core, human sin is a violation of our human *end*, which is to build shalom and thus to glorify and enjoy God forever.

Moreover, whether or not they believe in evolutionary naturalism, people who think of human beings as their own centers and lawgivers reject the whole idea of our dependence on a superior being. Indeed, they find this idea entirely distasteful. To them the proposal that we ought to worship someone who is better than we are, that we ought to study this person's will and then bend our lives to it, that we ought to confess our failures and assign life's blessings to him — to them, the notion that we ought to take this posture toward anybody else at all is humiliatingly undemocratic, an offense to human dignity and pride.

Not incidentally, the pride that resists God and God's superiority also resists objective moral truth. For such truth — the assertion that some acts are right and some wrong regardless of what we think

14. For an ingenious development of a suspicion in C. S. Lewis and others that naturalism and evolutionary theory are incompatible — that, in fact, evolutionary theory itself gives the naturalist a clinching reason for rejecting naturalism — see Alvin Plantinga, *Warrant and Proper Function* (New York: Oxford University Press, 1993), pp. 216-37.

15. Russell, "A Free Man's Worship," in *Why I Am Not a Christian* (New York: Simon & Schuster, 1957), p. 107. The larger passage that incorporates the quotation is one of the twentieth century's most eloquent statements of naturalistic atheism.

about the matter — stands against the freedom of human beings to create their own values, to make up moral truth as they go along.

Serious Christians view attitudes of this kind simply as modern instances of sin's age-old power to deceive. Humans notoriously suppress truth they dislike, says St. Paul.[16] In the biblical view, we not only sin because we are ignorant but we are also ignorant because we sin, because we find it convenient to misconstrue our place in the universe and to reassign divinity in it. (Of course, Christian believers engage in these misconstruals and reassignments, too; they simply do so less consistently than stable secular humanists.)

Interscholastic and Intramural Distinctions

Sin is *culpable* disturbance of shalom — that is, culpable in the eyes of God. In this way and others, sin distinguishes itself from many of its conceptual near-neighbors. Though partly overlapping with it, sin is distinct from crime, for example. A main reason for the distinction is obvious: crime is statute-relative in a way that sin is not. Thus, some sin, such as writing a no-account check in order to buy lottery tickets, probably breaks a criminal statute in every jurisdiction in which there are banks and lotteries. But a lot of sin (e.g., frittering your life away on trivial pursuits) is perfectly legal, and some (e.g., godlessness) is in certain legal jurisdictions even obligatory.

On the other side, though most crime offends God and therefore counts as sin, certain forms of civil disobedience in a righteous cause (e.g., sit-ins in protest of segregation) may offend Caesar but not God.

How about the relation of sin to immorality? If we follow a big and popular convention in restricting the scope of morality to, roughly, intra-creaturely behaviors, attitudes, rights, and obligations, then moral right and wrong are grasped and judged on a horizontal

---

16. "For the wrath of God is revealed from heaven against all ungodliness and wickedness of those who by their wickedness suppress the truth. For what can be known about God is plain to them, because God has shown it to them" (Rom. 1:18-19).

plane, so to speak. (In this convention, spirituality and spiritual evil are the vertical complements to morality and immorality.) From this perspective, all culpably immoral acts are sin: theft, for example, is both immoral and sinful. But not all sin is immoral: according to the convention, a person who broke the Sabbath, for instance, or who, despite years in the best seminaries, offered Jesus Christ only polite respect — and then only for his political courage — would have committed spiritual evil and would, if culpable, be guilty of sin but not of immorality.

But maybe this is the wrong way to cut the pie. Maybe we would do better to think of morality as applying to universal obligations that can also be universally accessed,[17] while reserving the concepts of sin and righteousness to cover special obligations that fall on particular persons or communities. If so, all idolatry is immoral, not just sinful, since (we might argue) all human beings have a built-in sense of God that they are obliged to respect and to translate into worship. On the other hand, Jonah's and Israel's disobedience with respect to specific commissions by God would count as sin but not as immorality.

The distinction between sin and immorality is knotty in lots of ways that need not delay us, and in the pages ahead I shall not fuss over it.[18]

Besides distinguishing sin from crime and immorality, we must also distinguish it from disease. True, sinful acts sometimes transmit

17. For a contemporary theory that moves strongly and intelligently along these lines, see Alan Donagan, *The Theory of Morality* (Chicago: University of Chicago, 1977), especially chaps. 1, 2, and 7.

18. The relation of sin to moral wrongdoing has attracted a growing and sophisticated literature. See, e.g., the debate in *Religious Studies* 20 (1984) involving Basil Mitchell, "How Is the Concept of Sin Related to the Concept of Moral Wrongdoing?" (pp. 165-73); Ingolf Dalferth, same title (pp. 175-89); and David Attfield, "The Morality of Sins" (pp. 227-37). See also Marilyn McCord Adams, "Problems of Evil: More Advice to Christian Philosophers," *Faith and Philosophy* 5 (1988): 121-43; and "Theodicy without Blame," *Philosophical Topics* 16 (1988): 215-45. What seems clear is that all *culpable* moral wrongdoing is sin but that not all wrongdoing is culpable (as in some cases of wrongdoing by children, mentally deficient or disturbed persons, or persons whose morally wrong acts are determined by outside influences). What is much less clear is how much of sin is morally wrong and, especially, what standard we have for making this judgment.

disease, or even cause it, as when illicit sex spreads syphilis or battery causes brain damage. Conversely, disease sometimes furnishes an occasion for or even inclines a person toward sin, as in cases of an invalid's malice toward the healthy. Disease is, moreover, a traditionally favorite image for sin. Still, the two evils remain distinct because sin is a spiritual and moral evil and disease a physical one. Sin makes us guilty while disease makes us miserable. We thus need grace for our sin but mercy and healing for our diseases.[19]

Further, we should not confuse sin with mere error (printing an inadvertently punning headline such as "DRUNK GETS NINE MONTHS IN VIOLIN CASE") or innocent folly (placing a highway sign that reads, "TAKE NOTICE: WHEN THIS SIGN IS UNDER WATER THIS ROAD IS IMPASSABLE").[20] Nor should we confuse sin with finiteness, let alone with mere awareness of finiteness. We are not to blame for being human instead of divine, and we are to be credited, not debited, for knowing the difference.

Besides distinguishing sin from other concepts that are, so to speak, in the same league and therefore count as interscholastic rivals, we also need a few intramural distinctions — that is, distinctions that clarify certain issues within the concept of sin itself.

Some sin is objective, some subjective. Let us say that an act is objectively sinful if it disturbs shalom and makes its agent guilty. An act is subjectively sinful if its agent thinks that it is objectively sinful (whether or not it is) and purposely (or in some other accountable way) does it anyhow. Thus, even if drinking wine is not objectively sinful, it would be quite wrong for a conscientious teetotaler to drink it. Even if volunteering for infantry duty in wartime is not objectively sinful, it would be quite wrong for a conscientious pacifist to volunteer. The reason in both cases is that by flouting the deliverances of his own conscience, a person breaks trust with God. For by doing what he thinks is wrong, a person does what he thinks will

19. In the age of AIDS, it is hard to think of a theological distinction that bears more pastoral, emotional, and spiritual urgency.

20. These examples come from Richard Lederer, *Anguished English* (New York: Laurel, 1989), pp. 66, 88. For an extended treatment of the relation of sin and folly, see Chap. 7 below.

grieve God, and the willingness to grieve God by one's acts is itself grievous.[21] Moreover, acting against one's conscience blunts and desensitizes it; indeed, repeated thwarting of one's conscience might eventually kill it. The subjective sinner therefore risks moral suicide.

But risking or actually committing moral suicide is objectively sinful. So in this way, all subjective sinners are also objective sinners — people who, so to speak, keep shooting themselves in the conscience. Making this distinction requires a commitment to a limited kind of moral subjectivism: some acts are genuinely (even if not objectively) wrong for one person but not for another, and they are wrong on account of what the person thinks about them. It also requires a commitment to a limited kind of moral absolutism: it is always wrong to act against one's conscience.

All sin is equally wrong, but not all sin is equally bad. Acts are either right or wrong, either consonant with God's will or not. But among good acts some are better than others, and among wrong acts some worse than others.[22] Christians believe that thinking deliciously about adultery is just as wrong as committing it and not a different offense in kind.[23] But Christians also know that adultery in one's heart damages others less, at least for the short term, than does adultery in a motel room and may therefore rank as less serious on the badness spectrum.[24]

Similarly for other offenses: given a choice, our neighbor would

21. I owe this point to Robert C. Roberts.

22. This distinction is standard in much of the Christian tradition, Protestant as well as Catholic. Consider the Second Helvetic Confession, chap. 8: "We . . . confess that sins are not equal; although they arise from the same fountain of corruption and unbelief, some are more serious than others. As the Lord said, it will be more tolerable for Sodom than for the city that rejects the word of the Gospel (Mt. 10:15;11:20-24)."

23. The source of this conviction is Jesus' Sermon on the Mount: "You have heard that it was said, 'You shall not commit adultery.' But I say to you that everyone who looks at a woman with lust has already committed adultery with her in his heart" (Matt. 5:27-28).

24. Still, adultery in one's heart damages oneself in subtle, progressive, and unpredictable ways, and damage to oneself may ripple out to affect others, so that the final tally in seriousness between adultery in one's heart and adultery in a motel room may be closer than we think.

rather have us covet her house than steal it. Neglecting to feed one's children seems clearly worse than neglecting to expose them to the fine arts (though that is bad enough). The badness or seriousness of sin depends to some degree on the amount and kind of damage it inflicts, including damage to the sinner, and to some degree on the personal investment and motive of the sinner. This is the heart of the distinction between mortal and venial sin in the Catholic tradition and a place where legal and theological thinking overlap. Most criminal codes acknowledge the relevance of motive in measuring the seriousness of an offense: the codes set higher penalties for premeditated murder than for involuntary manslaughter. And they acknowledge the relevance of the amount and kind of damage done by an offense: the codes set higher penalties for murder than for attempted murder. But, of course, both measurements count: a premeditated theft of the whole supply of paper towels in a restaurant rest room is a less serious offense than an involuntary vehicular manslaughter.

Where both crime and sin are concerned, involuntariness may mitigate, but it doesn't necessarily excuse. A thoroughly ungrateful person, for example, may be ungrateful without having in any way chosen to be so. Indeed, she may not even know that she is ungrateful. It may never occur to her that, where God, family members, and friends are concerned, she ought to feel some of the mixed sense of being blessed and indebted that spiritually healthy people feel. Her ingratitude is scarcely under her control in at least these respects and hence can be said to be involuntary. But it is also clearly sinful. If the ingrate were to detect her flaw and see its unloveliness, she would rightly feel obliged to confess and repent of it.[25]

Involuntary sins are surprisingly common. For example, the traditional seven deadly sins (pride, envy, anger, sloth, avarice, gluttony, and lust) are usually involuntary. They are desires, beliefs, and attitudes over which a person may have little or, at best, only variable control. Faithful warriors against these sins thus experience familiar failures, slight improvements, backslidings, painful conquests, Pyr-

25. See Robert Merrihew Adams, "Involuntary Sins," *Philosophical Review* 94 (1985): 3-31.

rhic victories, broken treaties, and humiliating compromises. The Scriptures claim that human beings need powerful outside intervention to control and eventually conquer their faults, but all veterans of the sin wars know this by personal experience as well. Where the deadly sins are concerned, a person may not want these states of mind (*nobody* wants to be envious), may not choose them, may not mean or try to have them.[26] In fact, just the contrary. Yet there they are. And we rightly call them sins even when they are involuntary.

Of course, some people *do* want some of these sins. Certain people want lust, for instance, and do what they can to excite it. They want not just sex but also the appetite for sex. Even then they may disappoint themselves. As St. Augustine knew, jaded appetites can be hard to freshen up. We cannot control lust very well at all: even people who want lust often cannot get it or, at least, cannot express it.[27] Much the same thing could be said about anger, sloth, and other deadly sins: they neither appear nor disappear on command.

Involuntary sin is not under a person's control in the ways just described. But in order to call it *sin,* we have to stipulate that its owner acquired it through some fault of her own, that she is responsible for having it — in short, that she is culpable. And here matters become murky.

Take the case of a white boy raised in a family of racists in Mississippi in the 1850s. Call him Jim Bob. The local cultural assumption of white superiority threads through all of Jim Bob's education, adult modeling, and training in etiquette. Jim Bob never

26. According to Adams, voluntary control includes at least one of the following: trying to do (or have) something, meaning to do it, or choosing to do it ("Involuntary Sins," pp. 8-9).

27. In *The City of God* 14.15-16, Augustine speculates that the enfeeblement of our will — shown in particular by its failure to govern the various forms of libido — is poetic justice: insubordination at the heart of our lives mirrors our insubordination to God. One dramatic instance of this, Augustine delicately suggests, is that male erections are no longer voluntary. Both tumescence and flaccidity have become (often unwanted) events rather than acts. The soul is so divided that impotence bedevils not only the godly who are earnestly attempting to beget children, but also lascivious playpersons who are impotent even to do evil. See also Garry F. Wills, *Under God: Religion and American Politics* (New York: Simon & Schuster, 1990), pp. 282-83.

encounters forceful alternatives to this assumption. He is dimly aware that some Yankees and certain Southern eccentrics are "nigger lovers," but the one time he asks about these unusual creatures, respected local authorities assure him that they are all either crazy or phony. Unless, like Huck Finn, extraordinary circumstances encourage in him the growth of a fugitive's independent mind, Jim Bob will simply absorb racism from his environment. The things he sees and learns will combine to corrupt his consciousness so that he simply adopts — without challenge or struggle and likely with only a little reflection — the assumption that the right posture of whites toward blacks is some patronizing blend of superiority, wariness, control, and apartheid.[28]

Biblically instructed Christians now know that a racist state of mind is wholly wrong, an offense to the aggrieved race and an offense to God. Racism is a breach of shalom and, seemingly, an excellent example of sin. But if a particular person has this state of mind so inadvertently that it would be true to say of him that he could not have helped acquiring it, that there is now no realistic way he could *avoid* having it, can we still call him guilty for having it? And if not, do we call his state of mind sin?[29] Is Jim Bob's racism sin? And is Jim Bob a sinner just because he has this state of mind?

Questions like these lead us, of course, into great philosophical and theological swamps. Fortunately, we needn't wade into them all the way up to our necks in order to stay on the route we have begun, but I do want to say at least something about the questions just

28. For a 1950s version of this story, see Melton A. McLaurin, *Separate Pasts: Growing Up White in the Segregated South* (Athens, Ga.: University of Georgia Press, 1987). McLaurin escaped the settled racism of his upbringing by profiting from the example of black friends whose lives exposed the racist lies McLaurin had been taught.

29. I am supposing that incompatibilism is true — i.e., that an agent's freedom, and hence his moral responsibility, with respect to some act (or, in this case, the acquisition of some evil state of mind) is incompatible with that act's being determined by causes other than the agent. For more on the relation of involuntary sin to blameworthiness and on the bearing of compatibilist and incompatibilist theories on the theory of involuntary sin, see Adams, "Involuntary Sins," pp. 28-31.

raised, both to secure a working use of the operative word *sin* and also to prepare the way for chapters to follow. Hence, three observations.

1. The suggestion that Jim Bob could not have helped acquiring his racism is speculative. Cultural influences, personal strengths and insights, the human capacity for self-deception, conscience as shaped by "the law of God written on the human heart," and numerous other factors combine in such intricate ways that we are seldom in a position to make accurate judgments about even our own blameworthiness, let alone someone else's. Judgments about degrees of culpability, unless they are demanded of people filling such special roles as that of parent, judge, or jury, may therefore wisely be left in the hands of God.

2. The Christian tradition has traditionally and plausibly reserved the word *sin* for culpable evil. The criterion of culpability distinguishes sin from certain natural evils, from simple errors and follies, and especially from moral evils (kleptomania, say, or necrophilia) that might have been blamelessly acquired. Thus, if Jim Bob is not to blame for acquiring his racism, we can characterize his wrongful state of mind as moral evil but not, strictly speaking, as sin. Still, we will tend to call Jim Bob's racism sin (a) because moral evil in a person is often sin, and we do not know that Jim Bob's is not, and (b) because, living in a no-fault culture, we fear the softness of self-deception more than the hardness of accusation.

3. Even if Jim Bob is not to blame for his racism, *somebody* is. Somebody in the chain of influences leading to Jim Bob's racism knew better, and this is true even if we have to follow the chain back to our first parents, who emerged good and innocent from the hands of God.[30]

What Jim Bob's racism shows us is that moral evil is social and structural as well as personal: it comprises a vast historical and cultural matrix that includes traditions, old patterns of relationship and behavior, atmospheres of expectation, social habits. Of course, culpability in social and structural evil is notoriously hard to assess.

---

30. See Robert C. Roberts, *Taking the Word to Heart* (Grand Rapids: William B. Eerdmans, 1993), p. 301.

Still, we know perfectly well that human pride, injustice, and hard-heartedness weave the web of social evil in which people like Jim Bob get caught and that this is true even when we cannot state with certainty *whose* pride, injustice, and hard-heartedness have produced the sticky strands. What we can state is that wherever people are to blame for these faults that generate racism, their racism itself renders them blameworthy and therefore additionally sinful. In case they infect others with racism (children, say, or pupils), that new and derived racism is often called sin because it is the fruit of sin and because it is morally evil. Accordingly, lots of Christians would simply call Jim Bob's racism sin, no matter how he acquired it.[31]

In so doing, they would be following a long tradition. The paradigm case is the doctrine of original sin. All traditional Christians agree that human beings have a biblically certified and empirically demonstrable bias toward evil. We are all both complicitous in and molested by the evil of our race. We both discover evil and invent it; we both ratify and extend it.[32] But in particular cases, including our own, only God knows the relevant degrees and even the relevant kind of blame for original and actual moral evil.[33]

Though we cannot always measure culpability for it, we do

---

31. Following suit, in the pages ahead I'll usually speak of moral and spiritual evil as sin without pausing to inquire into the perpetrator's degree of culpability for these evils. Usually, but not always. Sometimes the issue of culpability sticks its hand up and demands attention, as we've just seen in the case of involuntary sin, and as we shall see in the cases of addiction and of moral evils that look inevitable in particular social contexts.

32. See Paul Ricoeur, "'Original Sin': A Study in Meaning," in *The Conflict of Interpretations* (Evanston, Ill.: Northwestern University Press, 1974), p. 284.

33. If we are culpable for original sin, as the Augustinian and Calvinist traditions maintain (the Heidelberg Catechism says in answers 7 and 10 that "we are born sinners — corrupt from conception on" and that God is "terribly angry about the sin we are born with as well as the sins we personally commit"), we are culpable in some different sense of culpability than is used in ordinary discourse about actual sin. The major difference according to these traditions is that — whether because we were seminally present in Adam or because Adam was appointed by God as our "federal head" — we human beings inculpate ourselves before we are even born. Everybody is a sinner by second *nature*. Thus the Reformation contention that we are not only sinners because we sin; we also sin because we are sinners.

know that sin possesses appalling force. We know that when we sin, we pervert, adulterate, and destroy good things. We create matrices and atmospheres of moral evil and bequeath them to our descendants. By habitual practice, we let loose a great, rolling momentum of moral and spiritual evil across generations. By doing such things, we involve ourselves deeply in what theologians call corruption.

CHAPTER 2

Spiritual Hygiene and Corruption

"I don't want integrity to block my creative growth."

Oliver Stone

Among the first things the word *corruption* brings to mind for most people is municipal politics — the Tammany system, for instance, that Mayor Fiorello La Guardia inherited from Jimmy Walker in the city of New York in the 1930s. Walker's municipal authority rigged bids for city construction projects, hired lifeguards who could not swim, invented positions for party hacks ("Confidential Inspector, Examining Engineer [Refrigeration], In Charge"), built inaccessible piers, and jailed innocent teenagers to motivate their parents to bribe the presiding judge. In City Hall, graft from awarding municipal licenses enriched ordinary bureaucrats. Outside City Hall, dirty policemen who paid the going rate for promotion to sergeant sometimes discovered indignantly that the grafter was a con man who had taken their bribes and disappeared. The Tammany system adulterated public trust, perverted justice, and destroyed the credit of the richest city in America — all of it in an atmosphere at once flourishing and stifling, like some deadly garden.[1]

1. See Thomas Kessner, *Fiorello H. La Guardia and the Making of Modern New York* (New York: McGraw-Hill, 1989), pp. 209-10, 236-37.

28

None of this would have surprised the church father Athanasius. According to him, human beings east of Eden corrupt everything they touch, competing with each other in lawlessness and in "devising all manner of new evils."[2] In the works of Athanasius, Augustine, Luther, Calvin, and in classic Protestant confessional literature, corruption — an unhappy cluster of spiritual perversion, pollution, and disintegration — represents one of the two components of original sin (the other being guilt). In these sources, corruption and guilt present the problems that the gifts of sanctification and justification graciously address.

According to Scripture, God's original design included patterns of distinction and union and distinction-within-union that would give creation strength and beauty. In Genesis 1 and 2, God — who sometimes speaks there in tantalizing first-person plurals that helped kindle early Christian interest in the distinction-within-unity of the Holy Trinity — sets about to dig out oceans, build hills, plant forests, and stock lakes and streams. But the setting for these endeavors is a "formless void."[3] Everything in the universe is all jumbled together. So God begins to do some creative separating: he separates light from darkness, day from night, water from land, the sea creatures from the land cruisers. God orders things into place by sorting and separating them.

At the same time God binds things together: he binds humans to the rest of creation as stewards and caretakers of it, to himself as bearers of his image, and to each other as perfect complements — a matched pair of male and female persons who fit together and whose fitting harmony itself images God. (Older translations of Gen. 2:24 present the man as "cleaving" to the woman, a word that nicely suggests both distinction and union.)

Against this background of original separating and binding, we must see the fall as anti-creation, the blurring of distinctions and the rupturing of bonds, and the one as a result of the other. Thus,

2. Athanasius, *On the Incarnation of the Word* 5.3.

3. Genesis does not explicitly address the issue of whether God started from nothing. That claim, the doctrine of *creatio ex nihilo*, finds more plausible basis in such texts as Heb. 11:3 and 2 Macc. 7:28.

human beings who want to be "like God, knowing good and evil," succeed only in alienating themselves from God and from each other. Even the good and fruitful earth becomes their foe (Gen. 3:17-18; cf. 4:12-14).

Early biblical sin rises in ominous crescendo — Adam and Eve's juvenile pride and disbelief triggering disobedience, scapegoating, and flight from God (Gen. 3:4-5, 10, 12-13). Their first child then extends his parents' trajectory: Cain blames and kills his brother Abel, launching the history of envy and fratricide within the human family. Like his parents and the rest of the race, Cain becomes a fugitive in the land of wandering that lies east of Eden. There Lamech's macho homicidal boast echoes across the primitive civilization of cattle breeders, musicians, and metalmakers. Civilization grows, but evil multiplies: "Adah and Zillah, hear my voice; you wives of Lamech, listen. . . . I have killed a man for wounding me, a young man for striking me. If Cain is avenged sevenfold, truly Lamech seventy-sevenfold" (Gen. 4:23-24).

At last the great flood of Genesis 7, a terrible consequence of evil filling the earth, obliterates the created distinctions between water above and water beneath, between earth and dry ground. The flood overwhelms the safe space on which creatures may pass between the waters. The flood is thus uncreation, "only the final stage in a process of cosmic disintegration which began in Eden."[4]

The story of the fall tells us that sin corrupts: it puts asunder what God had joined together and joins together what God had put asunder. Like some devastating twister, corruption both explodes and implodes creation, pushing it back toward the "formless void" from which it came.

Along the generations, human nature itself, with its vast and mysterious amalgam of capacities to think, feel, supervise, love,

---

4. David A. J. Clines, *The Theme of the Pentateuch*, Journal for the Study of the Old Testament, Supplement Series 10, ed. David J. A. Clines, Philip R. Davies, and David M. Gunn (Sheffield: University of Sheffield, 1978), p. 75. For a rich interpretation of the plagues in Egypt (Exod. 7–12) as a similar threat to creation and its orders, a similar threat of chaotic excess, of hypernatural transgression of the bounds of nature, see Terrence E. Fretheim, *Exodus* (Louisville: John Knox, 1990), pp. 108-11.

create, respond, and act virtuously — that is, with its vast capacities for imaging God — has become the main carrier and exhibit of corruption. Human nature, says the Formula of Concord, has been *despoiled* of its powers by original sin. The image suggested by this language is that of stripping — stripping a tree of its bark, an animal of its hide, or an enemy army of its arms and provisions. To do these things is to remove the skin that protects against outside invaders and keeps one's innards from spilling out. In other words, to despoil is to remove that which preserves integrity.[5]

We human beings despoil each other in painful ways. In Pierre Van Paassen's *That Day Alone*, Nazi troops capture a rabbi, force him to remove all of his clothing including his wedding ring, bend him over a barrel, and beat him numb with a leather strap ("some [stripes] for Abraham, some for Isaac, and some for Jacob"). Then they unfasten and display him.

> The brownshirts ranged themselves in a semicircle around the table. One walked over and with a pair of scissors cut the left side of Rabbi Warner's hair away. Then he took hold of the Rabbi's beard and cut the right side of it away. Then he stepped back. The troopers laughed and slapped their sides.
>
> "Say something in Hebrew," the S.A. captain ordered.
>
> "Thou shalt love the Lord thy God with all thy heart," the Rabbi slowly pronounced the Hebrew words. But one of the other

---

5. The theological linkage among corrupting, stripping, and despoiling is suggested by the primary meanings of *spolio* (to strip) and *corrumpo* (to pervert, pollute, disintegrate, or spoil) and by the patristic and medieval traditions surrounding Gen. 3:21-22. According to these traditions, Adam and Eve's shame is a discovery of their threadbare souls: they suffer a metaphysical chill against which their own little tailorings are inadequate protection. The garments of skins that God then provides for these freshly fallen human beings represent the loss of animal life (hence mortality), a preview of cultic animal sacrifice, and a suggestion of transferred mortality to the human beings who, in v. 22, are escorted out of the garden in their new skins lest they eat of the tree of life and live forever. The skins thus symbolize both corruption (only dead animals are stripped) and grace: the animal mortality transferred to human beings sets a limit on exponentially increasing human sinfulness, and the skins that symbolize this mortality warm the newly chilled human beings.

officers interrupted him. "Were you not preparing your sermon this morning?" he asked him.

"Yes," said the Rabbi.

"Well, you can preach it here to us. You'll never again see your synagogue; we've just burnt it. Go ahead, preach the sermon," he cried out. "All quiet now, everybody. Jacob is going to preach a sermon to us."

"Could I have my hat?" asked the Rabbi.

"Can't you preach without a hat?" the officer asked him.

"Give him his hat!" he commanded. Someone handed the Rabbi his hat, and he put it on his head. The sight made the S.A. men laugh the more. The man was naked and he was shivering. Then he spoke.

"God created man in his image and likeness," he said. "That was to have been my text for the coming Sabbath."[6]

Mockery takes dead aim at our staunchest natural defense and tries to blow it away. Mockery aims to shred human dignity and therefore to despoil its victim in a specially devastating way. Accordingly, Nazis used mockery not only to entertain themselves but also to demoralize their victims. As William Styron brilliantly shows in *Sophie's Choice*, Nazis at their most demonic tried to slay not only the body but also the spirit, not only to slay the spirit but also to corrupt it so that it would recriminate and slay itself.

To despoil is to wreck integrity or wholeness, to strip away what holds a being together and what joins it to other beings in an atmosphere of hospitality, justice, and delight. As Augustine shows in *The City of God*, sin despoils persons, groups, and whole societies. Corruption disturbs shalom — twisting, weakening, and snapping the thousands of bonds that give particular beings integrity and that tie them to others.

Corruption is thus a *dynamic* motif in the Christian understanding of sin: it is not so much a particular sin as the multiplying power of all sin to spoil a good creation and to breach its defenses against invaders. Corruption is spiritual AIDS — the mysterious, systemic, infectious, and progressive attack on our spiritual immune

6. Van Paassen, *That Day Alone* (New York: Dial Press, 1941), p. 311.

system that eventually breaks it down and opens the way for hordes of opportunistic sins. These make life progressively more miserable: conceit, for instance, typically generates envy of rivals, a nasty form of resentment that eats away at the envier. "Sin," as Augustine says, "becomes the punishment of sin."[7]

Reformation documents offer a number of images for corruption: it is a despoiled nature, a diseased root, a contaminated spring, a foul heart.[8] According to these documents, we are wrong at the core. A bad strain has gotten into the stock so that we now sin with the ease and readiness of people born to the task. After the fall we sin by second nature: we are "born sinners" as some folk are born athletes. This fact, empirical as well as biblical, lies behind a broad consensus on original sin. Although, partly because of the silence of Scripture, Christians of various theological orientations differ on central issues in the doctrine of original sin — for example, how a child acquires the fateful disposition to sin, whether this disposition is itself sin, how to describe and assess the accompanying bondage of the will[9] — they agree on the universality, solidarity, stubbornness, and historical momentum of sin. That is to say, all serious Christians subscribe to the generic doctrine of corruption, the centerpiece of which is the claim that even when they are good in important ways, human beings are not *sound*.

---

7. Augustine, *De peccat. merit,* 2.22: "What is called 'sin' dwelling in our members is sin in this way: that it becomes the punishment of sin." Cf. *Ennar. in Ps.* [7]: "God so orders sins, that those that were a delight to man as he sins are instruments for the Lord as he punishes." (I am indebted to Mark F. Williams for these references and translations.)

8. See, e.g., the Formula of Concord 1.11 (neg.), the Second Helvetic Confession 8, the Belgic Confession 15.

9. In his anti-Pelagian treatises (e.g., "On Forgiveness of Sins, and Baptism"), Augustine stakes out the main debate on the acquisition of corruption, claiming that it is by propagation, not imitation (1.15). Main Reformers saw Augustine's bet on propagation and raised him — e.g., Calvin insisted that the disposition to sin is itself sin (*Institutes* 2.1.8).

Spiritual Hygiene

But what would a spiritually sound person be like? What sort of wholeness does corruption attack?

A spiritually sound person fits the universal design. She functions properly: in the range of her relationships to God, others, nature, and self we can spot impressive manifestations of shalom. Or, following one line of New Testament usage, we might call them impressive manifestations of *hygiene*.[10]

Although it sounds as if it might have something to do with the brushing and flossing away of small particles of vice, spiritual hygiene is actually wholeness of spirit — that is, wholeness of what animates and characterizes us. Spiritual hygiene is the wholeness of resources, motive, purpose, and character typical of someone who fits snugly into God's broad design for shalom. A spiritually hygienic person is one who combines strengths and flexibilities, disciplines and freedoms, all working together from a renewable source of vitality. This is a person who flourishes like a fine sapling rooted into the bank of a dependable stream.

What are some features of this flourishing? As Christians see her, a spiritually whole person *longs* in certain classic ways. She longs for God and the beauty of God, for Christ and Christlikeness, for the dynamite of the Holy Spirit and spiritual maturity. She longs for spiritual hygiene itself — and not just as a consolation prize when she cannot be rich and envied instead.[11] She longs for other human beings: she wants to love them and to be loved by them. She hungers for social justice. She longs for nature, for its beauties and graces, for the sheer particularity of the way of a squirrel with a nut. As we might expect, her longings dim from season to season. When they do, she longs to long again.

She is a person of character consistency, a person who rings

10. See Titus 1:13; 2:8. The Septuagint often uses cognates of *hygiainoo* to translate *shalom*. In general, I am using *shalom* in reference to social and cosmic wholeness, as in Chap. 1, and *hygiene* in reference to personal wholeness.

11. See Robert C. Roberts, *Spirituality and Human Emotion* (Grand Rapids: William B. Eerdmans, 1982), p. 93.

true wherever you tap her. She keeps promises. She weeps with those who weep and, perhaps more impressively, rejoices with those who rejoice. She does all these things in ways that express her own personality and culture but also a general "mind of Christ" that is cross-culturally unmistakable.

Her motives include faith — a quiet confidence in God and in the mercies of God that radiate from the self-giving work of Jesus Christ. She knows God is good; she also feels assured that God is good to her. Her faith secures her against the ceaseless oscillations of pride and despair familiar to every human being who has taken refuge in the cave of her own being and tried there to bury all her insecurities under a mound of achievements. When her faith slips, she retains faith enough to believe that the Spirit of God, whose presence is her renewable resource, will one day secure her faith again.

Since faith fastens on God's benevolence, it yields gratitude, which in turn sponsors risk-taking in the service of others. Grateful people want to let themselves go; faithful people dare to do it. People tethered to God by faith can let themselves go because they know they will get themselves back.

Grateful people overflow a little, especially with thanksgiving and passed-on kindnesses. But they do not therefore lack discipline. In fact, self-indulgence tends to suppress gratitude; self-discipline tends to generate it. That is why gluttony is a deadly sin: oddly, it is an appetite suppressant. The reason is that a person's appetites are linked: full stomachs and jaded palates take the edge from our hunger and thirst for justice. And they spoil the appetite for God.

The classic longings motivate a sound life; so do faith and gratitude. Of course, all these things fail from time to time. Spiritually healthy people know very well the drag of sloth and doubt. They know about spiritual depression. They know what it is like to feel keenly that the world has been emptied of God. That is why a spiritually sound person disciplines her life by such spiritual exercises as prayer, fasting, confession, worship, and reflective walks through cemeteries. She visits boring persons and tries to take an interest in them, ponders the lives of saints and compares them to her own, spends time and money on just and charitable causes. A person of spiritual hygiene covets the virtues and character strengths that Christians since Paul have always prized — compassion, for example, and patience. She seeks these and other excellences — endurance, hope, humility, forthrightness, hospitality. She then tries to work them into a regular practice routine, always aware that in order to grow in these excellences she needs both to strive for them and to fail in her striving.[12] She needs to persist through striving and failure and growth in order to become a free and joyful contributor to shalom.

Just as in sports and music, discipline in spiritual hygiene has a point. Anybody can play, but only a disciplined person can play freely. Discipline is the basis and presupposition of both freedom and power.

A basketball forward who does a spin move in the lane and a concert pianist who rips off a fortissimo run in octaves need strength to do these things, but they also need fluidity. They need what we might call powerful relaxation or relaxed power; they need strong fluidity or fluid strength. They are playing, but "playing within themselves." Behind their masterly mix of power and freedom lie hours and hours of painful, sweaty discipline. This is work for play. People who practice spin moves eventually make them part of their game. People who work for years on scales and arpeggios one day begin to play music.

Free and disciplined lives are a kind of music we offer to our parents, to our teachers, to friends and family and colleagues. By offering the music to them, we also offer it to God. As just suggested, the offerings differ from person to person and from culture to culture: they differ at least as much as violins do from saxophones, orchestras from a pair of back-to-back pianos. In any case, what makes them musical is that they bring peace and afford delight, that they please and "glorify" God.

The goal of human life, says the opening of the Westminster Shorter Catechism, is "to glorify God and to enjoy him forever."

---

12. More specifically, "Moral striving is both an essential part of spiritual growth . . . and a ground of self-despair which sensitizes the individual to the grace of Jesus Christ" (Roberts, *Spirituality and Human Emotion*, p. 56).

This famous claim, filed in language with all the "spareness, strength, and clarity of fine ironwork,"[13] was written as a kind of pre-life orientation for children. By writing documents like this, the church was trying to stake and guy a child's life so that it would point toward God: only then could it be sturdy, fragrant, and fruitful. A child must learn God's Word and speak of it tenderly, respect God's reputation and try to enhance it. She must place her very life in the hands of God and trust what those hands might do to it. She must shun emotional and religious junk food that might spoil her appetite for God and her hunger and thirst for righteousness.

Spiritual hygiene includes *ends* like these — goals, purposes, primary intended consequences. The point of our lives is not to get smart or to get rich or even to get happy. The point is to discover God's purposes for us and to make them our own. The point is to learn ways of loving God above all and our neighbor as ourselves and then to use these loves the way a golfer uses certain checkpoints to set up for a drive. The point is to be lined up right, to seek first the kingdom of God (Matt. 6:33), to try above all to increase the net amount of shalom in the world.

To glorify God is to do these things and, by doing them, to make God's intentions in the world more luminous and God's reputation more lustrous. To enjoy God forever is to cultivate a taste for this project, to become more and more the sort of person for whom eternal life with God would be sheer heaven.[14]

According to all traditional Christian wisdom, human flour-

---

13. Edward A. Dowey Jr., *A Commentary on the Confession of 1967 and an Introduction to "The Book of Confessions"* (Philadelphia: Westminster Press, 1968), p. 246.

14. According to John Henry Cardinal Newman, heaven is not for everyone: it is an acquired taste, and hard to acquire while our taste buds still resemble a crocodile's back. An unholy person would be restless and unhappy in heaven ("Holiness Necessary for Future Blessedness," in Newman's *Sermons and Discourses, 1825-39,* ed. Charles Frederick Harrold [New York: Longmans, Green, 1949], p. 24). C. S. Lewis develops this theme with characteristically powerful imagination in *The Great Divorce* (New York: Macmillan, 1946). Roberts also offers a fine discussion throughout his *Spirituality and Human Emotion,* but especially on pp. 87-90.

ishing is the same thing as glorifying God and enjoying him forever, and human wisdom is an inevitable, and human happiness a frequent, by-product of such flourishing. In the mystery of God's providence, those who do seek the kingdom find that various other flourishings often follow, but not when directly aimed at. Much of what we want in the way of happiness, wisdom, and general self-actualization cannot be gotten by trying for it. To try deliberately for self-actualization is like trying very hard to fall asleep or to have a good time. As C. S. Lewis reminds us, these things need to come by the way:

> Your real, new self (which is Christ's and also yours, and yours just because it is His) will not come as long as you are looking for it. It will come when you are looking for Him. Does that sound strange? The same principle holds, you know, for more everyday matters. Even in social life you will never make a good impression on other people until you stop thinking about what sort of impression you are making. Even in literature and art, no man who bothers about originality will ever be original: whereas if you simply try to tell the truth (without caring twopence how often it has been told before) you will, nine times out of ten, become original without ever having noticed it. The principle runs through all life from top to bottom. Give up yourself, and you will find your real self. Lose your life and you will save it.[15]

15. Lewis, *Mere Christianity*, paperback ed. (New York: Macmillan, 1960), p. 190.

CHAPTER 3

Perversion, Pollution, and Disintegration

Devotion to what is wrong is complex and admits of infinite variations.

Seneca

It is only the poor who are forbidden to beg.

Anatole France

According to the Scriptures, people who hold public office are divinely ordained ministers: God has assigned to their offices the solemn duties of administering justice and promoting the public good (Rom. 13:1-7). The main lines of Christian thinking have traditionally held that officials of this kind deserve respect and scrutiny because of the weightiness of their calling to protect and enhance civil shalom.

But, as a smoldering electorate knows, public officials often have vocational ideas of their own that sometimes wind themselves around ordinary provisions of the political system and ignoble expectations of voters in such a way that the net result is perverse. County prosecuting attorneys, for example, are ordinarily *elected* officials. The system turns prosecutors into politicians; their experience makes them savvy politicians. They come to know that many voters prefer bulging jails to nice distinctions between guilt and innocence and that voters in the market for a prosecutor therefore shop for one with an impressive string of convictions.

Predictably, prosecutors try to oblige them. They begin to hunger not for criminal justice (who could campaign on that theme?) but for guilty verdicts. In fact, they may try only those cases in which they are really confident of gaining a conviction, particularly near election time. If it takes a good prosecutor to convict a guilty party but a great prosecutor to convict an innocent one, then — judging by the number of persons annually released from prison because of the discovery that they had been unjustly convicted — the public is endowed with an impressive number of great prosecutors.[1] The justifying ideology for such perversion is simplicity itself: if you want to get elected, you have to sell what people are buying.

Perversion is an ends-and-purposes disease. Most broadly understood, perversion is the turning of loyalty, energy, and desire away from God and God's project in the world: it is the diversion of construction materials for the city of God to side projects of our own, often accompanied by jerry-built ideologies that seek to justify the diversion.

Specifically, to pervert something (such as the office of prosecutor) is to twist it so that it serves an unworthy end (such as merely gaining convictions) instead of a worthy one (such as achieving criminal justice) or so that it serves an entirely wrong end (such as humiliating one's political enemies). Examples abound: a journalist distorts an event in order to render it more controversial and thus more newsworthy; a clergyman uses his office and authority to bend children to his sexual wishes; a juror casts her vote to express her lifestyle preferences; a teenager uses a friendship to move up in the social pack; a head of state launches a short but lethal war against a tiny nation in order to boost the economy, raise his standings in the polls, and bury criticism of his domestic performance.

Sometimes we pervert our own longings, aiming them at the wrong objects (as in sexual perversions) or indulging them dispropor-

---

1. I draw this point from an unpublished manuscript by Henry Bouma entitled "Solving Crime without Seeking Justice" (1990). I got additional help on this matter from James Penning.

tionately so that they become dull where God and the things of faith are concerned but acute where various genuine but only proximate goods such as money, knowledge, and power are concerned. Many of our longings rise in us like a force of nature. Some of them seem to *be* a force of nature, as little under our control as a cramp.[2] Still, as every successful dieter knows, the discipline of desire is often merely difficult, not impossible. Whether or not we succeed depends in part on how much we are encouraged by others, including society as a whole. And, of course, contemporary society picks and chooses the desires it would like to see us discipline. In many settings, society seems far readier by various programs and prohibitions to help us discipline our desire for, say, cigarettes than our desire for our neighbor's spouse.

Good spiritual hygiene includes a practiced ability to assess goods (goods seldom come with their weights written on them) plus the power of will to pursue them with appropriate degrees of interest and to enjoy them with a fitting level of pleasure. Unhappily, involuntary longings lead us around a good deal, and ignorance and self-deception often skew our judgments about what is worth longing for in the first place.

Such perversions of judgment take a number of forms. Aleksandr Solzhenitsyn's 1978 commencement address at Harvard University, a defining moment in the twentieth-century culture wars, condemned Western godlessness, materialism, and consequent superficiality. The West has thrown away God, said Solzhenitsyn, as well as the accountabilities and depths of purpose that used to be attached to belief in God; it has substituted for these weighty things faddish variations on the pursuit of freedom and happiness. Any return to greatness must begin with a reappraisal of the goal of

2. See Augustine, *The City of God* 14.15, 16, 19, 28. Christian theologians have long used the term *concupiscence* in translating the Greek New Testament term *epithumia* and in reference to disordered longing generally. Although in classical Latin *concupiscentia* had no particularly wrongful or sexual overtones, Christian theologians (of whom Augustine is preeminent in this respect) have long used the word for indeliberate desire (desire that, after the fall, is no longer governed by will) and especially for one of its classic forms, lust. See, e.g., Augustine's equation of concupiscence with the Pauline *sarx*, or "flesh" (a similarly polysemous term), in *The City of God* 13.13; 15.7.

human life, a recognition of its spiritual nature, and the recovery of a sense of responsibility to God and for others.

Journalistic reaction to the speech was immense. A good deal of it was peevish and defensive. A *Washington Post* editorial interpreted Solzhenitsyn as proposing that he himself ought to become "the unifying inspiration" to correct American society![3] In this case, an editor twisted a speaker's meaning so hard that it ended up facing backward.

One of the most common perversions of judgment in American life appears in and around collegiate sports arenas. University athletic programs, especially men's football and basketball, often develop a life of their own that has little to do with higher education. Some of these programs might just as naturally be attached to meat-packing plants as to universities. Ordinarily the celebrity coaches of major sports programs claim to be teaching teamwork and building the kind of character that will prepare their protégés for careers as good citizens. Still, wise educators ask, how often in good society do you become a hero for knocking some other good citizen's helmet off? "How often is blind obedience taught in place of the courage of conviction? How often is intimidation taught under the guise of tenacity? How often is manipulation and deliberate rule violation taught as strategy? How often is composure and sportsmanship mistaken for lack of effort?"[4]

The conversion of sport to war is a perversion of ends. So is the conversion of war to sport. Benvenuto Cellini tells of a day he demonstrated to Pope Clement VII (1523-34) his skill with an artillery piece. Spying a brightly dressed member of the enemy army, Cellini selected just the right ordnance to dispatch him.

> I fired and hit my man exactly in the middle. He had trussed his sword in front, for swagger, after a way those Spaniards have; and my ball, when it struck him, broke upon the blade, and one could

3. See *Solzhenitsyn at Harvard: The Address, Twelve Early Responses, and Six Later Reflections*, ed. Ronald Berman (Washington: Ethics and Public Policy Center, 1980), p. 25.

4. John Massengale and James Frey, "American School Sports," *Journal of Physical Education, Recreation and Dance* 59 (August 1988): 43.

see the fellow cut in two fair halves. The Pope, who was expecting nothing of this kind, derived great pleasure and amazement from the sight, both because it seemed to him impossible that one should aim and hit the mark at such a distance, and also because the man was cut in two, and he could not comprehend how this should happen. He sent for me and asked about it. I explained all the devices I had used in firing, but told him that why the man was cut in halves neither he nor I could know. Upon my bended knees I then besought him to give me the pardon of his blessing for that homicide; and for all the others I had committed in the castle in the service of the Church. Thereat the Pope, raising his hand, and making a large open sign of the cross upon my face, told me that he blessed me, and that he gave me pardon for all murders I had ever perpetrated, or should ever perpetrate in the service of the Apostolic Church.[5]

Pollution

Perversion is sometimes ingredient in moral and spiritual pollution, a further dimension of corruption.[6] When a church uses hymns primarily as entertainment, for instance, it simultaneously perverts the hymns and pollutes worship by introducing entertainment into it. A married father's incest not only ruins his child but also perverts the gift of sex and pollutes his marriage.

5. Cellini, *The Life of Benvenuto Cellini*, trans. John Addington Symonds (New York: Scribner's, 1926), p. 73.

6. Certain theologians in the Reformed tradition use pollution as their *main* concept and image of corruption. In so doing, they follow and elaborate some of the typical imagery of the Reformation's confessional literature (see p. 33 above). See, e.g., Herman Bavinck, *Our Reasonable Faith*, trans. Henry Zylstra (Grand Rapids: Baker Book House, 1956), p. 243; Charles Hodge, *Systematic Theology*, 3 vols. (New York: Charles Scribner, 1874), 2:230; Louis Berkhof, *Systematic Theology*, 4th ed. (Grand Rapids: William B. Eerdmans, 1941), p. 246. Theologians who use *pollution* as their main corruption word, as Berkhof does, mean to include within it both "total depravity" (i.e., the fact that sin smudges every dimension of human life) and also "total inability" (i.e., the fact that unrenewed sinners impair their own consciousness so far that they become wholly unable to know or to love shalom or the God who intends it).

To pollute is to defile (the Latin roots of the word suggest dragging something through mud). Predictably, in Christian tradition the concept of pollution contains some residue of the biblical concept of uncleanness — an old and mysterious idea that certain diseases and substances (e.g., leprosy, blood, semen, and even mildew) possess the power to contaminate and thus to disqualify a person or thing from being in the presence of a God who is perfectly holy. In this setting, holiness implies not just otherness or transcendence but also wholeness, oneness, purity. In the ancient Near Eastern world, bodily discharges suggested the loss of vitality, of life itself, and hence of personal wholeness. Even animal and plant hybrids suggested it. In one remarkable passage in Leviticus (chap. 19), ceremonial uncleanness of this kind and moral uncleanness (idolatry, slander, double-dealing) appear together as instances of pollution.[7] The idea is that sin not only contaminates particular individuals and communities but also defiles their proper relation to God.

To pollute is to weaken a particular whole entity, such as a sound relationship, by introducing into it a foreign element. (In this respect, pollution brings together what God wants kept asunder.) "Fooling around," for example, pollutes both worship and marriage. Indeed, the biblical paradigm cases of pollution are idolatry and adultery, emblems of each other. In each case, some new commitment insinuates itself into an existing relationship and compromises it. In idolatry a third party gets in between God and human persons, adulterating an exclusive loyalty.[8] Idolatry violates both negative and positive law, both the first commandment's prohibition of idolatry ("You shall have no other gods before me" [Deut. 5:7]) and also the summary love command of the Deuteronomic code ("Love the LORD your God with all your heart, and with all your soul, and with all your might" [6:5]).

7. See Mary Douglas, *Purity and Danger: An Analysis of the Concepts of Pollution and Taboo* (New York: Praeger, 1970), p. 51; and Gordon Wenham, *The Book of Leviticus,* New International Commentary on the Old Testament (Grand Rapids: William B. Eerdmans, 1979), pp. 23-32.

8. Biblical writers accent the novelty of rivals to Yahweh. These, as in Deut. 32:17, are unknowns; they are recently immigrated, Johnny-come-lately gods.

But, of course, idolatry violates more than a law. In the Exodus literature, God's rescue of Israel from slavery and the ratification of his relationship to Israel at Mount Sinai place a covenant context around everything Israel says and does. As a worthy covenant partner, Israel must obey God's law. Sometimes she does and sometimes not, but when she fails to live up to God's covenant expectations, her failure is often described with words like "ingratitude" or "perversity" or "discontent" or "stubbornness."[9] These unhappy attitudes do break the summary law of love to God, but more basically they threaten the vital covenant relation. (That is why there is a general law against them.) Discontent, ingratitude, perversity, stubbornness — these attitudes and dispositions pollute filial loyalty to Israel's Creator, Deliverer, and Keeper. Ungrateful and refractory people at once foul their own character and their relation to God. They are like a child — willful, resistant, and adroit in self-defense by appeal to various legalisms — to whom an exasperated parent finally says, "Don't *be* that way!"

The image of pollution suggests bringing together what ought to be kept apart. To pollute soil, air, or water is to blend into them foreign materials — machine oil, for example — so that these natural resources no longer nourish or delight very well. Similarly, the introduction of a third lover into a marriage or an idol into the natural human relation to God adds a foreign agent to them; it corrupts these entities by addition.

Dividedness and Disintegration

But also by division. An adultery both pollutes and splits a marriage. An idolatry both contaminates human religious loyalty and divides it. In fact, the very reason for fencing off relationships like these from the approach of third parties is that these parties threaten to break the relationships down by dividing the loyalties of one of the principal parties. The danger of third parties in these cases is that they are always wedge-shaped.

9. George S. Hendry, "Is Sin Obsolescent?" *Princeton Seminary Bulletin* 6 (1985): 260.

Accordingly, in Scripture and much of the Christian tradition, a "pure" heart is an undivided one.[10] Scriptural writers fear "double-mindedness" not merely because it shows disloyalty and ingratitude but also because its perpetrator becomes its victim. Divided worship destroys worshipers. Divided love destroys lovers. To split the truly important longings and loyalties is to crack one's own foundations and to invite the crumbling and, finally, the disintegration of life itself. A divided house cannot stand.

But if so, how can civilized, let alone noble, life proceed? After all, surely everyone suffers from dividedness. Nobody loves God with a wholly pure and undivided heart. Nobody loves neighbors perfectly. Nobody's marriage is quite free of contaminants. If dividedness tends to break us down, how do we manage to hold up and go on?

Ideally, by repentance and renewal of mind and heart — that is, by the grace of God working through spiritual disciplines and the support of others. Actually, we often resort instead to various coping mechanisms that simply isolate the problem instead of addressing it. The chief of these is "compartmentalizing." A character that has lost its wholeness can undertake a partly effective program of damage control by storing conflicting materials in psychically well-insulated compartments.

In a book about her early life, Sylvia Fraser tells of the tributes paid at her father's funeral. He was a man of proper and regular habits — a Christian man "who didn't smoke or drink . . . who helped with the grocery shopping, who never took the Lord's name in vain." A polite and neighborly man, Mr. Fraser "kept his snow shoveled, his leaves raked, and his bills paid."[11] He also sexually molested his daughter Sylvia from age four to twelve, threatening

10. See, e.g., Ps. 24:4, in which the pure in heart are the non-idolatrous (they "do not lift up their souls to what is false"), a characterization echoed in Matt. 5:8 ("Blessed are the pure in heart, for they will see God"), and especially in James 4:8b: "Cleanse your hands, you sinners, and purify your hearts, you double-minded." For a thoughtful contemporary address to the theme, see Clifford Williams, *Singleness of Heart: Restoring the Divided Soul* (Grand Rapids: William B. Eerdmans, 1994).

11. Sylvia Fraser, *My Father's House: A Memoir of Incest and Healing* (New York: Ticknor & Fields, 1988), p. 239.

her first with the loss of her toys (he'd throw them into the furnace), then with killing her cat, then with sending her away to an orphanage — all this if she were to disclose their secret, a secret that not only divided him, but also split his daughter into two persons, the ordinary good girl and the evil daughter who submitted to her father's wishes. For almost forty years she successfully repressed the memory of the evil daughter, till it finally emerged in deep psychoanalysis.

"Integrity on one side of our character," as Newman once remarked, "is no voucher for integrity on the other side."[12] If Mr. Fraser was like the rest of us, he could live with his character inconsistencies only by sealing them off from each other, just as an ocean liner can sometimes keep sailing, even when damaged, if the crew seals off the flooded compartments. In both cases, business can continue for a time under emergency conditions.

Disintegration is the main event in corruption — the breakdown of personal and social integrity, the loss of shape, strength, and purpose that make some entity an "entirety" and make it *this* entirety.[13] As Sylvia Fraser's story reminds us, sin tends to disintegrate both its victims and its perpetrators. Disintegration is always deterioration, the prelude and postlude to death.

Amor Mortis

The association of sin with physical and spiritual death runs like a spine through Scripture and Christian tradition.[14] In commenting

12. John Henry Cardinal Newman, "Secret Faults," in his *Sermons and Discourses, 1825-39*, ed. Charles Frederick Harrold (New York: Longmans, Green, 1949), p. 5.

13. Robert C. Roberts, *The Strengths of a Christian*, Spirituality and the Christian Life series, vol. 2, ed. Richard H. Bell (Philadelphia: Westminster Press, 1984), p. 27.

14. The concept of corruption links sin and death in the Old Testament via the use of such words as *'abad*, which (as in Eccles. 7:7) often gets translated "to corrupt" but which also means "to cause to die." Exactly the same is true of *phtheiroo* in the New Testament. Consider also the biblical use of images of death (e.g., devouring and withering in Isa. 1:20, 30) to express the wages of sin and the explicit

on the story of the fall in Genesis 3, Athanasius remarks that we human beings, who were created out of nothing, corrupt ourselves back into nothing by our rebellion and defection. The Word of God that called us into being would have preserved us from our natural mortality if we had remained constant in fidelity and attentiveness, but, by spurning God's Word, we became "bereft of being." We began physically to disintegrate, to "abide in death and corruption."[15]

Unhappily, says Athanasius, deterioration has also spread through our soul, through our psychic governing center, making it internally lawless. Like some mad charioteer, we now run our lives with more speed than direction. We become off-track racers, amateurs who have lost sight of the finish line.[16] Even in little ways we keep corrupting others and ourselves. Worse, unless arrested by the graces and disciplines of God, we tend to gather momentum in this program: sinners who lose spiritual purpose and control eventually descend into a spiral of increasingly grave assaults on civic and personal integrity.

Of course, on a bluebird day in May, theological talk of this kind may seem alarmist, judgmental, or absurdly pessimistic. In other contexts we may find Athanasius no more pessimistic than the anchor of the evening news. Every day's news presents us with a new assortment of criminal cops, abusive parents, larcenous defense contractors,

---

statement in Rom. 6:23 that death is the wages of sin. Cf. *The City of God* 13.1-15, especially chap. 15, where Augustine states that the death of the soul consists in its being abandoned by God.

15. Athanasius, *On the Incarnation* 4.5. See also book 13 of Augustine's *City of God*, the whole of which is concerned in one way or another with the links among corruption, nothingness, and death. Further on, Augustine suggests that to live for oneself instead of for God "is not to be wholly nothing but to be approaching nothingness" (14.13). Following Augustine, C. S. Lewis extends the claim that goodness implies plenitude of being, and evil its bereavement, in *The Great Divorce* (New York: Macmillan, 1946). He describes heaven and its inhabitants as fiercely substantial, but hell and its population as almost inconceivably tiny, "for a damned soul is nearly nothing" (p. 123). Accordingly, one poor damned woman, a grumbler, keeps fading. Eventually she thins down from a grumbler to a mere grumble, "going on forever like a machine" (p. 75).

16. See Athanasius, *Against the Heathen* 5.2.

jailed corporate executives, and disgraced politicians. Though exposés of corruption on the newscasts often seem intended more to entertain than to inform — an end worth pondering — most citizens are not amused. They know what corruption does to society and what it does to corrupted persons — how it numbs them and hollows them out.

In *Castaways,* a book about teenage delinquents, George Cadwalader tells of juvenile behavior that seems wholly uncentered, sometimes random. Cadwalader's subjects are teenagers who have been neglected or assaulted by family members and who take their vengeance by following a career of casual, almost automatic, thuggery. They hurt others and wreck their own lives. But what frightens even professional observers of some of these delinquents is that they carry on their destruction as remorselessly as sharks. Here are rapists, killers, and thieves who appear to lack not only conscience but also emotion.[17]

Similarly, in a book about Joel Steinberg and Hedda Nessbaum, the central figures in a much-publicized trial in New York in the eighties, Joyce Johnson ponders "the archetypal features" of their evil. Through repeated cycles of beating and ignoring Lisa, Joel Steinberg's daughter, the two adults finally doused not only the life of a small girl but also some of the last sparks of humanity in themselves.

> It is the blank affectlessness of Steinberg and Nessbaum that we recognize with a shudder. It is this that causes us fear and trembling even more than the blows that descended upon a six-year-old girl. There is the sense that the blows were delivered with indifference . . . and that with the same indifference the two "educated" adults in the apartment let the child slip toward death before their very eyes over the next twelve hours, while, as it was later discovered, they smoked cocaine.[18]

At its nadir, the disintegrated human spirit moves beyond affectlessness to generate a demonic inversion of values, the sort of

17. See Cadwalader, *Castaways* (Post Mills, Vt.: Chelsea Green, 1988).
18. Johnson, *What Lisa Knew: The Truths and Lies of the Steinberg Case* (New York: G. P. Putnam's, 1990), p. 40.

upside-down morality we see in those mafia movies in which ruth-
lessness is respected and the refusal to accept a bribe taken as a sign
of contemptible self-righteousness. Movies of this kind disorient us;
at length, they can also seem suffocating. That is because serious
moral evil violates not only integrity but life itself: evil is first dis-
concerting and then lethal.

In a virtuoso discussion of the sexual madness of the Marquis
de Sade, Garry Wills remarks that Sade's determination to dominate,
to use, and to wear down the flesh of other human beings (Sade
specifically includes girls of any age) finally amounts to "an attempt
to seal up the universe, like some crypt in a Poe story." Sade's sex is
not for generating life but for suffocating it: "He tries to plug all the
human bodies present into each other's sockets to form a closed
system with no aspiration out."[19]

Of course, sin ordinarily tries to bag a good of some kind:
people want power or pleasure or wealth or self-esteem or happiness.
Their sin consists in seeking these things in hurtful ways or excessively or preeminently or even exclusively. But as human life degenerates, as people explore deeper and deeper recesses of evil, they begin
to seek pleasure not in such created goods as sex or material plenty
or the exercise of dominion. They seek it instead in the very dynamics
of sin. Like a hunter who, in a little flare of self-assertion, fires at
each letter of a No Hunting sign, sinners sometimes draw pleasure
from mere rebellion. They take satisfaction from showing who is
boss, from showing that no one else will legislate for them. Or they
take the vandal's pleasure in the destruction of beauty and wholeness.
This contrariety, as opposed to blank carelessness, is the first ingredient of sin done "for the hell of it."

People who joy in evil show that some wire has gotten crossed
in them; their moral polarity has switched. Such corruption climaxes,
as the Roman historian Livy says in a famous statement, in the
transforming of human love from a benevolent disposition to a fatal
attraction. Livy is describing the debauchery of the last century of
the Roman republic, but he might just as well have been describing

---

19. Wills, *Under God: Religion and American Politics* (New York: Simon &
Schuster, 1990), p. 294.

the hunger that makers of slasher films are trying to feed. What Livy describes is the inevitable destination of uninterrupted human evil. "Of late years," he says, "wealth has made us greedy, and self-indulgence has brought us, through every form of sensual excess, to be, if I may so put it, in love with death."[20]

20. Livy, *History of Rome* 1.1. Cf. Prov. 8:35-36: "Whoever finds me [wisdom] finds life and obtains favor from the LORD; but those who miss me injure themselves; all who hate me love death."

CHAPTER 4

The Progress of Corruption

If a man is allured by the things of this world and is estranged from his Creator, it is not he alone who is corrupted, but the whole world is corrupted with him.

Mesillat Yesharim

From the time they are children, most human beings come to understand, or at least to experience, the way in which one moral misstep leads to another.

- A fifth grader caught in the act of stealing a classmate's radio finds it easy to lie about the nature of the event ("I just wanted to know what size batteries it takes") and then to lie about the lie ("I'm telling you the truth!").
- A junior high school boy who prides himself on being tougher and more manly than other junior high school boys (especially those who are still mistaken for their mothers when they answer the telephone) bullies the beardless ones, calls them queers, and then crushes their soprano protests back into their faces with his fists.
- A high school girl watches television when she should be studying and snaps at a parent who gestures toward her unopened books. The next afternoon she cheats on the first of her

semester exams. Then, feeling irritable, she gets drunk with her friends, gossips more maliciously than usual about an acquaintance they all dislike, and — blood alcohol level still rising — aggressively drives her mother's car home. Indeed, she drives it part way through the end of the family garage. Afterward, she doesn't feel like studying.

Traditional presentations of sin, and particularly of corruption, feature a strikingly contrary pair of images. On the one hand, sin tends to despoil things. Unarrested, sin despoils even its own agents, eventually causing "the very death of the soul."[1] On the other hand, sin is remarkably generative: sin yields more and more sin. In a standard scenario, each episode of sin gets triggered by trouble from the last.

In Chapter 3 we noted some of the ways sin kills — by the kind of perverting, polluting, and dividing that breaks down persons and their vital relationships. Beyond this, sin breaks down great institutions and whole societies, or, in Augustinian terms, "cities." In this chapter I want to analyze some of the ways and settings in which this lethal process moves forward. After all, like virtue, sin is a dynamic and progressive phenomenon.[2] Hence its familiar metaphors: sin is a plague that spreads by contagion or even by quasi-genetic reproduction. It's a polluted river that keeps branching and rebranching into tributaries. It's a whole family of fertile and contentious parents, children, and grandchildren.

One more image, perhaps the biggest of the traditional ones: sin is "an evil tree" that yields "corrupt fruit."[3] Youngsters eventually

---

1. The General Council of Trent, fifth session.

2. In fact, sin may outstrip virtue in dynamism and progressivity. As Hag. 2:11-13 suggests, it is much easier to contaminate something than to decontaminate it. It is much easier to spread an oil slick than to clean one up.

3. The Second Helvetic Confession, 8. The allusion here is to Matt. 12:33-35 (cf. 7:17-18). See also Jer. 17:9 ("The heart is deceitful above all things, and desperately corrupt" [RSV]), which immediately follows an image familiar from Ps. 1:3 and elsewhere: a person is like "a tree planted by water, that sends out its roots by the stream." The psalmist uses the image to show the rootedness and fruitfulness of good; Jeremiah uses it to show the rootedness and fecundity of evil.

discover what the wise have known for millennia: people rarely commit single sins. Thievery and lies and lies about lies, macho pride and mockery and assault, laziness and snappishness and cheating, and alcohol abuse that empties back into laziness — these sins and products of sin keep on replicating and bunching together like clusters of grapes on the vine. The clusters show up in individual persons but also in groups (in family systems, for instance) and in the places where groups and individuals meet. Hence the corruption of persons, of communities, and of whole cultures.

History Echoes

In commenting on the "cultural mandate" of Genesis 1:28, in which God commands Adam and Eve to "be fruitful and . . . fill the earth," Augustine says that by their sin the first couple obeyed the command, albeit in a perverse and disastrous way. For this primal pair was the seed of the whole human race, and their sin contaminated the seed:

> Our nature was already present in the seed from which we were to spring. And because this nature has been soiled by sin and doomed to death and justly condemned, no man was to be born of man in any other condition. Thus, from a bad use of free choice, a sequence of misfortunes conducts the whole human race, excepting those redeemed by the grace of God, from the original canker in its root to the devastation of a second and endless death.[4]

When Augustine and the succeeding Christian tradition paired the nearly contrary motifs of death and fruitfulness in their theology of corruption, they were extending and intertwining lines from Scripture, but they were also disclosing their own observation of the character of sin. They knew that sin is both fatal and fertile. Like the drought that prompts a maple tree to announce its distress by producing hundreds of emergency seed pods, or like a man with AIDS who infects and impregnates a woman, so sin tends both to kill and to reproduce.

4. Augustine, *The City of God* 13.14.

Indeed, like cancer, sin kills *because* it reproduces. As every counselor knows, one of the most typical settings for this awful fruitfulness is the family. Apples do not usually fall far from the tree. Children not only look but often act like their parents. Alcoholics, for instance, often spring from alcoholic parents and tend, in turn, to marry alcoholic spouses and to produce still more alcoholic children.[5] Sexist families tend to reproduce sexism, to send it like a disease through the family tree so that in every spreading branch of it men want to control and patronize women. Similarly for racism, ethnic hatred, nationalism, xenophobia, hatred of homosexual persons, and many other bigotries.

Families transmit sin, including the distorted relational patterns of those families themselves. To help us think about this phenomenon, let's consider the "contextual" or "intergenerational" theory of Ivan Boszormenyi-Nagy.[6] According to Nagy, family systems thrive on basic justice. One of the most important forms of such justice is the give-and-take of the generations: in properly operating families, children take from parents and then give to their own offspring. Children have a right to expect a giving and nurturing posture on the part of their parents, and they have a right to take the nurture and care that parents give. Then, in turn, these children incur an obligation to provide similar attentiveness to their own children — which is not only the reasonable service they owe their children but also the most effective form of gratitude they can offer to their parents.[7] To be a healthy human being is therefore to exist "between give and take."

According to intergenerational theory, when family systems malfunction, the trouble often lies in some distortion or even reversal of this give-and-take dynamic. For instance, quarreling parents sometimes split a child's loyalty in such a way that the child cannot please

5. Alcoholism plainly qualifies as evil. In Chap. 8 I raise the question whether alcoholism and other addictions also qualify as sin.

6. Nagy, *Foundations of Contextual Therapy: Collected Papers of Ivan Boszormenyi-Nagy* (New York: Brunner-Mazel, 1987). For the introduction to Nagy on which my account is based, see Robert C. Roberts, *Taking the Word to Heart* (Grand Rapids: William B. Eerdmans, 1993), pp. 81-105.

7. Roberts, *Taking the Word to Heart*, pp. 99-103.

one parent without displeasing the other. A child who perceives the crazy wrongness of this setup may try to parent his parents — advising them, mediating between them, trying desperately to get them to stop their childish quarreling. Such "parentified" children may then grow into adults who feel, however subconsciously, that they have been cheated out of their own full and free childhood. One unhappy result is that parentified children, on becoming parents, try to restore the balance of payments by getting their own children to parent them! After all, doesn't *somebody* owe them a little parenting?[8]

Of course, families do not operate as closed systems. Peer and educational pressures on particular family members or the religious conversion of one or more of them or some particular trauma or triumph — these sorts of things might work their way into a family's life and change its chemistry. And sometimes families produce sheer anomalies. Still, in general, abuse predicts abuse. Abused children often grow up to abuse their children. Sometimes they grow up to abuse their parents. Pastors, social workers, clinical psychologists, and others testify to an eerie tendency in certain middle-aged children toward what the British call "granny-bashing." If a child irritates a parent by, say, wetting or whining and gets punished with uncontrolled anger and physical violence, this child may take her vengeance thirty years later when roles have been reversed, when the parent has grown old, incontinent, irrational, and childish. The parent's child, more beaten up than brought up, may return the compliment. She will have learned her lesson well.

Psychological explanations of family violence often focus on the dynamics of precedent and imitation within family systems or on the character disorders of arbitrary and domineering parents. Sociological interpretations, on the other hand, focus on such factors as poverty, ignorance, class and racial status, and powerlessness — factors that may dangerously raise the family stress level.[9] The predictable truth is that people living sorry lives often hate their lives, and people who hate their lives often hate the most intimate reminders of their lives,

8. Roberts, *Taking the Word to Heart*, pp. 86-87.
9. See Linda Gordon, *Heroes of Their Own Lives: The Politics and History of Family Violence — Boston, 1880-1960* (New York: Viking, 1988), p. 5.

including their parents and their children. For instance, the kind of blue-collar resentment in parents that Russell Banks portrays in his fiction — a flaring resentment of low wages, busted screen doors, cheap suits, doughy complexions, and greasy apartments — leaves little room for the large-hearted attentiveness that children thrive on.

On the contrary, in another variation of give-and-take disease, some socially voiceless and powerless parents demand unquestioning deference from their children by way of compensation. At least at home, socially humiliated parents "want some respect" and "don't want to take any guff." Filial failure to meet these demands (after all, children often harbor a few resentments of their own) rings a parent's bell and can start bouts of hand-to-hand combat. Parents beat up children, including babies; children beat up younger children (the junior high bully who isn't getting any respect at home brings his resentment to school); children beat up parents. Whether psychological or sociological explanations of family violence apply (political conservatives favor the former; political progressives, the latter),[10] or whether both or neither applies, the beating goes on generation after generation. Victims victimize others, who then send their own vengeance ricocheting through the larger human family. Nobody is more dangerous than a victim.

In an absorbing account of his years in the Middle East, Thomas Friedman pauses at one point to reflect on the character of Menachem Begin, prime minister of Israel from 1977 to 1983. Here was a man who had grown up in the middle of Polish and then German anti-Semitism, a man who from his youth knew what it was to be despised, marginalized, and targeted for spit. He longed so much for vengeance, says Friedman, that first the idea, and then the reality, of Jewish tanks, jets, and bombs became "his pornography," the cure for Jewish impotence. Begin saw Yasir Arafat as another in the long line of Israel's enemies and declared that the siege of Arafat's forces was the moral equivalent of going after "Hitler in his bunker."[11]

10. Gordon, *Heroes of Their Own Lives*, p. 5.
11. Friedman, *From Beirut to Jerusalem* (New York: Farrar, Strauss & Giroux, 1989), pp. 143-44.

What made Begin dangerous, says Friedman, is that even after years of military successes he never ceased thinking of himself as a victim. What makes victims dangerous is that they are unlikely to exercise stern self-control. They feel entitled.

> Begin [reminds] me of Bernhard Goetz, the white Manhattanite who shot four black youths he thought were about to mug him on the New York subway. Once you have been mugged enough times, as Goetz had, no one can tell you that you are not entitled to blow out the brains of some black kid for even thinking about mugging you. Begin, unfortunately, was a victim with more than a Saturday night special; he was Bernhard Goetz with an F-15.[12]

History echoes. For years in the late eighties and early nineties, Israeli soldiers in the West Bank and Gaza Strip terrorized Palestinian civilians, bulldozed their houses, and imprisoned their occupants, including children, and did a lot of it without due legal process. All along, they tried to block the access of journalists to the truth of these matters. Soldiers also fired teargas canisters at Palestinian teenagers — gas manufactured in the United States but rejected by U.S. domestic police because it was too toxic. "How easily," remarks one observer, "the Israelis throw gas canisters at people."[13]

During these years, violent Israelis would claim that they were answering Palestinian terrorists, and their claim was entirely plausible. On the other side, Palestinians who knifed Israeli civilians or shot up Israeli tourist buses would claim that they were answering the state terrorism of Israel. And, to distressed outsiders, *their* claim sounded entirely plausible too — though, of course, neither claim justified what had been done.

In a striking commentary on the echoing and re-echoing of sin in history, James Burtchaell remarks on the phenomenon of breaking the peace. Despite centuries of war, no one has ever done it, he notes: nobody has ever fired a first shot. All strikes are claimed to be counterstrikes. All shots are return fire. "For the Allies, World War II

---

12. Friedman, *From Beirut to Jerusalem*, p. 144.

13. Gary M. Burge, "Does History Not Echo?" *Reformed Journal* 40 (November 1990): 4.

began at the Polish border in 1939; for the Germans, hostilities dated back to Versailles. Your military operation is an attack; mine is a retaliation."[14]

Consider the way most of us look at terrorism. Most citizens of powerful nations think of terrorists as irrational persons. On this view, terrorists possess some wild and nameless malice that turns them into enemies of the peace that has been established by decent people. And, indeed, a few groups do seem to be fueled by what Burtchaell calls "nihilist rage." But such groups are rare. Terrorists nearly always think of their violence as retaliatory. True, the violence against which terrorists rage may be systemic rather than freelance like their own, but, as Solzhenitsyn knew, no matter how state violence is masked, euphemized, and defended, it may still be as grievous and unjust as any conventional war of aggression — or as any instance of terrorism. And terrorists do typically think of themselves as respondents to a history of state violence. Accordingly, "no one will ever comprehend or cope with [terrorism] without reconstructing the sense of the past that terrorists harbor."[15]

But who has the qualities of vision, fairness, and world-class responsibility to do some of this reconstruction? Which heads of state possess the maturity to reject the narrow self-interest that typically defeats any attempt to understand the motives of one's adversaries? As it is, powerful nations bomb to their deaths citizens of smaller and less powerful nations without bothering to understand the history of these citizens or their desperation and without trying very hard to understand their grievances in terms of this history. What we need in order to cut the loops of state violence and terrorist reprisal, says Burtchaell, is the kind of "great, patient statecraft" that relies less on sheer might than on a persistent determination to "inquire into the causes of grievances, think about them, and strive to allay them."[16]

The alternative is to keep the echo sounding:

14. Burtchaell, *The Giving and Taking of Life: Essays Ethical* (Notre Dame, Ind.: University of Notre Dame, 1989), p. 219.
15. Burtchaell, *The Giving and Taking of Life*, p. 220.
16. Burtchaell, *The Giving and Taking of Life*, p. 223.

If a man has seen his children die from malnutrition because of medical aid withheld, his village ravished by industry that underpaid and sickened the workers, his voice stifled by a dictatorship that tortured patriots, his priests shot for preaching justice and his wife raped by a plain-clothes death squad — if, after all this, he rises in wrath and bombs the vehicle of a government official with the official's innocent family inside, who has broken the peace? And can we, by military reprisal, restore the peace? Or will our reprisal only justify the rightness of his rage in his neighbors' minds and raise up ten more in his place?[17]

Motives, Contexts, and Causes

Why does sin ricochet down the generations, and why does history echo? What accounts for the fact that combatant ethnic groups and feuding clans lock themselves into round after round of hostilities that neither mend nor end? Where do the patterns of dysfunction in family systems come from, and why are they so miserably hard to fix? Why do even grade school students commit sins in sequence, each touching off the others like firecrackers in a string?

Of course nobody has full answers to such questions, and we should distrust people who pretend to have them. Still, we can learn something about the progress of sin if we inventory the answers we do have and describe the ones we lack.

What answers do we have? We know that where grievances are concerned people have long memories and short fuses. We know that injustice enrages people and makes them vengeful. We know that people who hate their lives often abuse those who incarnate what they hate and that the abused are then likely to abuse others. We know that nobody is more dangerous than a victim. We know that sin brings distress and that people often seek to relieve their distress with the same thing that brought it on — a dynamic, as we shall see in Chapter 8, that sin shares with addiction. Our fifth grade

17. Burtchaell, *The Giving and Taking of Life*, p. 221. See also William F. May, "Terrorism as Strategy and Ecstasy," *Social Research* (Summer 1974): 277-98.

radio thief, for example, lies to avoid the distress of getting caught. If his lie gets challenged by a skeptical teacher, he indignantly tells another lie — again, a short-term stress reliever that, like cigarette smoking, puts long-term stress on his heart.

At bottom, says Reinhold Niebuhr, we human beings want security.[18] We feel restless and anxious in the world because we are both finite and free, both limited and unlimited. We are persons of seemingly endless possibilities and of immense power, but we are also creatures utterly dependent on the good offices of our Creator. So we live on the edge of our finitude and freedom, anxious lest we miss opportunities and anxious anew when we have exploited them. For suppose we lose our advantage? Suppose somebody usurps our power or defrauds us of our money or defeats us in our reelection bid for office. Don't persons of eminence fear obscurity just as tyrants fear the approach of justice?

But anxiety, as Niebuhr observes, is only the context for sin, not its cause. Our base problem is unbelief. Failing to trust in the infinite God, we live anxiously, restlessly, always trying to secure and extend ourselves with finite goods that can't take the weight we put on them. We climb social ladders, buy securities, try to make a name for ourselves or leave a legacy. We deliberately put others in our debt (name a federal dam after somebody and he will listen with interest to your next request). We strive for raw power or for intellectual transcendence or for moral superiority. Alternatively, we try to escape all these strivings, calming our restlessness with flights into lust or drunkenness or gluttony. Unbelief, says Niebuhr, yields anxiety, which yields alternating pride and sensuality.[19]

But do the answers in our inventory, including Niebuhr's, fully explain the evils we have been discussing? Hardly. To start with what looks like the easiest case, take our radio thief. Suppose we interrogate him about his misdemeanor, seeking to learn from him its cause and motive. Why did he try to steal someone else's radio? A candid answer might be that he wanted the radio and concluded that theft

---

18. Niebuhr, *The Nature and Destiny of Man: A Christian Interpretation*, 2 vols. (New York: Scribner's, 1964), 1:182.

19. Niebuhr, *The Nature and Destiny of Man*, 1:183-86.

was the fastest way to get it. But why was he willing to break a law, trouble a schoolmate with an annoying loss, and disappoint his elders? Presumably because he wanted the radio more than he wanted shalom. But why? Because, in this respect, he is selfish: he would rather fulfill his personal desire than keep the peace. But if being selfish brings so much trouble to everybody, including oneself, why be that way? Because, as the filmmaker Woody Allen said in 1993, trying to explain his controversial affair with the young daughter of Mia Farrow, "The heart wants what it wants."[20]

But why doesn't the heart want God, trust God, look childlike to God for life's joys and securities? Why doesn't the heart seek final good where it can actually be found? Why turn again and again, in small matters and large, to satisfactions that are mutable, damaging, and imperiled?

Because the heart wants what it wants. That's as far as we get. That's the conversation stopper. The imperial self overrules all. Inquiring into the causes of sin takes us back, again and again, to the intractable human will and to the heart's desire that stiffens the will against all competing considerations. Like a neurotic and therapeutically shelf-worn little god, the human heart keeps ending discussions by insisting that it wants what it wants.

The trouble is that this is only a redescription of human sin, not an explanation of it — let alone a defense of it. Our core problem, says St. Augustine, is that the human heart, ignoring God, turns in on itself, tries to lift itself, wants to please itself, and ends up debasing itself. The person who reaches toward God and wants to please God gets, so to speak, stretched by this move, and ennobled by the transcendence of its object. But the person who curves in on himself, who wants God's gifts without God, who wants to satisfy the desires of a divided heart, ends up sagging and contracting into a little wad. His desires are provincial. "There is something in humility which, strangely enough, exalts the heart, and something in pride which debases it."[21]

20. See Jean Bethke Elshtain, "The Newtape File II," *First Things*, April 1993, p. 12.

21. Augustine, *The City of God* 14.13. Like Scripture writers, Augustine thinks of the heart not just as the seat of emotion or desire but also as the governing center

Returning to our radio thief, suppose we think of other possibilities in the attempt to find his motive. Maybe he isn't merely covetous and willful; maybe his motives are mixed with blue-collar resentments — resentment of his low-budget lifestyle, for example, and of the more prosperous radio owner. Maybe, to imagine a very different motive, our thief thinks he is clever and wants to see if he is clever enough to get away with a radio. Or maybe he and the radio owner will compete in next week's Middle Elementary Track and Field Day events, and the thief wants to upset the owner's concentration. Maybe lots of things. The point is that motives may be various, elusive, and mixed, and we cannot easily sift them.

Moreover, even when we have sorted and classified the motives of a sin, we still haven't fully explained it. Why not? The reason is that to identify a motive is to discern only what pushes a person in the direction of some act, not why he actually commits it. We still do not know why a person *succumbs* to the motive. After all, lots of people feel motivated to steal other people's possessions but manage to avoid giving in to these motives. They "resist temptation." Why doesn't a thief resist it too? Lots of people feel aggrieved by real injustice but manage to resist acting on their grievance in some way that creates new rounds of grievances. So why do terrorists act the way they do?

James Burtchaell says that we need great, patient masters of statecraft who will inquire into the causes of grievances, ponder them, and seek to allay them. Fair enough. And about those causes Burtchaell writes with great eloquence.

Still, as Burtchaell would no doubt acknowledge, to know the cause of a grievance is not yet to know the cause of all violence done by the aggrieved. Moreover, to know the cause of a grievance is not

---

of a human being — the human being at his center, at his core, considered in his fundamental orientation. From the heart "flow the springs of life" (Prov. 4:23). Hence, in Scripture, integrity is a pure heart (Matt. 5:8); where integrity is lacking, it is the heart that is "perverse" and "devious above all else" (Jer. 17:9). Accordingly, when Paul wants to describe the source of our new power, love, and integrity, he testifies that Jesus Christ has taken up residence at the governing center of human lives: he "dwells in our hearts" (Eph. 3:17). Depending on its orientation, then, the fact that "the heart wants what it wants" may be our shame or our salvation.

yet to know the cause of, let alone to justify, every specific means the aggrieved may employ to redress it. Indeed, we may dispute in some cases whether a violent person even has a grievance at all; maybe all he has is anger. At minimum, what we need here is a distinction between the context of an act and its cause. Jack Beatty offers it:

> Even poor youths, even poor, ill-educated youths, even poor, ill-educated youths who live in a society suffused by racism, must be responsible for their acts. To believe otherwise is to espouse an environmental determinism nearly as offensive to reason and morality as racism itself. Crime, arson, running amok in the streets, have social contexts, not social causes. The [media blare about] the contexts is an insidious distraction that rests on the presumption that society is responsible for the crimes against it. That is legal and moral nonsense.[22]

Is it? Doesn't society at least share in the responsibility for certain crimes against it? When society, via its legislatures, funds some of its schools twice as generously as others, when it provides poor schools for poor people, when its public schools clarify moral values instead of teaching them, when it invents gambling schemes and tries to entice its own citizens to wager their money on them, when it constitutionally and judicially protects rap lyrics that glamorize the killing of police officers and the terrorizing of women — when society does these things, can it completely wash its hands of crimes motivated by the very resentment, despair, and greed it has engendered?

To be fair-minded about sin — perhaps to be merely observant about it — is to concede that the forces within social and cultural contexts push, draw, stress, and limit human beings in countless ways. Contexts strain and constrain people. In fact, social and cultural dynamics exert their pressure regularly and powerfully enough so as to make certain subsequent behaviors predictable. That is why, with a fair degree of confidence, social scientists call certain behaviors or experi-

22. Beatty, "A Call to Order: Reflections on the Rhetoric of Evasion," *Atlantic Monthly*, August 1993, p. 18.

ences "predictors." Abuse, for example, predicts abuse: the fact that a person has suffered abuse is one predictor that he will engage in it.

Nonetheless, these forces do not fully explain or justify human evil. That is why, even if he has sharpened it excessively, Beatty has a point. Contexts, and even predictors, of bad behavior are much easier to identify than causes, and we should not confuse them. Nor should we judge personal responsibility on the basis of this confusion.

Consider gang rape, an urban horror. It is one thing to observe that a member of an urban wolf pack was himself sexually abused as a child or is poor and poorly educated and the product of a broken home. These are contextual factors for which other persons and society are answerable, and at least one is also a predictor. Together they weigh a lot. But it is another thing to assume that these significant burdens *cause* a wolf pack member to rape a young girl and then to stand on her neck to assure that she is dead. And it is still another thing to offer the rapist "lite" absolution for his horrific act on the ground that he has pre-atoned for it ("You are not guilty, for you have suffered much").

Environmental determinism and the no-fault morality that usually accompanies it are pretentious. Environmental determinists pretend to know what is almost always hidden from us — namely, the real causes of wrongdoing. The fact is that we know more contexts than motives of human evil, and we know more motives than causes, but we almost never know all three. A main reason is that although contexts, motives, and causes of evil certainly look as if they are linked, the linkage is hard to specify. In particular, even when we know the psychological or social context of someone's evil deed, and even its motive, we still might not know exactly what caused her to do it. In general, we do not know to what extent evildoers are themselves, as agents, the main cause of their evil and to what extent they have fallen into a trap set by others. Only God knows the percentages in these matters. Only God knows the human heart. Only God knows how much of our evil is chargeable to us as sin.[23] For example, only God knows when a psychological or social

---

23. Recall the definition of sin from Chap. 1: sin is any agential evil for which some person or group of persons is to blame.

account of a particular evil stretches past context and motive to describe its cause.

Given our ignorance along these lines, what should we call street rape? What should we call thievery and lying? How about a thoughtful piece of dental insurance fraud?

We ought to call these things sin. We know they are moral evils, and we know that most of these particular offenses are also crimes. As a working hypothesis, we ought to assume that anybody who has committed them has sinned. Why? The reason is that with this assumption we treat people as grownups. We start them off with a full line of moral credit. We deal with them as people who can accept their debts.

Of course, the assumption that someone's evil counts as sin may in particular cases have to be suspended or even abandoned — in the case of certain addicts, for example. In all cases the assumption must be held provisionally. But in the meantime, and in general, we ought to pay evildoers, including ourselves, the "intolerable compliment" of taking them seriously as moral agents, of holding them accountable for their wrongdoing. This is a mark of our respect for their dignity and weight as human beings. After all, what could be more arrogant than treating other persons as if they were no more responsible than tiny children or the mentally maimed? What could be more offensive than regarding others not as players but only as spectators in human affairs, including their own? What could be more condescending, stultifying, and inhumane? What could be more patronizing than the refusal to blame people for their wrongdoing and to praise them for their rightdoing, and to ground this refusal in our assumption that these people have not caused their own acts or had a hand in forming their own character?

In his Lyman Beecher lectures, William Muehl recalls the humanist passions of Arthur Koestler, a onetime defender of communism who later became its critic. What began to distress Koestler was that in the Soviet communist system the concept of blame disappeared. Nobody blamed reluctant communists. Nobody blamed peasants who resented the loss of their freedoms or who resisted conversion to communism, for surely they had been corrupted by faulty social and economic conditions. Nobody blamed critics of the party line, for surely they had been brainwashed by capitalist propaganda. Instead of blame, party officials offered their opponents pity and reeducation. Of course, the cradle of such pity often turned out to be a mental hospital, and the school for such reeducation a concentration camp — places at least as confining and dehumanizing as any conventional prison. But at least none of the inmates was to blame for being there. Koestler found all this blamelessness progressively disturbing. "Before long it began to become clear that those whom we do not blame we do not regard as responsible. Those whom we do not regard as responsible we do not see as fully human. And those whom we do not see as fully human we are willing to twist and manipulate to suit our own convenience."[24]

Human rights and prerogatives depend on human responsibility, on citizenship in a *community* of responsibility. People in this community properly hold each other accountable. People who respect each other's full humanity and responsibility refuse to explain moral evil with reference to a psychological or social "root cause" or with appeals to the authority of some party official or professor of victimology. In other words, until they are moved by evidence to the contrary, respectful people assume that evildoers are responsible citizens like themselves and that they are answerable for their evil.

The Great Law of Returns

We do not finally know why evildoers do evil. At last the origin and explanation of human evil belong to what St. Paul calls "the mystery of iniquity" (2 Thess. 2:7, KJV). We may observe the contexts and speculate about the force of contributing factors in other people's wrongdoing, and we may rationalize our own wrongdoing, but a lot of the time we cannot be sure we know what we are talking about. In particular, motives and causes elude us. At bottom, the heart wants what it wants, and the heart has its reasons that reason does not know.

24. Muehl, *Why Preach? Why Listen?* (Philadelphia: Fortress Press, 1986), p. 65.

Still, as we have seen, people do discern patterns in evil and can even predict new rounds of these patterns. Moreover, experts offer plausible theories of the dynamics that generate such patterns (recall Nagy's theory of generational give-and-take). While theories of this kind do not give us causal explanations of sin and thus do not demystify it or excuse it (carefully stated theories do not even pretend to do so), they do help us see and think about some of the movement and rhythm of sin.

Many accounts of the rhythmic progression of sin finally amount to variants on one account — an account so old and deep in the knowledge of our race that it has seemingly arisen from the very soil of the universe. The classic New Testament statement is in Galatians 6:7-8: "God is not mocked, for you reap whatever you sow. If you sow to your own flesh, you will reap corruption from the flesh; but if you sow to the Spirit, you will reap eternal life from the Spirit."

Of course, people sometimes state the general dynamic here some other way: Like yields like. You get back what you put in. What goes around comes around. The measure you give is the measure you get. Garbage in, garbage out.

Paul states the great law of returns agriculturally, because that image is apt in the context of the life-and-death issue he is discussing. Paul knew that everything depends — life itself depends — on what we sow and what we reap. If we sow wheat, we get food. If we sow poison ivy, we get a nasty weed. Similarly, if we sow to the flesh, we get corruption and death; if we sow to the Spirit, we get eternal life.

No matter what we sow, the law of returns applies. Good or evil, love or hate, justice or tyranny, grapes or thorns, a gracious compliment or a peevish complaint — whatever we invest, we tend to get it back with interest. Lovers are loved; haters, hated. Forgivers usually get forgiven; those who live by the sword die by the sword. "God is not mocked, for you reap whatever you sow."

This text is a proverb, a wisdom saying that distills the observations of alert people across many centuries. It is also a cry from the depths in much of the world's great fiction and drama. And it is a nightmare of tyrants. Perhaps their violence will one day return to haunt them. Perhaps they have sown the seeds of their own destruction. Perhaps, having sown the wind, they will reap the whirl-wind.

As we shall see in Chapter 7, the wise person knows the laws, rhythms, and dynamics of reality. Sometimes the wisdom writers of Scripture speak of physical reality along these lines and sometimes of the social lives of human beings, but usually the rhythms and dynamics apply both places. Thus, the great law of returns is true not only for the person who on a September afternoon walks out into her garden with a bushel basket in her hands; it's also true of respectful persons who are much respected, and of hostile persons who find hostility coming right back at them.

Of course, like other proverbs, the great law of returns gener-alizes: it summarizes the regular but not the uniform experience of the race. For example, although good and bad parents tend to re-produce in kind, they sometimes raise surprises. Some rotten parents produce good children; some terrific parents produce awful children. But outcomes of this kind strike us as extraordinary. The reason is that, generally speaking, you reap what you sow. This is simply how things are in the universe. There is no explaining it, no use railing against it, usually no way to get around it. We might as well try to get around the law of gravity. We might as well argue with our body's need for sleep.

What Paul describes as life "in the flesh" extends beyond what people often call the sins of the flesh — namely, lust, gluttony, and drunkenness. Paul uses "flesh" as an image for any kind of life that is turned away from God, even if it is intellectually turned away, and especially if it is willfully turned away. Thus, just as sowing to the Spirit yields such dispositions and states of mind as love, joy, peace, and patience, so, on the other side of the field, sowing to the flesh brings a crop of attitudinal sins and miseries as well as bodily ones: idolatry, sorcery, enmity, anger, and envy as well as fornication, li-centiousness, drunkenness, and carousing (Gal. 5:19-20, 22-23). In both instances, the dynamics of sowing and harvesting go on down the ages with awesome inevitability.

A main reason is that people not only reap what they sow but also sow what they reap. Abusive parents who then get abused by their children reap what they have sown. But abused children who abuse *their* children sow what they have reaped. The same goes for terrorized terrorists, swindled swindlers, and jilted lovers who even the score with their next partner.

Inside a given human life, the dynamics of sowing, reaping, and resowing lie behind the process of character formation. As we saw from the life of our high schooler at the beginning of this chapter, even the low-energy sin of laziness can replicate itself by starting a round of acts and attitudes that peters out into laziness. Dispositions and acts form character, which then forms dispositions and acts. A mere state of mind can eventually swell to become a person's destiny (as *hybris* often does in classic Greek tragedy), but meanwhile it may spiral down to produce more states of mind like itself. A fuller statement of the great law of returns would therefore go something like this: sow a thought, and reap a deed; sow a deed, and reap another deed; sow some deeds, and reap a habit; sow some habits, and reap a character; sow a character, and reap two thoughts.[25] The new thoughts then pursue careers of their own, but they, plus their produce, also intersect and cross-fertilize with similar life cycles from hundreds and thousands of other persons. All these persons exist in families and other group systems that they influence and that influence them. Hence the progress of both good and evil is more like a spiral than a shuttle and, more than that, like waves of intertwined and self-replicating spirals.

Where the waves meet, cultures form. A culture, the pattern of beliefs, social forms, dispositions, and values "that are institution-alized in a people's collective life,"[26] stands in the same relation to individual character as character does to thoughts and deeds. That is, character forms culture, which then forms character. Rock video culture, for example, both depicts and excites lust. Political culture both represents and exacerbates public cynicism. Popular religious culture both reflects and deepens the conviction that worship ought to entertain worshipers.

One of the most familiar debates in the United States teeter-

---

25. I am indebted to Joseph C. Aldrich for some of this sowing and reaping.
26. David F. Wells, *No Place for Truth; or, Whatever Happened to Evangelical Theology?* (Grand Rapids: William B. Eerdmans, 1993), p. 167.

totters over this character and culture issue. What about the social impact and responsibility of the heroes du jour of pop culture? Are these folks leaders or followers? By behaviors that range from the exotic to the vile, do these heroes simply give a hungry culture what it already wants, or do they corrupt the appetites of American youth with new menus of lust and violence?

Parents and community leaders suspect the latter. Recognizing that youngsters not only idolize but also imitate their heroes, noting that imitation is one of the main ways children sow what they have reaped from these fertile figures, parents and community leaders ask indignant questions. If the world's greatest basketball players bed hundreds of sex partners, if they gamble away hundreds of thousands of dollars, if they curse other players in public and brawl with fans in bars, if they appear in TV commercials to sell the idea that the purchase of a particular brand of sneakers is a career move — if they do these things, what ripples of influence spread to their millions of immature fans? If rap stars publish albums filled with unlyrical desires to bust vaginal walls, to break women's backbones, and to force fellatio on "bitches" till they "puke," what wreckage might such grunted depravity leave in its wake? How realistic is it to expect fair and respectful treatment of women by young men whose stereos, ears, and brains are full of hostile, sexist sludge? How realistic is it to expect from them, instead, sexual "wilding" — the gang rapes, bludgeonings, and casual, remorseless murders of women that startle, and eventually numb, a whole nation?[27] In short, shouldn't we hold some of the heroes of pop culture responsible for the sins of their fans?

27. In one of his most searing columns, George F. Will remarks that "America's slide into the sewer is greased by praise." Execrable "lyrics" by rap groups — lyrics that exult in hurting and humiliating women — get defended by the nation's most prestigious newspaper editors. Do rap groups celebrate busting and sucking and puking? Do they package the celebration and sell it to teens? "Not to worry, yawn the New York Times editorialists. 'The history of music is the story of innovative, even outrageous styles that interacted, adapted, and became mainstream.'" When busting the walls of vaginas becomes "mainstream" entertainment, says Will, "this will be an interesting country." George F. Will, "America's Slide into the Sewer," *Newsweek,* 30 July 1990, p. 64.

These are sensible questions, but they also have sensible responses. The main one, of course, is that these heroes are in significant measure themselves the products of their culture. Sports and rap stars do not invent themselves. They extend a culture that has feted and formed them.

Consider the extraordinary status of athletes. From the time they are junior high school players, top athletes ride waves of adulation. It's only one of their full rides. Passing through high school and college as social elites, athletes often enjoy special dorms, special meals, special scholarships, special curricula that feature courses in "Leisure Living" and "Adapting to Modern Life," and, for stud players, special young women to welcome and escort them on their recruiting visits to famous universities. These specialties plus cheerleaders who compete to do cartwheels for them, deans who doctor transcripts for them, moneyed alumni who obligingly gamble with them ("Bolenciecwicz," says an alumnus, "I'll bet you a thousand dollars you can't jump over that beer bottle!"), and grownup coaches who implausibly defend them ("OK, so Jones *was* driving 123 miles per hour, but he told me he was trying to get some bad gas out of his tank, and I, for one, believe him")[28] — all these things tell athletes that, for them, behavioral limits are negotiable and social boundaries movable. When athletes, spawned by such a culture, gang rape coeds or scorn their fans or batter their girlfriends or dope themselves into incoherence, where is the surprise?

Other Causes?

The great law of returns and other dynamics of corruption describe, illuminate, and even predict the progress of sin, but they do not fully explain it. As we have seen, the reason is that the contexts and dynamics of sin do not necessarily amount to causes of sin. Thus, while some athletes move in the direction their culture is pushing them, many do not. Many athletes lead quiet and sober lives. In searching for the root of sin, we have to reckon with the human

28. See Rick Telander, "Something Must Be Done," *Sports Illustrated*, 2 October 1989, p. 102.

heart, the active control center of a human agent. And here our search runs into trouble, for the heart of even a pretty good person is divided.[29] An evil heart is a maze. In commenting on the overwhelming character pathology that psychiatrists have to struggle with in some patients, M. Scott Peck describes it as a "labyrinthine mass of lies and twisted motives and distorted communications."[30] That's just one patient. Let him and his kin, plus ordinary sinners and pretty good persons and everybody else, sow and reap and sow again; let them fertilize and cross-fertilize each other, and the resulting culture will defy rational analysis.

In every culture good and evil combine and recombine in so many ways that even agricultural experts lose track of all the new hybrids. Such growth is not only complex but also partly hidden. In fact, secrecy fertilizes evil: in and around incestuous relationships, for example, everybody has secrets. Incest could not survive without them.

Ultimately, the only human beings we know are people who have been created to please God and build shalom but who, to a greater or lesser degree, mysteriously live against the purpose of their existence.[31] The folly, fecundity, and endurance of such life in the flesh, such life against the grain, have always tempted human beings to look for some explanation outside the human heart and its motives and outside the cultural pressures created by human beings themselves. After all, why *do* human beings persist in sin despite the notorious miseries of this program? Why *does* the heart want what it wants? Could it be that, with some obscure purpose, God causes people to sin? Does the Devil make them do it? How about the "powers" that are mentioned, but not really described, in the New Testament (e.g., in Rom. 8:38; Eph. 6:12; Col. 1:16)?

The main voices in the Christian tradition have always com-

---

29. See Lewis B. Smedes, *A Pretty Good Person* (San Francisco: Harper & Row, 1990), p. 2: "Pretty good people still sweat it out against some wild and some mild corruptions that inhabit their frail spirits."

30. Peck, *People of the Lie: The Hope for Healing Human Evil* (New York: Simon & Schuster, 1983), p. 64.

31. Hendrikus Berkhof, *Christian Faith* (Grand Rapids: William B. Eerdmans, 1980), p. 188.

bined to reject these suggestions as rationalizing evasions.[32] The first
of them (God made me sin) smears the center of the biblical portrait
of God: "God is light and in him there is no darkness at all" (1 John
1:5).[33] God is perfectly just, holy, and good. According to the massed
testimony of Scripture, God therefore hates sin. God outlaws sin,
judges it, redeems people from it, forgives it, and suffers to do so.
Naturally, then, the Christian church overwhelmingly rejects as
blasphemous any proposals that God authors, encourages, nurtures,
or otherwise sponsors sin. If some "hard saying" of Scripture hints
that, to the contrary, God's hands are not wholly clean where sin is
concerned (that, e.g., in the events preceding the Exodus, God
"hardened Pharaoh's heart"), Christians strive to find some plausible
way of interpreting the saying that preserves the portrait of God's
holiness.[34] For in the Christian religion, God's holiness is strictly
nonnegotiable.

Not so for the one the New Testament calls Satan or the Devil.
This is a figure who deceives, accosts, seduces, accuses, and destroys
— a figure of such power and wiliness that New Testament writers
grudgingly title him "the prince of demons" (Matt. 12:24, RSV), or
even "the god of this world" (2 Cor. 4:4; cf. John 12:31).[35] Nonetheless, Satan is no match for Jesus Christ the exorcist, the destroyer
of the destroyer, the one who rebukes, plunders, and intimidates
Satan. Nor can Satan detach and harm those who faithfully cling to
Christ. Satan can tempt but not coerce. Satan can accuse but not
convict. Satan can accost but not destroy — or, at any rate, cannot

32. G. C. Berkouwer summarizes and extends the tradition in a sequential
treatment of these evasions in *Sin*, trans. Philip C. Holtrop (Grand Rapids: William B. Eerdmans, 1971), pp. 11-148.

33. Berkouwer calls God's holiness "the biblical a priori" (*Sin*, pp. 27-66),
and describes 1 John 1:5 as its "superscription" (p. 32).

34. This is never an artificial task, and not always an arduous one. See
Berkouwer, *Sin*, pp. 44-66. For insight into Pharaoh's hard heart, see Brevard S.
Childs, *The Book of Exodus: A Critical, Theological Commentary* (Philadelphia: Westminster Press, 1974), pp. 170-75. Does God harden Pharaoh's heart (Exod. 10:1),
or does Pharaoh harden his own heart (9:34), or does Pharaoh's heart simply harden
all by itself (9:7)? Childs observes that the Hebrew texts are casual on this question
and that the interest of the passage clearly lies elsewhere.

35. See Berkouwer, *Sin*, pp. 99-129.

destroy those who "put on the whole armor of God" (Eph. 6:11). A central New Testament conviction is that the evil one gains no ground that we do not give him. Satan seduces only those who are in the market for seduction. Satan deceives only the self-deceived.

In other words, Satan does not compel people to sin. Nor do the "powers."[36] Whatever these mysterious things are — whether spirits or forces or both, whether demons or dynamics or some dark hybrid of them, whether persons or personifications, whether structures of society or their patterns of influence — most Christians who hear of "the powers" react with a shiver of recognition. They have discovered that sin is not only personal but also interpersonal and even suprapersonal. Sin is more than the sum of what sinners do. Sin acquires the powerful and elusive form of a spirit — the spirit of an age or a company or a nation or a political movement. Sin burrows into the bowels of institutions and traditions, making a home there and taking them over.[37] The new structure that is formed by the takeover is likely to display some combination of perversion, formlessness, or excessive rigidity.[38] Law, for example, may be bent to end the freedoms of selected pariah groups. Whole companies

36. Richard J. Mouw provides an excellent short discussion of the powers in *Politics and the Biblical Drama* (Grand Rapids: William B. Eerdmans, 1976), pp. 85-116. See also the following three volumes by Walter Wink: *Naming the Powers: The Language of Power in the New Testament* (Philadelphia: Fortress Press, 1984); *Unmasking the Powers: The Invisible Forces That Determine Human Existence* (Philadelphia: Fortress Press, 1986); *Engaging the Powers: Discernment and Resistance in a World of Domination* (Minneapolis: Fortress Press, 1992).

37. One of the standard representations in American literature of the maddening force and elusiveness of the powers appears early in Steinbeck's *Grapes of Wrath* (a novel that tells us a lot about the sowing and reaping of good and evil). The banks that foreclose on struggling tenants, those monsters that "eat interest" and "breathe profits," have a life of their own but apparently no center of responsibility. No specific individuals within them are responsible for wrenching the poor from their land. It's the times that are responsible. It's progress. It's the necessity of showing profit. It's orders from the parent bank back east. How can an outraged tenant shoot any of *those* things? Steinbeck, *The Grapes of Wrath*, ed. Peter Lisca (New York: Penguin Books, 1976), pp. 43, 52.

38. See Marguerite Schuster, *Power, Pathology, Paradox: Dynamics of Evil and Good* (Grand Rapids: Zondervan, 1987), pp. 140-44.

may dissolve in an orgy of intertwined deceit and neglect.[39] Whole nations may join in lockstep with brutal dictators.

No traditional Christian wants to admit that the powers rob us of all freedom and accountability, that they cause us to sin. In fact, every traditional Christian wants to affirm that the powers have already been deeply compromised by the greater power of God. Don't the victory texts of the New Testament cry out that Jesus Christ has disarmed the powers, made a spectacle of them, and triumphed over them in such a way that they can never separate believers from the love of God (Col. 2:15; Rom. 8:38-39)? Still, the powers are aptly named. As Hendrikus Berkhof says, personal goodness cannot lick them. In fact, their force has the feel of inevitability.[40]

Why did millions of German Lutheran Christians hand over their lives to Hitler and his band of criminals, thrilling themselves with their new status as vindicators of national greatness? Where in race and *Volk* and ethnic identity (those vital centers of treasure and particularity) do we find the switch that, once thrown, turns neighbor against neighbor in a nightmare of bigoted violence? What forces in stock brokerages, banks, insurance companies, legal firms, and real estate agencies move people to attempt not only the defeat but also the humiliation of rivals — a goal that, as individuals, these people shun?[41] Why do military procurement officials and defense contractors invariably lock themselves into mutually corrupting relationships that millions of cheated taxpayers simply cannot break?

In Chapter 1 we saw that sin qualifies as the worst of our troubles because, among other things, it corrupts what is peculiarly human about us. Sin attaches to intention, memory, thought, speech, intelligent action — to all the special features of personhood — and transforms them into weapons. Thus, the same gift that enables a scientist to conquer a disease also enables her to manufacture one

39. For one classic story of such dissolution, see James Sterngold, *Burning Down the House: How Greed, Deceit, and Bitter Revenge Destroyed E. F. Hutton* (New York: Summit, 1990).

40. Berkhof, *Christian Faith: An Introduction to the Study of the Faith*, trans. Sierd Woudstra (Grand Rapids: William B. Eerdmans, 1979), pp. 208-9.

41. This is one version of the central question in Reinhold Niebuhr's *Moral Man and Immoral Society* (New York: Scribner's, 1932).

and to sell it to terrorists. Using the same thoughtful expressions of praise and caring, a man may inspire a woman he wants to marry or seduce one he wants to conquer. The same obedience to authority that binds children to parents, pupils to teachers, and citizens to governments may also turn these children, pupils, and citizens into easy victims, or even tools, of evil.

Why? What accounts for turns and ironies of this kind? What central feature of evil must we examine in order to explain these things?

CHAPTER 5

Parasite

There is a sort of moth that lives only on tears. That's all they eat or drink.

Thomas Harris, *The Silence of the Lambs*

You cannot have power for good without having power for evil too. Even mother's milk nourishes murderers as well as heroes.

Bernard Shaw, *Major Barbara*

During the Montgomery bus boycott of 1955, Martin Luther King Jr. and the Montgomery Improvement Association led thousands of local blacks through months of hardship in an attempt to break municipal bus segregation. Blacks rode bicycles, trudged miles to and from work, and formed car pools that local police regularly harassed. Police would stop and interrogate drivers, make them demonstrate their wipers and lights, and then write them up for tiny and, often, bogus violations. Drivers adapted. According to one historian, they "crept along the road and gave exaggerated turn signals, like novices in driving school."[1]

1. Taylor Branch, *Parting the Waters: America in the King Years, 1954-1963* (New York: Simon & Schuster, 1988), p. 159.

Under these difficult conditions, many black citizens of Montgomery supported the boycott single-mindedly and with a spirit of mutual help and accountability. Even those who had little to sacrifice nonetheless sacrificed what they had in order to bring down city walls of injustice. Remarkably, a number of blacks also figured out ways to defraud their own movement. By submitting phony reimbursement claims, they hustled the Montgomery Improvement Association for "oceans of gasoline and truckloads of imaginary spare tires." The MIA, says Taylor Branch, was constantly trying to "plug the holes in the reimbursement system."[2] The hustlers were living on tears.

Ironies and Hybrids

An often-noted irony of history, including the history of the Christian church, is that people bring dirty weapons to holy wars. Ambitious preachers libel secularists and caricature their positions. Crusaders force conversions. Orthodox believers light fires under the heretical. Then, after the war, the winners sometimes reintroduce the very evil — despotism, for example — that they had fought to overthrow.

The sobering fact is that reforms need constant reforming. Rescuers need rescue.[3] Amendments need amendment. Repentant sinners need to repent even of some dimensions of their repentance, such as their pride in the humility that has driven them to their knees.[4] Evil contaminates every scalpel designed to remove it. Even

---

2. Branch, *Parting the Waters,* p. 189.

3. Richard Lovelace comments on the end of William Golding's *Lord of the Flies:* "The young hero is saved from death at the hands of his companions, former choirboys, by the forces of law and order — the crew from a warship designed to kill men from rival nations. This says it all. The very powers which keep us from killing one another . . . are ultimately part of systems which are engaged in the planetary equivalent of gang fights" (*Renewal as a Way of Life: A Guidebook for Spiritual Growth* [Downers Grove, Ill.: InterVarsity Press, 1985], p. 115).

4. So the veteran demon Screwtape instructs his apprentice Wormwood in the art of snaring a new Christian: "Catch him at the moment when he is really poor in spirit and smuggle into his mind the gratifying reflection, 'By jove! I'm being humble,' and almost immediately pride — pride at his own humility — will

the Montgomery bus boycott — as just a cause as any — had to fight corruption within as well as without.

Nobody studies sin very long without discovering that the subject is full of depths, turns, ironies, and surprises. Some of these arise from the inventiveness of the human will, and some from its intractability; some from the oddities and pressures generated by group evil, and some from the sovereignty of the individual conscience, struggling to uncinch its burdens. At its depths, sin corrupts religion itself, its public enemy. All of the turns and ironies of sin arise in some way from the fact that evil does not — indeed cannot — appear alone. Even in our sin, said Augustine, we imitate God whose image we bear. Our willfulness, for instance, shows "a dim resemblance to omnipotence."[5] Evil always appears in tandem with good. Thus, in wartime espionage and in movements to harbor persecuted fugitives, the person likeliest to do well and to achieve a measure of justice is one who means well and who can also lie and cheat convincingly. In general, good and evil grow together, intertwine around each other, and grow out of each other in remarkable and complicated ways.

Biographers make themselves students of this phenomenon, particularly when it goes on display in human character. Good biographers find character ironies irresistible. Hence the attraction of Martin Luther, one of the three or four most prominent Christians after Paul, a doughty champion of the gospel of grace and a ghastly anti-Semite who wanted his readers to break down Jewish homes and house their occupants in stables. Other ironies appear in other characters, including Luther's most famous modern namesake. Martin Luther King Jr., one of the noblest and most eminent Americans of the twentieth century, adulterated his marriage and plagiarized some of the work that made his reputation. Thomas Jefferson held slaves. The Bible itself gives us such alloyed heroes as King David,

---

appear. If he awakes to the danger and tries to smother this new form of pride, make him proud of his attempt — and so on, through as many stages as you please. But don't try this too long, for fear you awake his sense of humour and proportion, in which case he will merely laugh at you and go to bed." C. S. Lewis, *The Screwtape Letters and Screwtape Proposes a Toast,* rev. ed. (New York: Macmillan, 1982), p. 63.

5. Augustine, *Confessions* 2.6.14.

a great and godly and wicked man whose name has been blessed by centuries of Jews and Christians.

Observing character ironies of these kinds, we naturally conclude that human beings are inexpressibly complex creatures in whom great good and great evil often cohabit, sometimes in separate and well-insulated rooms and sometimes in an intimacy so deep and twisted and twined that we never get to see the one moral quality without the other. "What we are," says Lewis Smedes, "is a set of walking contradictions":

> Our inner lives are not partitioned like day and night, with pure light on one side of us and total darkness on the other. Mostly, our souls are shadowed places; we live at the border where our dark sides block our light and throw a shadow over our interior places. . . . We cannot always tell where our light ends and our shadow begins or where our shadow ends and our darkness begins.[6]

As a result, except where a particular person has become a symbol of good or evil, rendering qualifying judgments trifling and perverse (we do not blame Mother Teresa for small theological lapses or praise Hitler for shunning profanity), our judgments of most everybody, including ourselves, are bound to be mixed.

The same is true of certain emotions and states of mind. Anger, for example, can take the form of righteous indignation, a virtue of the just. Anger can also take the form of smoldering resentment of competitors, the vice of the envious. Pride comes in at least two editions as well. Pride can take the form of proper satisfaction in the achievement of excellence, the virtue of the diligent. But pride can also take the form of inordinate self-congratulation, the vice of the pompous. Significantly, cultural decay shows up wherever the first form of pride gives way to the second.

Roughly until the Enlightenment, sinful human pride — that blend of narcissism and conceit that we detest in others and sometimes tenderly protect in ourselves — was widely regarded as the first of the seven deadly sins. What sin, after all, causes more wars,

---

6. Smedes, *Shame and Grace: Healing the Shame We Don't Deserve* (San Francisco: HarperCollins, 1993), p. 116.

envies, fratricides, tyrannies, ethnic cleansings, and general subversions of fellowship? What sin makes God seem more irrelevant? God wants to fill us with his Holy Spirit, but when we are proud we are already full of ourselves. There's no room for God. Augustine characterized pride as the great *political* enemy in the City of God, the usurper that wants to unseat God and enthrone itself.[7]

But now winds are shifting. Of course, pride itself is still with us. People still have affairs with themselves. Professors still leave faculty meetings feeling less enlightened by what they heard than by what they said.[8] People still feel injured when admirers offer them the sort of sincere but moderate praise that limits their merit. What has changed is that, in much of contemporary American culture, aggressive self-regard is no longer viewed with alarm.[9] Instead, people praise and promote it. This is a culture in which schoolchildren outrank Asian schoolchildren not in math ability but in self-confidence about their math ability;[10] a culture in which prophets of the New Age and gurus of pop psychology (who are sometimes the same) package transcendence and sell it to consumers, advising them that they are superconscious beings, Higher Selves growing toward godhood, "one with the One," and thus in line for the

7. *The City of God* 14.13.

8. An observation made by Patrick G. Henry, executive director of the Institute for Ecumenical and Cultural Research, to a group of uneasy professors in Pasadena, California, in December 1992.

9. Standard discussions of this change include Christopher Lasch, *The Culture of Narcissism: American Life in an Age of Diminishing Expectations* (New York: W. W. Norton, 1978); Amitai Etzioni, *An Immodest Agenda: Rebuilding America before the Twenty-first Century* (New York: New Press, 1983); Robert N. Bellah et al., *Habits of the Heart: Individualism and Commitment in American Life* (Berkeley and Los Angeles: University of California Press, 1985). For analysis of the impact of the self-fulfillment movement on American religion and theology, see Paul Vitz, *Psychology as Religion: The Cult of Self-Worship*, 2d ed. (Grand Rapids: William B. Eerdmans, 1994); James Davison Hunter, *Evangelicalism: The Coming Generation* (Chicago: University of Chicago Press, 1987), especially pp. 50-75; and David Wells, *No Place for Truth; or, Whatever Happened to Evangelical Theology?* (Grand Rapids: William B. Eerdmans, 1993), especially pp. 137-86, and the literature they cite.

10. "Hey, I'm Terrific!" *Newsweek*, 17 February 1992, p. 48.

ultimate job promotion.[11] In this culture, avant-garde literary critics teach "imperial readers" that what they bring to a Milton text is more important than what the text brings to them, and trendy preachers imply that the main problem with savings and loan embezzlers is that they do not love themselves unconditionally. After all, didn't Jesus and Paul talk a good deal about love? "I can see it now," says John Alexander, "Jesus gently saying, 'Woe to you, poor scribes and Pharisees! Nice guys — but your self-esteem is low' (Matt. 23:13-36). Or Paul writing the Judaizers, 'Neither circumcision counts for anything nor uncircumcision, but feeling good about yourselves' (I Cor. 7:17)."[12]

In an ego-centered culture, wants become needs (maybe even duties), the self replaces the soul, and human life degenerates into the clamor of competing autobiographies.[13] People get fascinated with how they feel — and with how they feel about how they feel. In such a culture and in the throes of such fascination, the self exists to be explored, indulged, and expressed but not disciplined or restrained. Self-centered religion, says David Wells, crowds out theology and objective truth:

> Theology becomes therapy. . . . The biblical interest in righteousness is replaced by a search for happiness, holiness by wholeness, truth by feeling, ethics by feeling good about one's self. The world shrinks to the range of personal circumstances; the community of faith shrinks to a circle of personal friends. The past recedes. The Church recedes. The world recedes. All that remains is the self.[14]

11. See Douglas J. Groothuis, *Unmasking the New Age* (Downers Grove, Ill.: InterVarsity Press, 1986), p. 53; and Russell Chandler, *Understanding the New Age* (Dallas: Word Books, 1988), pp. 175-79.

12. Alexander, "Self-Esteem as Salvation," *The Other Side,* March 1988, p. 44.

13. Madeleine L'Engle remarks that one of the casualties of an egocentric culture is the very meaning of the word *integrity,* which has "slowly been coming to mean self-centeredness" (*A Circle of Quiet* [New York: Seabury Press, 1979], p. 130). L'Engle has in mind people who conflate their wants and their obligations. Hence someone who says "I can't do this and keep my integrity" may mean little more than that he doesn't want to do it.

14. Wells, *No Place for Truth,* p. 183.

The Bible and Christian tradition tell us that sinful pride *(hybris)* is an enemy of God.[15] And so it is, no matter whether in fashion or out. According to traditional Christian wisdom, a main problem with pride is that it recognizes neither sin nor grace; in fact, pride hammers them flat and discards them.

Still, those of us who think that *hybris* is a deadly sin (and a wondrous folly) must also acknowledge a couple of complicating realities — realities that do not nullify the old Christian word on pride but do qualify the way we say and receive it. Let's say that pride is a blend of self-absorption — that is, narcissism — with an overestimate of one's abilities or worth — that is, conceit. So a proud person thinks a lot *about* herself and also thinks a lot *of* herself. But one familiar complication is that in some people the narcissistic aspect of pride arises from insecurity; such a person may think a lot about herself just because she's worried that she isn't making it, that she doesn't measure up in some way. She may then overinflate her self-appraisal in order to compensate, especially if she has a guru at her elbow, and most especially if she thinks she has to present a high profile in order to attract the kind of attention she wants. Take as an absolutely typical example the following ad from the "Strictly Personals" section of *New York* magazine, placed by a woman who wants to meet a man as remarkable as herself:

> **Strikingly Beautiful** — Ivy League graduate. Playful, passionate, perceptive, elegant, bright, articulate, original in mind, unique in spirit. I possess a rare balance of beauty and depth, sophistication and earthiness, seriousness and a love of fun. Professionally successful, perfectly capable of being self-sufficient and independent, but I won't be truly content until we find each other. . . . Please reply with a substantial letter describing your background and who you are. Photo essential.[16]

Anyone who describes herself publicly as possessing "a rare balance of beauty and depth" naturally throws her friends into a

15. See Prov. 8:13; Jer. 50:31; James 4:6; and Augustine, *The City of God* 11.15; 14.11-15.
16. *New York* magazine, 8 June 1992, p. 111.

quandary. How do they respond to a statement of this kind? With rebuke for its swelling spirit of self-admiration? Or with pity for its childish confidence that self-admiration will look like self-confidence to readers? Maybe with wariness that splits the difference between rebuke and pity?

Sinful pride is an exceedingly unstable compound, one that looks alternately grandiose, desperate, and foolish. Or, put it like this: *hybris* is a hybrid. It might be titanic or pathetic, or it might wobble in between. A name-dropper, for example, who casually and irrelevantly mentions his recent phone conversation with the governor may sound a little wobbly in this way.

A second complication — or, perhaps, irony — of pride is that it may afflict the great as well as the would-be great. Pride is often the sin of the noble and accomplished, the sin of prime ministers and generals and Nobel Prize winners, of people who really have something to be proud *of.* How poignant it is, then, and what a plum for biographers, that towering achievement often appears with trimmings of childish vanity. In William Manchester's *The Last Lion*, Winston Churchill, for example, emerges as one of the two or three most significant men of his generation. Churchill apparently thought so, too. "His idea of a good dinner, he said, was to dine well and then to discuss a good topic — 'with myself as chief conversationalist.'" He admired his own speeches so much that he used to lie in bed listening to recordings of them. "Once he and his valet had words. Afterward, Churchill rumbled: 'You were rude.' His manservant, forgetting his station, said, 'You were rude too.' Churchill pouted. After a moment he said: 'But I am a great man.'"[17]

Significantly, as a child Churchill had been brutally ignored by his self-absorbed parents (who, despite his pleading, wouldn't visit him at boarding school or stay home for his Christmas visits). Carrying childhood self-doubt like a backpack, the adult Churchill was determined to throw it off — and did a pretty good job of it.

Consider another of Manchester's subjects. Douglas MacArthur, supreme commander of American forces in the Pacific during World

17. Manchester, *The Last Lion: William Spencer Churchill — Visions of Glory, 1874-1932* (Boston: Little, Brown, 1983), p. 25.

War II, was "the best of men and the worst of men," an extraordinarily brave and resourceful soldier who also used fifteen-foot mirrors to heighten his image and who came to speak of himself in the third person ("MacArthur will be leaving for Fort Meyer now"). "His belief in an Episcopal, merciful God was genuine, yet he seemed to worship only at the altar of himself. He never went to church, but he read the Bible every day and regarded himself as one of the world's two great defenders of Christendom. (The other was the pope.)"[18] Pride and a vanity trim package come as standard equipment on some models of greatness. "It is an egalitarian fiction," says Manchester, "that the great are modest."[19] Some are; many aren't.

A third complication is that the same tradition that held pride to be a sin and humility a virtue has often been dominated by whites who have preached humility to blacks, by men who have preached submissiveness to women, by rigid and unimaginative persons who have regarded every creative impulse, every struggle for personal dignity, as a shameful show of arrogance. In the eyes of such persons, anyone who wanted mere self-respect was cheeky. What is troubling is that the advocates of humility and submissiveness have often had a personal stake in the popularity of these virtues and have therefore made adopting them look like the project of a special-interest group.

In general, the proud love humility in *others* and often try to sell it to them. Then, in one of the tragic ironies of sin, the humbled sometimes reply by usurping the very pride they had hated. They reach for proper self-respect but end up overreaching — as in the case of oppressed people who revolt against tyranny and then become tyrants or the case of certain feminists who respond to the pride of dominant males by searching for God in themselves and somehow end up believing that they, or their abilities, are actually identical with God.[20] In sin as on ice, people coming out of a skid tend to oversteer.

18. William Manchester, *American Caesar: Douglas MacArthur, 1880-1964* (Boston: Little, Brown, 1978), pp. 3, 145.
19. Manchester, *The Last Lion*, p. 25.
20. Naomi R. Goldenberg, e.g., reports (with respect) that in feminist witchcraft "worshipers name each other Goddess and God," signifying "a close bond — even an identity — between the Goddess and self" (*Changing of the Gods: Feminism*

Privation and Parasite

The intertwining of good and evil, and the ironies and complexities that proceed from their union, assume somewhat sharper outline when we stand back and look at them from a biblical point of view. The Bible's big double message is creation and redemption. Sin intervenes, but never as an independent theme. Thus St. Paul, the Bible's chief theologian of sin and grace, speaks of sin in terms of what it is *against*. Sin is anti-law, anti-righteousness, anti-God, anti-Spirit, anti-life. Paul's message is that God has shown free and lavish grace to sinners in the death and resurrection of Jesus Christ. Faith in this God, in this Christ, and in their grace is the only hope for human justification. Accordingly, grace, faith, and righteousness, together with the means of expressing and acquiring them — cross, resurrection, Spirit, justification, baptism into Christ — these topics cluster in the center of Paul's interest. As for sin, Paul knows that sin lures, enslaves, and destroys, that Christ died to redeem us from it, and that our sin must therefore be dreadful, but he never does tell us exactly where sin comes from. Nor does he try to define the nature of its power or the means by which it is transmitted.[21]

Perhaps one reason for this omission is that, in the biblical worldview, even when sin is depressingly familiar, it is never normal.

---

and the End of Traditional Religions [Boston: Beacon Press, 1989], p. 89). Note also Carol Christ's much-repeated cry of triumph: "I found God in myself, and I loved her fiercely" ("Why Women Need the Goddess: Phenomenological, Psychological and Political Reflections," in *Womanspirit Rising: A Feminist Reader in Religion,* ed. Carol Christ and Judith Plaskow [San Francisco: Harper & Row, 1979], p. 277).

21. See Stephen Westerholm, *Israel's Law and the Church's Faith* (Grand Rapids: William B. Eerdmans, 1988), p. 160. As many commentators recognize, even Rom. 5:12-21, the *locus classicus* of the doctrine of original sin, says much more about the scope of sin and the divine solution to it than it does about the origin or transmission of sin. Specifically, the passage does not educate us about the nature of the link between Adam's primal sin and the subsequent sin and death of his successors, nor does the passage say anything at all about how Adam himself became a sinner. The weight of the passage lies elsewhere. In typical style (citing Adam as a type of Christ), Paul uses Adam and sin in order to highlight Jesus Christ and the lavishness of grace (vv. 15-17).

It is finally unknown, irrational, alien. Sin is always a departure from the norm and is assessed accordingly. Sin is deviant and perverse, an *in*justice or *in*iquity or *in*gratitude. Sin in the Exodus literature is *dis*order and *dis*obedience. Sin is faithlessness, lawlessness, godlessness. Sin is both the overstepping of a line and the failure to reach it — both transgression and shortcoming. Sin is a missing of the mark, a spoiling of goods, a staining of garments, a hitch in one's gait, a wandering from the path, a fragmenting of the whole. Sin is what culpably *disturbs* shalom. Sinful human life is a caricature of proper human life.

So the biggest biblical idea about sin, expressed in a riot of images and terms, is that sin is an anomaly, an intruder, a notorious gate-crasher. Sin does not belong in God's world, but somehow it has gotten in. In fact, sin has dug in, and, like a tick, burrows deeper when we try to remove it.[22] This stubborn and persistent feature of human sin can make it look as if it has a life of its own, as if it were an independent power or even a kind of person. Indeed, St. Paul uses language that suggests as much, as when he says that sin "exercised dominion in death" (Rom. 5:21), that "sin deceived me and . . . killed me" (7:11), that "if I do what I do not want, it is no longer I that do it, but sin that dwells within me" (7:20).

Still, one must always read on. Victory passages typically follow the big Pauline sin passages, and these (especially Rom. 8:31-39, in which all the trumpets are sounding) present the main biblical teaching: sin is a fearfully powerful spoiler of the good, but it cannot finally overpower either the original or the renewed project of God in the world. It could not overpower even the Montgomery bus boycott.

Why not? How do we explain that sin is both dominant and doomed, both a "power" and a "nothing," both formidable and negligible? "The works of sin are real enough," says Geoffrey Bromiley, "but they carry no solid achievements."[23] Why?

22. Geoffrey W. Bromiley, "Sin," in *The International Standard Bible Encyclopedia*, vol. 4, ed. Geoffrey W. Bromiley (Grand Rapids: William B. Eerdmans, 1988), p. 522.
23. Bromiley, "Sin," p. 519.

The reason is that sin is a parasite, an uninvited guest that keeps tapping its host for sustenance. Nothing about sin is its own; all its power, persistence, and plausibility are stolen goods. Sin is not really an entity but a spoiler of entities, not an organism but a leech on organisms. Sin does not build shalom; it vandalizes it. In metaphysical perspective, evil offers no true alternative to good, as if the two were equal and opposite qualities. "Goodness," says C. S. Lewis, "is, so to speak, itself: badness is only spoiled goodness. And there must be something good first before it can be spoiled."[24] Here Lewis reproduces the old Augustinian idea that evil "has no existence except as a privation of good."[25] Good is original, independent, and constructive; evil is derivative, dependent, and destructive. To be successful, evil needs what it hijacks from goodness.

In one of his novels, Stephen Vizinczey gives us William T. MacArthur, "the most infamous defense attorney in the whole city of New York." The interesting thing about MacArthur, says the narrator, is that he could bribe judges and suborn witnesses successfully just because in these endeavors he was entirely dependable: "William T. MacArthur's word was his bond. It was precisely for this reason that he could obstruct justice so effectively." The narrator comments that the only people who really succeed at judicial corruption are those that can be trusted.[26]

The smartest blows against shalom are struck by people and movements of impressive resourcefulness, strength, and intelligence — that is to say, by people and movements gifted by the very God and with the very goodness that their sin attacks. Additionally, and paradoxically, though sinners attack what's good, they usually intend to *gain* something good by sinning. The defiant "Evil, be thou my good!" of Milton's Satan is dramatic because it is perverse. As I suggested in Chapter 3, people do sometimes rebel literally for the hell of it, but this is rare. Usually they are after peace of mind, security,

24. Lewis, *Mere Christianity*, paperback ed. (New York: Macmillan, 1960), p. 49.

25. Augustine, *Confessions* 3.7.12.

26. Vizinczey, *An Innocent Millionaire* (Boston: Atlantic Monthly, 1983), pp. 307-8.

pleasure, *Lebensraum*, freedom, excitement. Evil wants good; in fact, evil needs good to be evil. Satan himself, as C. S. Lewis explains, is *God's* Satan — a creature of God who can be really wicked only because he comes from the shop of a master and is made from his best stuff.

> The better stuff a creature is made of — the cleverer and stronger and freer it is — then the better it will be if it goes right, but also the worse it will be if it goes wrong. A cow cannot be very good or very bad; a dog can be both better and worse; a child better and worse still; an ordinary man, still more so; a man of genius still more so; a superhuman spirit best — or worst — of all.[27]

The parasitic nature of sin accounts for certain facts that otherwise puzzle us. It accounts for the fact that, in various complicated and ironic ways, good and evil keep showing up, and even growing up, together. Take, for example, the "fruitfulness of sin" that we encountered in Chapter 4. This expression strikes us as an oxymoron because we rightly associate fruitfulness with goodness, with abundance, with life itself. We associate it with the fruit of the Spirit, the fruit of the womb, even the fruit of the loom. We associate fruitfulness with the divine word of Genesis 1:28, "Be fruitful and multiply, and fill the earth," a wonderful encouragement to do what comes naturally.

How peculiar, then, that sin multiplies right along with goodness. Faithful parents tend to reproduce themselves, but so do faithless ones. Generous acts congeal into character traits, but so do selfish ones. People who long for God want to satisfy their appetite and also to sharpen it, but the same is true of sex addicts.

Sin is fruitful just because, like a virus, it attaches the life force and dynamics of its host.[28] Sowing and reaping, human longing,

---

27. Lewis, *Mere Christianity*, p. 53.

28. In describing HIV, Geoffrey Cowley remarks that "viruses are the ultimate parasites . . . mere shreds of genetic information, encoded in DNA or RNA, that can integrate themselves into a living cell and use its machinery to run off copies of themselves." Moreover, when confronted by its enemies, HIV acts like sin: it "mutates out of range," even assuming "different personalities in different settings" ("The Future of AIDS," *Newsweek*, 22 March 1993, pp. 48-50).

children's natural trust of their parents — such things belong among the springs and roots of a good creation. Sin does not remove these things; it attaches them and converts them to new uses. A faithful father, for instance, accepts his small daughter's trust and love, strengthens them, and tries to extend them toward God and out toward the world. A sexually abusive father also accepts his daughter's trust and love, but he uses them to bind his daughter to his lust. Sooner or later, he converts trust to fear and love to resentment. He strengthens *these* emotions with each episode of abuse, and, whether he wants to or not, may extend them toward God and out toward the world.

The parasitic nature of sin accounts for the fruitfulness of sin. Does it also account for those instances in which human beings find themselves strangely drawn to pictures and accounts of sin? According to Wallace Stegner, spectators would rather look at cruelty than at kindness, and painters and poets (perhaps because of their own inclinations along this line) use their artistry to oblige them. Moreover, they do a better job of portraying evil than of portraying good. Dante, for example, knew his business when it came to depicting evil (his inferno "boils with hot life") but flopped when he tried to portray goodness: he turned paradise into "theological meringue" full of simpering saints and characterless angels. "If you were walking down the Tornabuoni," Stegner hypothesizes, "and saw, at the same instant, Beatrice with her beneficent smile and Ugolino gnawing on Ruggieri's skull, which would catch your eye?"[29]

Fair enough: evil fascinates people who walk down the Tornabuoni and also those who channel surf across daytime television. The fastest way to kill the dramas on daytime television would be to rewrite the scripts so that shows would begin to dwell on moral stabilities — on marital fidelity, loyal friendship, and generous cooperation in the workplace. Nobody would watch. People want to see the seven deadly sins, not the seven deadly virtues. Ian Fleming once went so far as to claim that without the seven deadly sins, our lives would go flat.

29. Stegner, *Crossing to Safety* (New York: Penguin, 1987), pp. 267-68.

How drab and empty life would be without them, and what dull dogs we all would be without a healthy trace of many of them in our makeup! And has not the depiction of these sins and their consequences been the yeast in most great fiction and drama? Could Shakespeare, Voltaire, Balzac, Dostoevsky, or Tolstoy have written their masterpieces if humanity had been innocent of their sins? It is almost as if Leonardo, Titian, Rembrandt, and Van Gogh had been required to paint without using the primary colors.[30]

But, once more, complications arise. The "attractiveness of evil" thesis needs qualification. First, not nearly all sin is as colorful and yeasty as Fleming suggests. Some sin attracts us about as much as an unlubricated wheel bearing. Think, for example, of the aggressive irritability that fills unhappy households, the relentless bitchiness that grinds on and on. Surliness, bureaucratic indifference, whining self-pity, sebaceous forms of gluttony, petty resentments and petty larceny — none of these dreary things quickens our pulse.

Second, when people relish dramatic presentations of evil, maybe it's the drama they like and not the evil. After all, they also relish dramatic presentations of good. They find Dostoevsky's Alyosha just as fascinating as his Raskolnikov, Hugo's Jean Valjean just as intriguing as Shakespeare's Iago. They savor accounts of daring rescues and of conspicuous grace as well as accounts of daring bank robberies and conspicuous treason. In 1984, the world watched with just as keen an interest when Pope John Paul II met and forgave Mehmet Ali Agca, his would-be assassin, as they did, three years earlier, when the Pope was felled by his bullet.

Moreover, in certain conventional forms of drama, people enjoy the presentation of evil only because they know that, according to convention, someone will eventually detect and penalize the evil. Mystery and detective genres are as predictable along these lines as a morality play. That is one reason we like them. We know that goodness will end up triumphant and that we will therefore end up contented. Thus, from soap operas to old Westerns to contemporary

30. Fleming, introduction to *The Seven Deadly Sins,* ed. Angus Wilson (New York: Morrow, 1962), p. x.

whodunits and cop programs, the winning formula persists: let sin threaten, enrage, and enthrall, but make sure it is satisfyingly punished at the end of the day.

Third, in assessing the relative attraction of good and evil characters, we need to factor in the level of the artistry that is used to present them. A truly skillful portrait of a dreary evil person (or, for that matter, of a boring good person) may fascinate us even if, outside the life of our mind, we would never want to spend a weekend with these characters. C. S. Lewis reminds us that "the imitation in art of unpleasing objects may be a pleasing imitation."[31] This old critical discovery explains, in part, why generations of readers, especially modern ones who tend to applaud rebellion, have thought that Milton's Satan steals the show in *Paradise Lost*.[32]

Still, we want to know why writers and artists often seem to exercise their artistic gifts more strenuously and bestow their characterizing riches more lavishly on evil characters than on good ones. Granting the possibility that they and we simply know less good than evil, that we know less of Eden than of the lands that lie to the east of Eden, the question persists: Why do artists and their audiences find evil characters so interesting?

A dark reason is that we sometimes identify with these characters. We might not dare to imitate them, but we do secretly admire them. Why? Perhaps because the characters act out the rebellions of our own hearts. Nobody tells them what to do. Everybody has to "respect" them. They write their own rules. Bonny and Clyde, for instance, strike us as extraordinary and interest us for that reason alone. Beyond that, they may also strike us as audacious, even courageous. Bank robbery, after all, takes guts. Further, given their

31. Lewis, *A Preface to Paradise Lost* (New York: Oxford University Press, 1961), p. 94.

32. William Blake admired Milton's Satan as a sympathetic, not just as a skillfully depicted, figure. In "Satan Rousing His Legions," one of his illustrations for Milton's *Paradise Lost*, Blake pictured Satan as "a blond, well-built Saxon, naked, defiant, and tumescent," and surrounded him with a corps of similarly well-muscled and healthy-looking Adonis types (Robert Pattison, *The Triumph of Vulgarity: Rock Music in the Mirror of Romanticism* [New York: Oxford University Press, 1987], p. 111).

Depression context with its hungers and resentments, the two out-laws may look to us a little like Robin Hood, another purveyor of alternative justice in hard times. Still further, like all rebels, robbers invade forbidden territory, and forbidden territory attracts us. We identify with the invaders of such territory, with people who thumb their noses at Keep Out signs, and we can do it safely because the identification is merely vicarious.

Finally, we want outlaws to "get away with it," because *we* would want to get away with it. If nothing else, our nightmares tell us this. Before we awaken in relief, before we discover that we are not criminals and fugitives, we spend half the nightmare trying to escape pursuit. Indeed, if we combine an attraction to forbidden fruit with a streak of contrariness and a voyeur's desire just to watch, we have the very profile of an armchair rebel. Perhaps armchair rebellion lies on about the same moral plane as an adulterous fantasy — not usually as bad as the real thing but nonetheless a revelation and corruption of its author's heart.

Remarkably, it's not only the evil in sin that attracts us; it's also the goodness in it. Sin attracts us whenever it is *vital.* Daring thieves, dashing rogues, renegade police detectives, disobedient angels, charm-ing psychopaths — these figures attract us because they are bold, urbane, witty, energetic, or imaginative. They seem so full of life. Their sin interests us because it leeches the color, wit, and energy out of normal life and presents these things to us in a novel, risky, and therefore dramatic form. Even rebellion against God, as in the case of Milton's Satan, looks good to rebels not just because it expresses their rejection of divine sovereignty but also because the rebellion borrows boldness, imagination, and creativity from the very God it attacks. All of Satan's virtues, as Mary Midgley says, are traditional.[33]

Of course the world has needed some of its rebellions, and has said so by calling them revolutions. Even Calvinists, those lovers of order, have endorsed vigorous and, in some cases, forceful opposition to evil social structures.[34] On the other hand, rebellions against justly

33. Midgley, *Wickedness: A Philosophical Essay* (London: Routledge & Kegan Paul, 1984), p. 151.

34. See Nicholas Wolterstorff, *Until Justice and Peace Embrace* (Grand Rapids: William B. Eerdmans, 1983), pp. 8-10.

constituted authority damage the stability, security, and good order that protect creaturely happiness. They offend God, disturb shalom, and leave victims. But in a romantic, revolutionary frame of mind, we choose not to notice such fallout. When we thrill to demonic rebellion or cheer for fleeing bank robbers, we do not focus on any of the damage, disturbance, or offense. We notice only those features that sin has pirated from goodness — energy, imagination, persistence, and creativity. Everything sin touches begins to die, but we do not focus on that. We see only the vitality of the parasite, glowing with stolen life.

CHAPTER 6

Masquerade

Hypocrisy is an homage that vice pays to virtue.

La Rochefoucauld, *Maxims*

Mistakes were made.

A federal agency head's confession
of massive fraud, 1991

In a book called *Unholy Matrimony: A True Story of Murder and Obsession,* John Dillman tells of a homicide he investigated as a New Orleans police detective in the early eighties. Two men had hatched a scheme to fatten their wallets from life insurance fraud. According to plan, one of them scouted, courted, and married an innocent young woman. He was an attentive man, and she found him irresistible. Then, on their honeymoon, he coaxed his bride out for an evening walk, maneuvered her to a prearranged position, and shoved her into the street, where his accomplice skillfully drove over her with a rented Chevrolet, crushing her skull. Shortly afterward, the widower filed an insurance claim for the life lost to the hit-and-run driver.

During the process in which these men were caught, tried, and sentenced, Dillman saw that they were not sorry for their crime. They were not even very interested in it. In fact, pointing to the way police kept interfering in their lives by pursuing, interrogating, and

96

charging them, the two men complained that they were themselves the real victims in this whole affair and implied that they ought to be not punished but consoled.

The Mask of Sanity

Mental health experts describe people of this kind as possessors of an antisocial personality disorder, or, more specifically, as psychopaths.[1] Remarkably, such persons are often intelligent and attractive, even charismatic — qualities that make them superb players of confidence games. Psychopaths wear the mask of a genial and trustworthy human being, but underneath it everything is self-protective chaos. Here are people without a core — loveless, guiltless, and wholly unreliable. As Daniel Akst remarks, a psychopath will look you in the eye, smile winningly, swear from the depths of his soul to stay by your side, and simultaneously take from you everything you cherish, including your self-respect and maybe your life.[2] Afterward he will copulate promiscuously, sleep soundly, and awaken refreshed and ready for a new day of challenges and opportunities.

Observation of the psychopathic phenomenon reminds us that the lack of a sense of guilt is both dangerous and deviant. People without an active conscience and a capacity for remorse threaten the general population like a speeding car without brake linings. They

1. See, e.g., Irwin G. Sarason and Barbara R. Sarason, *Abnormal Psychology: The Problem of Maladaptive Behavior*, 6th ed. (Englewood Cliffs, N.J.: Prentice Hall, 1989), pp. 244-46, 257-63. Though "antisocial personality disorder," "sociopathy," and "psychopathy" are often used as rough synonyms, it is helpful to think of the first as broader than the second and third (which are more genuinely synonymous). Thus, antisocial personality disorder is a disturbance characterized by chronically manipulative, dishonest, and disloyal behavior, whereas psychopathy (or sociopathy) is antisocial personality disorder marked by lovelessness and general guiltlessness. Hervey Cleckley provides the classic description of the psychopath in *The Mask of Sanity*, 5th ed. (St. Louis: C. V. Mosby, 1976). Significantly, Cleckley's eight-point syndrome of the disorder starts with "superficial charm and good intelligence."

2. Akst, *Wonderboy Barry Minkow: The Kid Who Swindled Wall Street* (New York: Scribner's, 1990), pp. 4, 270-71.

might do anything; they might end up anywhere. Besides jail, one place they regularly end up is in the section of abnormal psychology textbooks that describes personality disorders. The reason is pretty basic: healthy people feel guilty when they know they have done wrong just as they feel pain when they grasp a hot pan handle. Psychopaths do not. In fact, they "know they have done wrong" only disinterestedly, only in the same way that they know they have rented a Chevrolet while someone else has rented a Ford. That is why they are disordered, and that is why we find them alarming.

But we find them alarming only when we understand who they are and what they have been doing. Until then, until the mask of sanity slips, psychopaths flash their killer smiles and make their way through the lives of other human beings, charming them out of their clothing, their marriages, their money, and their sense of security.

To do its worst, evil needs to look its best. Evil has to spend a lot on makeup. Hypocrites have to spend time polishing their act and polishing their image. "Hypocrisy is an homage that vice pays to virtue." Vices have to masquerade as virtues — lust as love, thinly veiled sadism as military discipline, envy as righteous indignation, domestic tyranny as parental concern. And this is so whether the masquerade takes the form of putting on an act or making up a cover story. Either way, deceivers learn how to *present* something falsely, and they exert themselves to make the presentation credible. Even Satan, who looks heroic to rebels, must masquerade "as an angel of light" (2 Cor. 11:14) in order to look merely plausible. This infernal embarrassment (Satan must appeal to our God-given appetite for goodness in order to win his way) suggests a significant feature of evil: to prevail, evil must leech not only power and intelligence from goodness but also its credibility. From counterfeit money to phony airliner parts to the trustworthy look on the face of a con artist, evil appears in disguise. Hence its treacherousness. Hence the need for the Holy Spirit's gift of discernment. Hence the sheer difficulty, at times, of distinguishing what is good from what is evil.

Not surprisingly, then, as M. Scott Peck keeps pointing out in *The People of the Lie*, evil people (and he has in mind people of overwhelming moral and emotional pathology) try to keep up appearances. They seek at least the form of godliness, if not its substance. They are "acutely sensitive to social norms and what others might think of them." Hence the constant attempt to explain, justify, rationalize, and scapegoat evil. These people do not want to be good people, but they do want to appear to be good people. "This is why they are 'the people of the lie.'"[3]

The heart of personal evil, in Peck's view, is not so much the usual run of wayward thoughts, cutting words, and damaging acts. Nor is it the absence of a sense of sin: not all evil people are conscienceless psychopaths. The heart of sin is rather the persistent refusal to *tolerate* a sense of sin, to take responsibility for one's sin, to live with the sorrowful knowledge of it and to pursue the painful way of repentance. Evil people are simultaneously aware of their evil and desperately trying to resist that awareness.[4]

A Public Resistance Movement

Remarkably, some main players in American public life have lately been fighting on the side of the resistance movement. Public high school teachers, for example, used to show students something of the moral drama of the universe. They wanted students to know good and evil, to describe the wars between them, and to judge the outcome of the wars. Most of these teachers took it for granted that good and evil could be known and that, with guidance and persistence, students could know them — perhaps by studying *Macbeth,* for instance, or the history and setting of the Civil War. Didn't Shakespeare show us how deeply murder stains everybody around it, including the murderer? In his Second Inaugural Address, didn't President Lincoln show us how to reject gloating, how to seek "charity for all," and, especially, how to think of suffering as expiatory?[5]

3. Peck, *People of the Lie: The Hope for Healing Human Evil* (New York: Simon & Schuster, 1983), p. 75.

4. Peck, *People of the Lie*, p. 76.

5. See Garry F. Wills, *Under God: Religion and American Politics* (New York: Simon & Schuster, 1990), pp. 217-18.

Fondly do we hope — fervently do we pray — that this mighty scourge of war may speedily pass away. Yet, if God will that it continue, until all the wealth piled by the bond-man's two hundred and fifty years of unrequited toil shall be sunk, and until every drop of blood drawn with the lash, shall be paid by another drawn with the sword, as was said three thousand years ago, so still it must be said, "the judgments of the Lord are true and righteous altogether."[6]

As admirers of Lincoln, as heirs and custodians of the broad spiritual tradition he expressed, public school teachers used to undertake not merely to transmit knowledge and skills but also to refine the character and sharpen the judgment of students, to make them deeper people and better citizens, and to do so by using national heroes as models. Teachers saw moral education as part of their job description.

Nowadays, "moralizing" is a dirty word in public education, and the consensus on what constitutes good and evil has contracted: for a regnant educational elite, moral tolerance is now the only good, and moral intolerance the only evil.[7] In the kingdom of the elite, classroom wars between good and evil thin down to angry border skirmishes between the politically correct and the politically challenged. The politically challenged are, of course, those doofuses who still use short words when they talk — words like *good, bad, right,* and *wrong.* The politically correct, on the other hand, prefer more leisurely and ironic expressions. To be sure, the politically correct (e.g., those who describe a lazy person as "motivationally dispossessed" and prostitutes as "sex care providers")[8] are still willing to make moral judgments — but only of those who make moral

6. *Abraham Lincoln: Speeches and Writings, 1859-1865,* ed. Don F. Fehrenbacher (Washington: Library of America, 1989), p. 687.

7. See Charles L. Glenn and Joshua Glenn, "Schooling for Virtue," a review of William Kilpatrick's *Why Johnny Can't Tell Right from Wrong,* and of Edward A. Wynne and Kevin Ryan's *Reclaiming Our Schools,* in *First Things,* August/September 1993, pp. 45-46.

8. Henry Beard and Christopher Cerf, *The Official Politically Correct Dictionary and Handbook* (New York: Villard, 1992), pp. 82, 87.

judgments. They say things like this: "It is always wrong to make moral judgments."[9]

Contemporary politicians, too, miss opportunities where the acknowledgment of wrongdoing is concerned. Let us acknowledge straightforwardly that many politicians faithfully serve the public good and that cynicism about these people is just as destructive as anything the cynics charge them with. Still, it remains true that public servants seldom confess that they have done wrong. Do they regard public contrition as a sign of character weakness? Do they see it as politically lethal? Do they in fact view themselves as impeccable? Whatever the reason for their reluctance, scandalized public officials rarely say, "I did wrong. I'm heartily ashamed of myself. I have betrayed you and disgraced my high office, and I therefore resign."

No, that's not the drill these days. Of course, it's not as if public servants avoid the confessional altogether. Tarred by scandal, they will confess to being misunderstood. They will confess to being victimized by the media. They will confess the sins of other public servants. They will also humbly confess to being victims of their own virtues, as when President Nixon claimed that in the Watergate scandal he had used his heart, not his head, and had tried to do what he thought was "best for the nation." He then resigned, he said, as a "personal sacrifice."

In late 1992, sixteen women charged a U.S. senator with flagrant sexual harassment. The senator's response was typical and revealing. He first denied the charges outright. He then attacked the credibility of his accusers. Next, he issued an extraordinary apology. Faced with charges that for years he had been kissing and groping his staff members, sometimes standing on their feet while attempting to remove their clothing — faced with such charges from sixteen women, the senator declared that he had never intended "to make anyone feel uncomfortable." Still, he advised the media that he would

9. Mary Midgley, *Can't We Make Moral Judgments?* (New York: St. Martin's Press, 1991), p. x. Midgley wrote her book in response to an earnest student who stood up in philosophy class and said, "But surely it is always wrong to make moral judgments!"

"seek professional help to see if his alleged behavior was related to his use of alcohol."[10]

Here is an apology of major, almost metaphysical, elusiveness. According to the senator, nothing happened, but in any case he meant no harm by it, and, regardless, he might have been loaded at the time and so missed the significance of the nonevent in question. To a sober observer, all this is a little hard to follow. (The senator's apology brings to mind a time Winston Churchill sent a pudding back to the kitchen, complaining that it lacked a *theme*.)

Educators and wayward politicians have been missing the seminars on sin. Even some preachers in contemporary American culture sidestep the acknowledgment of sin, at least where traditionally recognized forms of it are concerned. Some of them resort to euphemism ("I'd just like to just share that we need to target holiness as a growth area") and some to psychological sin-substitutes. For instance, Robert Schuller's book *Self-Esteem* (modestly subtitled *The New Reformation*) defines sin as anything that robs people of their self-esteem. Sin, according to Schuller, is "psychological self-abuse with all of its consequences."[11]

A number of preachers dispense altogether with the confession of sin. Perhaps they think people already know they are sinners and needn't be reminded. Or maybe these preachers have gained a reputation for putting a high shine on people's self-esteem and see public confession of sin as a smear on this reputation. Or perhaps they want to attract secularist seekers and assume that such frank and traditional acts as confessing sin will seem gauche, painful, and generally off-putting to them.

Avoidance behavior in the sin department has begun to appear even in Calvinist precincts. In this way Calvinists (Robert Schuller

---

10. *Newsweek*, 7 December 1992, p. 28.

11. Schuller, *Self-Esteem: The New Reformation* (Waco: Word Books, 1982), pp. 14, 99. Schuller helpfully adds that hell is "the loss of pride that naturally follows separation from God." Not surprisingly, salvation is the move from psychological self-abuse to self-esteem (p. 99). Lest we worry that such a conflation of salvation with self-esteem might tempt people to give in to self-centeredness, Schuller offers a remarkable reassurance: "The Cross will sanctify your ego trip," he says, just as it did for Jesus (pp. 74, 75).

is a minister of the Reformed Church in America) have been neglecting one of their specialties. Surely it is extraordinary for Calvinists to lose a traditional sense of sin. What if the French forgot how to cook or the Italians how to sing? Calvinists have long been regarded (*honored* would put it too strongly) as some of the world's experts on sin. Doesn't the Heidelberg Catechism go so far as to describe us as "born sinners"? Isn't the Calvinist doctrine of total depravity the one Christian doctrine that can be *proved?*

No doubt a good historian of culture could account for contemporary slippage in the acknowledgment of sin. Perhaps she would observe that teachers, preachers, and politicians reflect as well as shape general cultural trends where sin is concerned. Perhaps our historian would point, for example, to academic acceptance of sociological and psychological determinism, according to which we lack morally significant freedom: if we are not free, we cannot be guilty of abuse of our freedom. Or perhaps she would mention, on the other side of campus, the cultural residue of those existentialist doctrines of human freedom according to which we are so awesomely free that we constantly reinvent ourselves by our choices. Each time I make a choice I am, in effect, a new person. (This fact could come in handy when it comes time to pay back a loan, for clearly it was some other person — an earlier one — who promised to repay, and I am responsible only for *my* debts.) Either way, determined or radically free, I am off the hook.

Maybe our cultural historian would also speak of cultural hedonism and hedonist resistance to moral brakes and curbs. Likely she would add some comments on moral relativism and subjectivism: if no moral borders are objectively fixed, either culturally or personally, then the biblical concepts of transgression and shortcoming fade away. If moral lines keep moving, how will people know when they have overstepped a line or fallen short of one?

Still, modern people clearly know where *some* lines are drawn. Most contemporary North American people know, for example, that date rape, sexual harassment, child abuse, racism, ecological attack and neglect, and gay bashing are all out of line. Remarkably, people who take a casual attitude toward, say, pornography, tax evasion, or mockery of religion can at the same time show a fierce (even legalist) opposition to sexism, racism, self-righteousness, and air pollution (especially by cigarette smoke). Such people resist moral judgment and rebuke of traditionally recognized sins — the seven deadly sins, for example — at the same time that they try commendably to sharpen our awareness of ecological violence and of such anti-egalitarian sins as sexism.[12]

So what we now have in some of the elite precincts of contemporary North American culture is a simultaneous evasion of the big, old understandings of sin and a heightening awareness of a number of newer ones. We also have large pockets of anti-egalitarian traditionalists who resist the heightening of their awareness: they think society, church, and private life were better ordered in the old days when Asian-Americans didn't cluster at the top of first-year classes at Harvard and Stanford; when if you handed a bag to a uniformed African-American at the airport you could assume he was a porter, not a pilot; when women in church quietly accepted their subordination to men; and when companies that wanted to rearrange the landscape didn't first have to go to the trouble of submitting an environmental impact study.

12. Mary Midgley observes how difficult it is for modern moralists to reject traditionally objectivist moral judgments and standards while reserving the right to criticize those sins that are currently unfashionable (*Can't We Make Moral Judgments?* especially pp. 71-103). Such people often jumble together relativism (roughly, the view that moral judgments, like fashions and manners, are validated by and limited to the culture that generates or adopts them) and subjectivism (roughly, the view that moral judgments are validated by and limited to the particular person who generates or adopts them), even though the two positions are jarringly incompatible and each by itself breeds remarkable paradoxes. In particular, the modern moralist who in her heart really (and rightly) thinks that sexism is just plain wrong is also committed to a jumbled theoretical position in which she can say only, on her relativist side, that this sin is "wrong for *them*" (referring to some culture) or, on her subjectivist side, "wrong for *her*" (referring to some person). Given this theoretical position, how can she consistently try to influence sexists to reform? What is she to make of cross-cultural clashes between sexists and gender egalitarians in some culture other than her own? (After all, according to her premise, sexism in a sexist culture is "right for them," and egalitarianism in an egalitarian culture is "right for *them*.") Whose side shall she take? Indeed, what entitles her, as an outsider, to any judgment whatsoever on these matters?

Self-Swindling

But whether it is older or newer understandings of sin we resist, and however preachers, teachers, and politicians may assist us in the resistance movement, each of us possesses one last defense against the knowledge of sin — a defense so strong, supple, mysterious, and private that even veteran sinners cannot track its ways.

Self-deception is a shadowy phenomenon by which we pull the wool over some part of our own psyche. We put a move on ourselves. We deny, suppress, or minimize what we know to be true. We assert, adorn, and elevate what we know to be false. We prettify ugly realities and sell ourselves the prettified versions. Thus a liar might transform "I tell a lot of lies to shore up my pride" to "Occasionally, I finesse the truth in order to spare other people's feelings." We become our own dupes, playing the role of both perpetrator and victim. We know the truth — and yet we do not know it, because we persuade ourselves of its opposite.[13] We actually *forget* that certain things are wrong and that we have done them. To the extent that we are self-deceived, we occupy a twilight zone in which we make up reality as we go along, a twilight zone in which the shortest distance between two points is a labyrinth.

13. Several of these modest-looking claims conceal questions and problems beyond the scope of this study. One of the claims is noticeably paradoxical: "We know the truth — and yet we do not know it." Is that even logically possible? It all depends on how we translate informal claims of this kind. Take the case of a father (call him Smith) who knows that his daughter accepts cash and luxurious gifts from each of a sequence of men with whom she has sex. Suppose Smith knows p: My daughter is a prostitute. But suppose he keeps telling himself b: My daughter just has lots of generous boyfriends with whom she keeps eccentric visiting hours. Smith rightly takes b to be the denial of p — which is, indeed, why he tries to persuade himself of b. In sum, he knows p, but gets himself to believe b. The right description of this state of affairs is not, strictly speaking, that Smith both knows and doesn't know p. That, at any given time t, is indeed impossible: the proposition *Smith knows p at t* cannot be both true and false. The right analysis is rather that at t Smith both knows p and also believes b. In other words, Smith holds inconsistent views of his daughter. For the base of this analysis and a helpful introduction to the philosophical literature and issues in the area of self-deception, see Bruce S. Alton, "The Morality of Self-Deception," *Annual of the Society of Christian Ethics* N.S. 5 (1984): 123-55.

In a book on the psychology of self-deception entitled *Vital Lies, Simple Truths,* Daniel Goleman tells the story of John Dean, President Nixon's counsel and a central figure in the Watergate scandal. Dean's testimony before the Senate Watergate Committee was lengthy, articulate, and remarkably detailed. Dean amazed committee members with his ability to remember precisely who said what, to remember it verbatim, and to do this after many intervening months.

The trouble was that when the Watergate tapes were pried loose from Nixon and played for the committee, Dean's testimony turned out to be mostly "wishful memory." Like many of us who keep aging, Dean had remembered a lot of stuff that hadn't happened. Not surprisingly, most of his mistakes and distortions of recall had the effect of placing him in a much more favorable light than the one in which he actually stood. His testimony turned out to have described not the critical presidential meetings themselves but Dean's fantasy of those meetings — the way he dreamed they went. And Goleman adds that Dean's memory conversion may have proceeded at largely a subconscious level.[14]

The same is true for others. Do Mafia wives, for example, *work* at achieving a virtuoso level of self-deception?[15] The godfather's wife doesn't seem to know where his money comes from and somehow doesn't ask. She doesn't ask why his chauffeur looks like a piece of heavy farm machinery with sunglasses. She doesn't ask why the FBI never stakes out other houses in her neighborhood. She doesn't dwell on the fact that she routinely places a lot of intriguing oddities in the Do Not Ask file.

14. Goleman, *Vital Lies, Simple Truths: The Psychology of Self-Deception* (New York: Simon & Schuster, 1985), p. 95. Whether and to what degree self-deception is conscious and intentional and the relevance of judgments on this matter to the morality of self-deception are parts of the philosophical debate described by Alton in "The Morality of Self-Deception," especially p. 136.

15. Or do they perhaps work at sustaining ignorance? Willed ignorance, as Calvin P. Van Reken has pointed out to me, falls short of and remains distinct from self-deception. Willed ignorance is the deliberate avoidance of truth and of avenues to it. Self-deception is manipulation (by minimizing, say, or outright denial) of truth already known. Of course, if we successfully suppress or deny a truth, it becomes a fresh candidate for willed ignorance.

Self-deception is "corrupted consciousness," says Lewis Smedes. Whether fear, passion, weariness, or even faith prompts it, self-deception, like a skillful computer fraud, doubles back to cover its own trail. "First we deceive ourselves, and then we convince ourselves that we are not deceiving ourselves."[16]

A moment's reflection reminds us that self-deception has long been a growth industry. Why do alcoholics and other drug abusers typically go through years of denial? Why is the revelation of incest an astonishment to people who are living right in the middle of it? How did reigning Nazis convince themselves that their killing programs served the best interests even of their victims? Why do battering husbands offer minimizing and euphemistic accounts of the beatings they administer, and why do battered wives sometimes accept and repeat those accounts?

Not even encounter groups that have been designed for candor and self-discovery can insulate themselves against such self-swindling. "Surely there are few moments," Stephen Crites remarks, "more ripe for self-deception than those in which people are puffing and straining to be honest."[17] Or, significantly, those in which people are puffing and straining to be religious.

Nothing, said Martin Buber, hides the face of our fellowman more than morality, and nothing hides the face of God more than religion.[18] When we are most religious, we may be most at risk of losing touch with God. The corruption of the best is the worst. Certainly religious beliefs and practices may illuminate the face of God, just as people intend. Confessing sin and giving thanks to God, reading Scripture, celebrating sacraments, giving money for the relief of suffering, preaching and listening to sermons, fighting injustice, caring for animals as a deliberate act of stewardship, singing hymns of praise, educating children to revere Jesus Christ as king of the whole creation — such practices and the beliefs that sponsor them tie us to the living God in such a way that, by repeating these

16. Smedes, *A Pretty Good Person* (San Francisco: Harper & Row, 1990), p. 74.

17. Crites, "The Aesthetics of Self-Deception," *Soundings* 62 (1979): 111.

18. Buber, *Between Man and Man* (New York: Macmillan, 1965), p. 18.

practices and rehearsing these beliefs, we may come to know God more keenly, to love God more deeply, and to serve God more efficiently. Honest religious practice thus builds spiritual momentum: "To those who have, more will be given" (Mark 4:25).

But not nearly all religious practice is honest. Evil perverts religion as well as everything else that is vital and momentous. When it does, religious beliefs and practices may mutate into a self-serving substitute for the service of God. People start to use their religion to get rich or to get happy or to feel good about themselves. They use it to build a power base or simply to secure and enrich a middle-class life. Some versions of popular Protestantism look as if they could go right on, long after Christianity has been forgotten. We believers are entirely capable of using mutant religion to conceal from ourselves the character of God; we are entirely capable of using our religion to *oppose* the project of God in the world.

Part of the hazard in such an undertaking is that there is every possibility that nobody will warn us about the mistake we're making. People find religious perversions hard to track. Religious people are often slow to judge a movement that carries a cross or repeats the name of the Lord. And, of course, every con artist who chooses religion as his vehicle depends on this fact.

In a trio of penetrating works, Merold Westphal ponders the difference between the truth of religion and the *use* of religion.[19] Trouble lies on both sides of the difference. For one thing, it is not only secularists who "suppress the truth" about God. This famous Pauline characterization of sinners in Romans 1:18 — the characterization that Calvin develops memorably at the start of his *Institutes of the Christian Religion* — indicts believers as well. After all, how many believers really believe in *God,* as opposed to some deified image of themselves? How many, for example, really do attend to the countercultural images of God in Scripture — the ones that

---

19. Merold Westphal, "Taking Suspicion Seriously: The Religious Uses of Modern Atheism," *Faith and Philosophy* 4 (1987): 26-42; "Taking St. Paul Seriously: Sin as an Epistemological Category," in *Christian Philosophy,* ed. Thomas P. Flint (Notre Dame, Ind.: University of Notre Dame Press, 1990), pp. 200-226; and *Suspicion and Faith: The Religious Uses of Modern Atheism* (Grand Rapids: William B. Eerdmans, 1993).

judge and condemn as well as the ones that affirm and comfort? How many of us would rather fashion God in our own image so that God's pleasures and peeves will merge conveniently with our own? Believers, not just secularists, exchange "the glory of the immortal God for images resembling a mortal human being" (Rom. 1:23).[20]

Why else do new revised versions of God keep appearing? Why else does God emerge as racist, sexist, chauvinist, politically correct, legalist, socialist, capitalist? If we are intellectuals, God is a cosmic Phi Beta Kappa; if we are laborers, God is a union organizer (remember, his Son was a carpenter); if we are entrepreneurs, God is for free enterprise (didn't his Son say, "I must be about my father's *business*"?); if we are poor, God is a revolutionary; if we are propertied, God is nightwatchman over our goods. The gods of the Persians always look like Persians. "Unbelief is not the only way of suppressing the truth about God," says Westphal. "It is only the most honest."[21]

Corrupt and self-serving uses of religion naturally follow false ideas of religion and of religion's God. A racist God presides over racist religion. An American God sponsors the kind of red, white, and blue religion that recites the Pledge of Allegiance to the Flag at patriotic Sunday worship. A politically correct God cares much more for the lives of seals and snail darters than for the lives of unborn children: to slay the latter is your personal and legal right; to slay the former is unforgivable speciesism.[22]

Corrupt and self-serving uses of religion naturally follow false ideas of religion and of religion's God, but, alarmingly, they may also follow true ones. For example, Christians have often used the sternness of the law of God to hamstring and scorn the lives of others, and the loveliness of the grace of God to exculpate and adorn their own. Picking and choosing from the testaments of Scripture, Chris-

20. See Westphal, "Taking St. Paul Seriously," pp. 202, 213-14.
21. Westphal, "Taking St. Paul Seriously," p. 214.
22. Robert P. George has noted that at an early stage a fetus is phenotypically equivalent to a snail darter, and he wonders whether pro-life advocates ought therefore to concentrate their energies on appealing to the federal law that protects snail darters ("Where Babies Come From," *First Things*, October 1990, p. 12).

tians have walled off the liberties of others (to prevent libertinism) while making plenty of allowances for themselves (to promote Christian freedom). Preachers have used sermons to humiliate enemies and to justify friends, to construct ecclesiastical fiefdoms, to vent personal prejudices, and to gratify childish desires to be the center of attention. Christians have used benevolent donations to elicit the gratitude of others, and then used their gratitude to control them. Even those dark Christians who despair of their sins and shortcomings may become "fiercely aware" of this despair and curious as to its merit.[23] As Helmut Thielecke somewhere observes, every mature Christian knows that even when we are at worship the wolves may be howling in our souls.

Merold Westphal suggests that Marx, Nietzsche, and Freud, the three main architects of the "atheism of suspicion" in the modern age, have much to teach us about the corrupt uses of religion — even of true religion.[24] Haven't believers sometimes used their religion to defend and even to enforce the exploitation of others? Recall that in the nineteenth century, Christians in the American South devised an elaborate justification of slavery, complete with proof texts from the Bible. Recall that in the gilded age, Northern churches preached the gospel of wealth, complete with an economic Darwinism, and expressed an almost savage opposition to the nation's young labor movement — and this in a time of twelve-hour work days, sweatshops, and child labor.[25] Doesn't our "love of economic liberty" sometimes look a lot like greed and our "hunger for distributive justice" a lot like envy? Do we never honor the power of God in a way that domesticates it or turns it to our own purposes?

Perhaps we ought to notice, says Westphal, that the critique of "useful religion" by the atheists of suspicion sounds a lot like what

23. See Geoffrey W. Bromiley, "Sin," in *The International Standard Bible Encyclopedia*, vol. 4, ed. Geoffrey W. Bromiley (Grand Rapids: William B. Eerdmans, 1988), p. 522.

24. Westphal, *Suspicion and Faith*, pp. 13, 16-17.

25. See *Slavery Defended: The Views of the Old South*, ed. Eric L. McKitrick (Englewood Cliffs, N.J.: Prentice Hall, 1963); and Winthrop S. Hudson, *Religion in America: An Historical Account of the Development of American Religious Life* (New York: Scribner's, 1965), pp. 305, 309.

the biblical prophets and Jesus had to say. He advises that before we seek to score points against the genetic fallacies and ad hominem arguments of modern atheists, before we "turn suspicion against the suspicious," perhaps we ought to adopt *self*-suspicion "as the hermeneutics of Lent." We ought to consider the possibility that in our own religion, "what presents itself as an altruistic virtue may be, in terms of motive and function, only an egoistic vice dressed up in its Sunday-go-to-meetin' clothes."[26]

Just because religion emerges from the depths of our existence, just because it possesses such enormous power to express our purposes and longings, just because it focuses our very worship, the evil that clings to our religion can corrupt us to the core. Religious sin shows us sin "in its full range and possibility," remarks Geoffrey Bromiley. Hence the strength of Jesus' opposition to the Pharisees:

> The inward corruption to which Jesus refers in the scathing denunciation in Mt. 23 is not the corruption of deliberate and calculated insincerity. It is the corruption of a sincere and sincerely practiced religion, which is ultimately a supreme manifestation of religious pride. . . . The frightening picture opened up here is that when one recognizes obvious sin one has hardly begun to reckon seriously with this adversary. The open and blatant sinner, the oppressor or the harlot, is indeed a sinner. But it is not here that the genuine depth of sin is revealed, not even if the oppressor be ever so grasping or the harlot ever so shameless. It is in religious persons that the depths are to be seen.[27]

How striking it is, says Joseph Butler, that we make ourselves strangers to ourselves. We blunt our own conscience, darken our own judgment by self-interest, and rebuke in others the very vices for which we are famous. Each of us carries around a "deep and calm source of delusion, which undermines the whole principle of good."[28]

---

26. Westphal, "Taking Suspicion Seriously," pp. 34, 37.

27. Bromiley, "Sin," p. 522.

28. Butler, "Upon Self-Deceit," in *Fifteen Sermons Preached at the Rolls Chapel and a Dissertation upon the Nature of Virtue,* ed. W. R. Matthews (London: G. Bell, 1914), p. 163.

Yes and no. The drafting of cover stories, the refusal to inquire into our motives, the filing of our own lies under the heading of finesse, the phony understandings and uses of religion — all these moves do corrupt. As Butler contends, they introduce falseness into the heart of our lives. At the same time, they testify to our almost desperate desire to keep up appearances, even within our own psyche. We want to keep up at least our *image* of the image of God. We want to keep up the masquerade even within our own hearts. Remarkably, the phenomenon of self-deception testifies that we human beings, even when we do evil, are incorrigibly sold on goodness. At some level of our being we know that goodness is as plausible and original as God, and that, in the history of the human race, goodness is older than sin.

CHAPTER 7

Sin and Folly

Fear and love must always go together; always fear, always love, to your dying day.

John Henry Cardinal Newman

For Thee all the follies of sin I resign.

William R. Featherstone,
"My Jesus I Love Thee"

Reports of murders in the newspapers and on television often use the adjective *senseless*. Observers use the term to describe not only drive-by homicides and the methodical shooting of strangers by a crazed killer in a fast-food restaurant but also the first-degree murder of a businesswoman by her greedy partner and the enraged slaying of a wife by her jealous husband. The term also routinely shows up in descriptions of murders committed in the course of robberies and rapes. We keep reading and hearing observers say — of almost any murder — that it was "a senseless slaying," "a senseless act," an example of the "senseless violence" that keeps threatening society.

But why *senseless*, particularly? After all, unless the killer was grossly impaired, the killing probably made sense to *him*. He was trying to silence a witness or gain revenge or express his power or act out his racist hatred or stimulate and satisfy his lust. In a culture in which up-to-date intellectuals often drift toward moral subjectivism, how can an act that makes perfectly good sense to its perpetrator be judged senseless by outsiders? The outsiders cannot mean that the act was irrational in the sense that it lacked a motive. Are they saying, then, that the act was unintelligent? That it lacked alertness, say, or foresight? Are they suggesting that the killer stupidly miscalculated the odds of getting away with murder?

Not likely. The truth is that, when pressed, even the most avant-garde observer drops his moral subjectivism, forgets all Nietzschean attempts to get "beyond good and evil," and joins the rest of us in expressing shock, indignation, and the metaphysical judgment that a murder *does not belong in the world*, no matter what its author thinks of it. The murder of a human being is not the way it's supposed to be. This act is out of order. It is a senseless act because it saws against the grain of the universe, because, as Christian believers would say, it doesn't fit the design for shalom.

Senseless is only one word people use to express this conviction. Haven't we all noticed that people who prefer not to judge or confess sin will nonetheless concede that some objectionable act was stupid, tragic, shortsighted, mistaken, unfortunate, miscalculated, erring, regrettable, or out of line? Suppose a white-collar criminal, for example, confesses to a "lapse in judgment" or "inappropriate behavior" after cheating thousands of retirees out of their life savings. Despite the ludicrous and cowardly nature of his euphemism, the criminal has nonetheless admitted that he was wrong in an important way: he has admitted that he was out of order, out of line — that he was, in a word, *foolish*. He will not concede that he has been a knave, but he feels obliged to concede, in effect, that he has been a fool.

By so doing, ironically enough, he enters a mainstream of biblical thought, and a route to the biblical concept of sin. For biblical writers think of sin as the main species of folly. Indeed, if a person confesses folly, and then admits that she is to blame for her folly, she has as good as confessed her sin. A person who calls her theft of two packages of AA batteries from a supermarket checkout display "inappropriate" or a "lapse in judgment" puts us in position to reflect not only on folly but also on the nature of sin, and then to deepen our understanding of both by exploring the relationship between them. That, in fact, is the agenda for this chapter.

To follow it, we should try to get a sense for the biblical concept of wisdom, contrast it with the notion of folly, and conclude with some observations about the foolishness of sin.

Fitting into the World

In the literature of Scripture, wisdom is, broadly speaking, the knowledge of God's world and the knack of fitting oneself into it. The wise person knows creation. She knows its boundaries and limits, understands its laws and rhythms, discerns its times and seasons, respects its great dynamics.[1] She understands that creation possesses its own integrity and significance quite apart from her claim on it and quite apart from any possibility that creation will make her happy. The wise person *gives in* to creation and to God — and she does the first because she does the second. She knows that the earth is the Lord's, and so is its fullness. She knows that wisdom itself is the Lord's, and so is its fullness.[2] She knows some of the deep grains and textures of the world because she knows some of the ways and habits of its maker.[3]

In the biblical view, the wise are righteous and the righteous are wise: these are people who love and fear God, affirm God's world, live gladly within its borders, and make music there according to divine time and key signatures. The wise are always "in order."[4] Insofar as they live right, they also live well. The book of Proverbs usually doesn't even bother to distinguish between righteousness and wisdom: it pairs up

1. See Gerhard von Rad, *Wisdom in Israel,* trans. James D. Martin (Nashville: Abingdon Press, 1984), especially pp. 74-176; Raymond C. Van Leeuwen, "Enjoying Creation — within Limits," in *The Midas Trap,* ed. David Neff (Wheaton, Ill.: Victor Books, 1990), pp. 23-40; and "Liminality and Worldview in Proverbs 1–9," *Semeia* 50 (1990): 111-44.

2. Proverbs 8:22-36 pictures wisdom as God's blueprint for creation and also personifies her as mediator of creation.

3. Von Rad, *Wisdom in Israel,* p. 67.

4. Von Rad, *Wisdom in Israel,* p. 79.

righteousness with wisdom and wickedness with folly in such a way that the distinction between a moral judgment and a prudential judgment fades.[5] In Scripture more generally, the standard for judging the course of a human life includes a blend of morality, prudence, metaphysics, and religion. Thus the Scripture writers exhort but they also instruct. As Frederick Buechner once pointed out,

> the Bible is not first of all a book of moral truth. I would call it instead a book of truth about the way life is. Those strange old scriptures present life as having been ordered in a certain way, with certain laws as inextricably built into it as the law of gravity is built into the physical universe. When Jesus says that whoever would save his life will lose it and whoever loses his life will save it, surely he is not making a statement about how, morally speaking, life *ought* to be. Rather, he is making a statement about how life *is*.[6]

Wisdom is a reality-based phenomenon. To be wise is to know reality, to *discern* it. A discerning person notices things, attends to things, picks up on things. She notices the difference between tolerance and forgiveness, for example, and between pleasure and joy, and between sentimentality and compassion. She can spot real humility and keep it distinct in her mind from its thinner cousin, unpretentiousness. (Consider the ambiguity of the assertion "He's a humble man," which might mean either that the man virtuously sees others as his equals or that he leads a lowly life and never pretends otherwise.)

Discernment is a mark of wisdom: it shows a kind of attentive respect for reality. The discerning person notices the differences between things but also the connections between them.[7] She knows creation — what God has put together and what God has kept asunder — and can therefore spot the fractures and alloys introduced

5. Raymond C. Van Leeuwen makes this point in an unpublished essay entitled "Proverbs" (1991), pp. 1-2.

6. Buechner, "The Two Loves," in *The Hungering Dark* (New York: Seabury Press, 1981), pp. 85-86.

7. See Lewis B. Smedes, *A Pretty Good Person* (San Francisco: Harper & Row, 1990), p. 123.

by human violation of it. She knows, for instance, the way a particular sort of request can contaminate a friendship. The discerning person, moreover, possesses an eye for the details and oddities of reality — the anxieties, for example, that sometimes lie behind overbred chit-chat, name-dropping, and the overuse of foreign phrases at dinner parties. She knows that kindness sometimes coexists with stupidity and integrity with humorlessness. She knows that people full of shadows may also be full of a light that causes them. In such and other respects, Lewis Smedes remarks, "a discerning person has the makings of a connoisseur."[8]

But such "cognitive discernment," as Smedes calls it, isn't enough. The really discerning person, the one whose discernment marks genuine wisdom, does not merely inspect reality or analyze it: the one who discerns also loves. She possesses what Jonathan Edwards called "benevolence to being in general."[9] At some level, she *affirms* the reality she knows and even commits herself to it. Just as the knowledge of God in the theology of Calvin includes active engagement with God (what students of Calvin call *ac*knowledgment of God, or existential knowledge of God),[10] so knowledge of God's creation requires the commitment of the knower.

To discern realities at their deeper levels, we have to become engaged to them. The deeply discerning person brings empathy and care to what she knows. Discernment of the hopes and fears of other persons, for example, depends on compassion for them; knowledge of these persons comes into us only if our hearts go out to them. Only so, Smedes remarks, could Steinbeck have written as he did of Ma Joad or of Rose of Sharon in *The Grapes of Wrath*. Only so can we see behind the status of divorce or homosexuality to discover complex persons who possess gifts greater than their troubles, gifts unseen by the unloving.[11]

8. Smedes, *A Pretty Good Person*, p. 124.

9. Edwards, *The Nature of True Virtue* (Ann Arbor: University of Michigan Press, 1960), p. 3.

10. See Nicholas Wolterstorff, *Until Justice and Peace Embrace* (Grand Rapids: William B. Eerdmans, 1983), p. 13; and Edward A. Dowey Jr., *The Knowledge of God in Calvin's Theology* (New York: Columbia University Press, 1952), p. 26.

11. Smedes, *A Pretty Good Person*, pp. 133-36.

To be wise is to know and affirm reality, to discern it, and then to speak and act accordingly. The wise *accommodate* themselves to reality. They go with the flow. They tear along the perforated line. They attempt their harvests in season. Ordinary people proceed with such a program no matter whether they have derived their wisdom from Scripture or from more general revelation. From Proverbs or from genuine attention to the life played out before them or even from their grandmother, the wise eventually learn and then accommodate themselves to such truths as the following:

- The more you talk, the less people listen.
- If your word is no good, people will not trust you, and it is then useless to protest this fact.
- Trying to cure distress with the same thing that caused it only makes matters worse.
- If you refuse to work hard and take pains, you are unlikely to do much of any consequence.
- Boasting of your accomplishments does not make people admire them. Boasting is vain in both senses of the word.
- Envy of fat cats does not make them slimmer and in the end will rot your bones.
- If you scratch certain itches, they just itch more.
- Many valuable things, including happiness and deep sleep, come to us only if we do not try hard for them.

Against the Grain

In a famous incident, the World Health Organization once tried to help residents of Borneo exterminate houseflies, which were widely suspected of spreading disease there. Officials sprayed the insides of houses with large quantities of DDT, an action that triggered an unforeseen and nearly disastrous sequence of events. As the flies died, local gecko lizards (their natural predator) feasted on the fly corpses and sickened from the DDT concentrated in them. Their sick condition made the geckos easy prey for house cats, who ate their fill of the DDT-poisoned geckos and likewise sickened and died. The loss of the cats gave rats free run of people's houses. When the rats began to devour house food and to threaten people with serious disease — in particular, with bubonic plague — panicky government officials scrambled for solutions. At last they resorted to *feles ex machina:* they arranged for large numbers of foreign cats to be parachuted into the area in order to mend the break in the food chain![12]

If wisdom is knowledge of God's world and the knack of fitting oneself into it, then, predictably, folly is contrariness or destitution in these areas — a kind of witlessness with respect to the world and a tendency either to bang one's shins and scrape one's elbows on it or else to miss its opportunities and waste its gifts.

Many but not all instances of folly count as sin. Suppose a person unthinkingly places a subway ad that reads, ILLITERATE? WRITE TODAY FOR FREE HELP! Suppose, in one of his speeches, a politician says with an air of significance, "Things are more like they are now than they have ever been." Small campaign bloopers, playful nonsense, inadvertent puns ("Grandmother of Eight Makes Hole in One"), portentously delivered commonplaces or confusions, and other such gentle mischief scarcely qualify as evil, let alone as sin. These small follies do not disturb shalom; some of them may even contribute to it.

We find such follies amusing, not blameworthy. Even such industrial-strength folly as the food chain foul-up in Borneo may have been wholly innocent, at least the first time. Common sense tells us that a lot of things human beings do are loopy but not sinful, and that the right response to those things is a guffaw, not a rebuke. Common sense also tells us that some things human beings do are *both* loopy and sinful (a bank robber, responding to a teller's inspired request, fills in a withdrawal slip with his real name and address) and that the right response is amazement.

In the kingdom of folly we find a whole circus of wonders — carelessness, for example, and other attention deficit disorders. We find discernment deficits. In a familiar lapse of discernment, certain contemporary fiction (Josephine Hart's novel *Damage* is a good example) adolescently conflates love, romance, and sexual obsession

---

12. Paul and Anne Ehrlich, *Extinction: The Causes and Consequences of the Disappearance of Species* (New York: Random House, 1981), p. 79.

as if they were all the same thing. We find poor judgment. Consider middle-aged parents who want to become chums with their teenage children or who try to buy their children's love. Consider parents who sense some deficiency in themselves and try to get their children to fill it. Whether in peer popularity or athletics or money-making or intellectual achievement, parents who have come short of their own expectations often double them for their children. Then, when children resist, these parents feel wounded.

Of course, poor judgment may handicap the learned as well as the ignorant. Some of us have met people who can speak three or four languages but cannot say anything sensible in any of them, including their own. There is no contradiction, said C. S. Lewis, in being a Master of Arts and a fool.[13] The reason is that intelligence and education are only raw materials for good judgment. The same is true of knowledge, attentiveness, and discernment. Using them, a person must also estimate, appraise, and infer. She must conclude, choose, and act — all in a way that is firmly based in reality and relatively undistorted by personal whim and bias.

Folly includes poor judgment, lack of discernment, inattentiveness. These deficiencies may be innocent or partly innocent: perhaps God distributes common sense and alertness as gifts, and distributes them as unequally as physical agility and good looks. Perhaps common sense and alertness can also, to some degree, be taught by family members and teachers. Indeed, writers in Scripture sometimes talk as if wisdom is a gift and sometimes as if it is an acquired discipline.[14] No doubt, in either case people vary widely in their mere access to it.

But they also vary widely in their *attitude* toward wisdom. Some attend to a parent's teaching and some ignore it. Some listen with interest to the Word of God, and some scoff at it. Some welcome

13. Lewis, *Mere Christianity*, paperback ed. (New York: Macmillan, 1960), p. 10.

14. E.g., 1 Kings 3:5-15; Prov. 2:6; and 2 Pet. 3:15 speak of wisdom as a gift, whereas Prov. 1:2-7 (the prologue to the book) says that wisdom is to be taught and learned. Of course these ways of looking at wisdom need not be incompatible: the wisdom a teachable child gains from an attentive parent may be both given and learned. Moreover, a person may possess a large capacity for wisdom as a native gift but then have to work hard to fulfill this capacity.

criticism and seek to learn from it; others automatically assume that every criticism is unjust or even irrelevant.

These facts lead us to consider another: while some folly is relatively innocent and some pretty funny, a good deal of it is neither. Teachers and preachers who would rather be fashionable than faithful; parents who prefabricate a child's life in order to fulfill their own dreams; undiscerning Christians who prefer comfort to compassion, who cannot be bothered to look at human trouble and cannot be provoked to feel it because they have closed the door to their hearts — some of these folk have involved themselves in culpable folly.

As this last example suggests, the foolish gain their status not only by what they do but also by what they fail to do. Carelessness concerning one's health, neglect of one's marriage or children, obliviousness to one's calling, disregard of one's faults, and other inattentions to duty and opportunity belong in the large class of follies of omission. Naturally enough, because wisdom is essentially a practical matter — less a body of knowledge than a way of applying it, less a fine art than a knack — the follies of omission often take the form of simple failure to "follow through." People know what's right, but simply don't do it — like all those well-educated libertines who have become AIDS encyclopedias without ever practicing either chastity or "safe" sex.[15]

The Main Event

The shortest and clearest way to state the relation between sin and folly is to say that not all folly is sin, but all sin is folly. Sin is both wrong and dumb. Indeed, wherever the follies are playing, sin is the main event. Sin is the world's most impressive *example* of folly.

What is it about sin that makes it so foolish? Sin is the wrong recipe for good health; sin is the wrong gasoline to put in the tank; sin is the wrong road to take in order to get home. In other words, sin is finally futile.

15. See Katie Leishman, "Heterosexuals and AIDS: The Second Stage of the Epidemic," *Atlantic Monthly*, February 1987, p. 45.

Pride, for example, is futile because self-fascination is so often unrequited. Moreover, pride is subject to the tolerance effect, the law of diminishing returns: the more self-absorbed we are, the less there is to find absorbing. Commenting on some themes in Ernest Becker's *Denial of Death,* Robert C. Roberts adds that the pride project in human life — the attempt to become our own first cause — is carried on by people who are riven with the knowledge that though they may be gods, transcendent above the rest of creation, they are also worms and food for worms. We live with "the dreadful contradiction lying drugged and groggy in our bosoms: the need to be heroes and the fact of being worms."[16]

What's more, we try to resolve this contradiction by adopting another: we try to exalt ourselves by meeting other people's standards of acceptability. What would be the point of doing thunderous slam dunks or of performing rock songs if everybody just yawned? Our godness (being known, admired, envied) depends on the standards and opinions of people just as riven as we are. "Stars" are really only moons, says Roberts, drawing upon and reflecting the light of others.

> Apart from the values which we breathe cozily in our social environment, our behavior and our self-esteem would suffocate, and our psychological identity would expire. Anyone who opens his eyes will see how contradictory is the project of divine self-creation on the basis of what other people think; and yet this is what we do. Few of us are in a position to make ourselves as obviously absurd as King Elvis, but in our "humbler" ways our project is the same.[17]

Hybris is the first and most popular form of idolatry. But all forms of idolatry involve us deeply in folly. All idolatry is not only treacherous but also futile. Human desire, deep and restless and seemingly unfulfillable, keeps stuffing itself with finite goods, but these cannot satisfy. If we try to fill our hearts with anything besides the God of the universe, we find that we are overfed but under-

16. Roberts, "The Transparency of Faith," *Reformed Journal,* June 1979, p. 12.
17. Roberts, "The Transparency of Faith," p. 12.

nourished, and we find that day by day, week by week, year after year, we are thinning down to a mere outline of a human being.

Sad to say, this kind of thing happens all the time. People hungry for love, people who want to "connect," will often open up a sequence of shallow, self-seeking relationships with other shallow, self-seeking persons and find that at the end of the day they are emptier than when they began. The whole project has been as idle and dehumanizing as the conversations on those dating-and-mating TV programs that explore the sump level of lubriciousness. Beneath all their surface liveliness, the sadness of these programs is that they reduce their participants to mere leering silhouettes.

Sin is futile and therefore foolish. Georges Bernanos's country priest remarks that Satan has involved himself in a hopeless program of swimming against the stream of the universe, of "wearing himself out in absurd, terrifying attempts to reconstruct in the opposite direction the whole work of the Creator."[18] Thus, while moral evil is destructive, and sometimes infuriating, it is also in some ways ludicrous. *Mere Christianity*, says C. S. Lewis, commits us to believing that "the Devil is (in the long run) an ass."[19]

Sin is folly. No matter what images they choose, the Bible writers say this again and again. Sin is missing the target; sin is choosing the *wrong* target. Sin is wandering from the path or rebelling against someone too strong for us or neglecting a good inheritance. Above all, at its core, sin is offense against God.

Why is it not only wrong but also foolish to offend God? God is our final good, our maker and savior, the one in whom alone our restless hearts come to rest.[20] To rebel against God is to saw off the branch that supports us. As Richard Lovelace remarks, to flee from God to some far country and to search for fulfillment there is to find only "black-market substitutes":[21] instead of joy, the buzz in

18. Bernanos, *The Diary of a Country Priest*, trans. Pamela Morris (London: John Lane, 1937), p. 81.

19. Lewis, *A Preface to Paradise Lost* (New York: Oxford University Press, 1961), p. 95.

20. Augustine, *Confessions* 1.1.

21. Richard Lovelace, *Renewal as a Way of Life: A Guidebook for Spiritual Growth* (Downers Grove, Ill.: InterVarsity Press, 1985), p. 36.

your temples from four or five martinis; instead of self-giving love, sex with strangers; instead of a parent's unconditional enthusiasm for you as a person, only the professional support of a fashionable therapist who will indeed pump up your ego whenever it loses pressure but only while his meter is running. Rebellion against God and flight from God remove us from the sphere of blessing, cutting us off from our only invisible means of support.

Thus sin dissipates us in futile — and self-destructive — projects. Sin hurts other people and grieves God, but it also corrodes *us*. Sin is a form of self-abuse. Promiscuous persons, for example, coarsen themselves. They disqualify themselves for the deepest forms of intimacy, the ones bonded by trust, and "condemn themselves to social superficiality," as one of my friends once put it. Something similar is true of liars and cheats. As Christopher Lasch remarks, "Whoever cheats his neighbor forfeits his neighbor's trust, imprisons himself behind a wall of enmity and suspicion, and thus cuts himself off from his fellows."[22] Envy — the displeasure at another's good and the urge to deprive her of it — traps and torments the envier, turning her life into a hell of resentment. Proud persons isolate themselves. Pride aborts the very possibility of real friendship or communion — namely, "benevolence toward being in general."

More basically, pride amounts to a kind of phantom wisdom. Pride renders fools unteachable. They know it all. You can't tell them anything. They are "wise in their own eyes" — a sure sign of folly. Badly educated ministers who are both vague and dogmatic, off-key singers who insist on contending for solo parts, children of Israel who wander forty years in the wilderness because even then the men were unwilling to ask for directions, pinball enthusiasts who devote ten years of their adult lives to becoming the best player in their neighborhood tavern, rejecting every inquiry about the worthwhileness of this project with the remark that the inquirer must be envious — these and other standouts from the ranks of the foolish display one of human life's most wondrous combinations: a stubborn com-

22. Lasch, *The True and Only Heaven: Progress and Its Critics* (New York: W. W. Norton, 1991), p. 268. Lasch is here characterizing the central theme of Emerson's essay "Compensation."

bination of ignorance and arrogance. The foolish, as the saying goes, are often in error but never in doubt. Moreover, when their dogmatism is challenged, they increase it. Some of them give you a piece of their mind they can hardly afford to lose.

Willfulness of this kind causes the foolish a good deal of misery and also prevents their escape from it. For to escape from a foolish line of thought or a destructive course of action, a person has to stop, admit he is wrong, turn around, head back to safe ground, and then try a new route. As C. S. Lewis once said, when we have gotten a wrong sum at the beginning of a sequence of calculations, we cannot improve matters "by simply *going on.*"[23]

A proud person tries to reinvent reality. He tries to redraw the borders of human behavior to suit himself, displacing God as the Lord and boundary keeper of life.[24] At bottom, the fool is out of touch with reality. For, of course, our wills are not sovereign. We are not really our own centers, anchors, or lawgivers. We have not made ourselves, cannot keep ourselves, cannot ultimately oblige or forgive ourselves. The image of ourselves as center of the world is fantasy — perhaps, in its sheer detachment from reality, even a form of madness. This is especially clear at the most ruinous levels of evil. Only a fool, Milton believed, would rise from his flaming ruins, look out across a "dismal Situation waste and wild," filled with "huge affliction and dismay," and declare: "Better to reign in Hell than serve in Heav'n."[25]

Sin corrupts. Corruption spreads and kills. Hence the note of urgency, even of desperation, in many of the biblical prophecies. The prophets rebuke sin in Israel not just because it breaks God's law but ultimately because it breaks the peace, because it breaks even the people who do it. Israel is a nation constituted, redeemed, and regulated by the acts and covenant of God. Israel depends for her very existence on her gracious benefactor. In the prophetic view, sin against God is therefore outrageous folly: it's like pulling the plug

23. Lewis, *The Great Divorce* (New York: Macmillan, 1946), p. 6.
24. See Van Leeuwen, "Liminality and Worldview in Proverbs 1–9," pp. 116-17, 121-22; and "Enjoying Creation — within Limits," p. 29.
25. Milton, *Paradise Lost* 1.57, 60, 98, 263.

on your own resuscitator. When Nathan accuses King David of selfish encroachment on gentle lives; when Micah cries out against injustice, or Hosea against idolatry; when Isaiah warns against national pride, or Amos against phony worship, the complaint is never generic and the context never abstractly legal. The complaint is always particular (e.g., "The official and the judge ask for a bribe" — Mic. 7:3) and the context always a crisis: the nation has committed itself to jackassery. It's carrying on like a damned fool and is in danger of self-destructing.[26] In this role, the prophet acts as seer and wise man. He sees that in sin the stakes are higher, the reverberations wider, and the corruption deeper than people suspect. And he tells them so, often in disagreeable ways.

Because it is futile, because it is vain, because it is unrealistic, because it spoils good things, sin is a prime form of folly. And, of course, folly has its fashions. This, indeed, is one of the reasons folly is so foolish. It's just as foolish to have fashions in folly as to have them in burps or in cockroaches. Predictably, fashions in folly reflect the characteristic sins of the age — in our own case, impatience, hedonism, narcissism, flight from accountability, and the deifying of the self and its choices. "Corrupted modernity" chafes under restraint and accountability, says Thomas C. Oden: it displays a kind of "adolescent refusal of parenting."[27] If we know the characteristic sins of the age, we can guess its foolish and fashionable assumptions — that morality is simply a matter of personal taste, that all silences need to be filled up with human chatter or background music, that 760 percent of the American people are victims,[28] that it is better to feel

---

26. See Claus Westermann, *What Does the Old Testament Say about God?* ed. Friedemann W. Golka, trans. Julian Grinsted and Friedemann W. Golka (Atlanta: John Knox Press, 1979), p. 57.

27. Oden, *Agenda for Theology: After Modernity, What?* (Grand Rapids: Zondervan, 1990), p. 50.

28. John Leo has observed that a lot of Americans qualify for victim status in multiple ways: they are victims of AIDS, the press, rock music or pornography, warped upbringing, anti-nerd bias, public hostility toward smokers, addiction, patriarchy, being black, being white, belonging to male bonding groups that beat drums in the woods, and so on ("A 'Victim' Census for Our Time," *U.S. News and World Report*, 23 November 1992, p. 22).

than to think, that rights are more important than responsibilities, that even for children the right to choose supersedes all other rights, that real liberty can be enjoyed without virtue, that self-reproach is for fogies, that God is a chum or even a gofer whose job is to make us rich or happy or religiously excited, that it is more satisfying to be envied than respected, that it is better for politicians and preachers to be cheerful than truthful, that Christian worship fails unless it is fun.

How do we recover from bad judgment of this kind? We have to go back to basics. A much-defeated basketball team goes back to layup and footwork drills. An out-of-shape violinist — one who can play the Praeludium of Bach's E Major unaccompanied Partita either in tune or else up to tempo, but not both — goes back to scales and arpeggios. A husband and wife who are trying to shore up their crumbling marriage may have to relearn elementary forms of courtesy to each other.

The same is true for all would-be conquerors of folly. Where unteachableness, presumption, general bad judgment, and lack of discernment are concerned, the prescription is to gain wisdom. And "the fear of the LORD is the beginning of wisdom" (Prov. 9:10). Wisdom begins with awe. As C. S. Lewis knew when he characterized Aslan in *The Lion, the Witch, and the Wardrobe,* God is good, but God is not safe. God is "good and terrible at the same time."[29] That is why only a foolish person would describe a meeting with God as "fun."

God-fearing people have a dreadful love for God, an awe-filled love that knows God is not mocked, that we reap whatever we sow, that God is not to be fooled with, scorned, or ignored but trusted, loved, and obeyed. Everything wise and righteous is built on this unshakable foundation. "Fear and love must go together," said Newman; "always fear, always love, to your dying day."[30] God-fearing

29. Lewis, *The Lion, the Witch, and the Wardrobe* (New York: Scholastic Books, 1987), p. 123.

30. John Henry Cardinal Newman, "The Religion of the Day," in *Sermons and Discourses, 1825-39,* ed. Charles Frederick Harrold (New York: Longmans, Green, 1949), p. 137.

people know that God's first project in the world is not to make us happy and that we will gain happiness only after we have renounced our right to it. "For those who want to save their life will lose it, and those who lose their life for my sake, and for the sake of the gospel, will save it" (Mark 8:35). As Frederick Buechner reminds us, when Jesus says these words, he is not telling us how, morally speaking, life ought to be; he is telling us how life *is*.

CHAPTER 8

The Tragedy of Addiction

"Master, I am in great distress! The spirits that I conjured
up I cannot now get rid of."

Goethe, *The Sorcerer's Apprentice*

One respectable way to sharpen our vision of a big, messy reality
is to compare it with near neighbors. Thus, in Chapter 1 we
briefly considered the relation of sin to crime, disease, folly, and
immorality, and in Chapter 7 we took a longer look at the relation
of sin and folly. The idea, of course, is to isolate and clarify the nature
of sin by comparing and contrasting it with other realities in its
neighborhood. Naturally, any illumination of its near neighbors sheds
light on sin as well, particularly along shared borders.

Nowhere is a border survey more helpful and more needed than
it is in the case of sin and addiction. For here the borders are long,
disputed, and sometimes indiscernible. Principally, to look at addiction is to look at significant dynamics of sin. Moreover, to discuss
addiction is dramatically to raise, once more, the hard questions of
human freedom and responsibility in the assessment of human behavior. To identify these dynamics, raise these questions, and thus
to deepen our understanding of the nature of sin is the project in
this chapter. What we want to explore, most generally, is the *relationship* between sin and addiction.

The Wide World of Addiction

Addiction is a complex, progressive, injurious, and, often, disabling attachment to a substance (alcohol, heroin, barbiturates) or behavior (sex, work, gambling) in which a person compulsively seeks a change of mood. The addictor might be a good staple of life, such as food and drink, or a slimy little vice, such as voyeurism. It might be almost anything, if one defines addiction loosely enough. Indeed, addiction writers in recent decades have impressively lengthened the list of possible addictors so that it now includes not only alcohol and other drugs but also sex — and not only sex but also love and romance.[1] Also on the growing list are shopping, religion, exercise, video games, money, and going to the movies. One writer who follows the trends in fashionable dependencies cites a confession in Pittsburgh of a "sewing or fabric addiction."[2]

Leaving aside the question of how seriously to take some of the more exotic addictions, we are safe in assuming that the genesis of addictions and the number and blend within them of contributing factors (chemical, neurological, psychological, cultural, social, spiritual) vary among addictors and from one addict to another. Furthermore, addictive dependencies range along a spectrum from mild to devastating.[3] By themselves such variables guarantee the complexity of the addictive phenomenon, but in addition to this some addicts also struggle with cross-addictions and multiple addictions. Some even appear to get hooked on the cures for their addictions. (In certain cases, government methadone prescriptions are roughly as helpful to heroin addicts as school suspensions are to truants.) Recovering addicts often come to believe that their addictions, whether single or grouped, whether predominantly

1. See Anne Wilson Schaef, *Escape from Intimacy: The Pseudo-Relationship Addictions* (San Francisco: Harper & Row, 1989), p. 3.

2. Scott McKenzie, "Addiction as an Unauthentic Form of Spiritual Presence," *Studies in Formative Spirituality* 12 (1991): 325.

3. See Stanton Peele, *The Meaning of Addiction: Compulsive Experience and Its Interpretation* (Lexington, Mass.: Lexington Books, 1985), p. 2; and Archibald D. Hart, "Addicted to Pleasure," *Christianity Today*, 9 December 1988, p. 40.

chemical or psychological, include a spiritual dimension that can only be called "demonic."[4]

No matter how they start, addictions eventually center in distress and in the self-defeating choice of an agent to relieve the distress. In fact, trying to cure distress with the same thing that caused it is typically the mechanism that closes the trap on an addict — a trap that, as just suggested, might be baited with anything from whiskey to wool.

But what moves an addict to the bait? At every stage, addiction is driven by one of the most powerful, mysterious, and vital forces of human existence. What drives addiction is longing — a longing not just of brain, belly, or loins but finally of the heart.[5]

Because they are human beings, addicts long for wholeness, for fulfillment, and for the final good that believers call God. Like all idolatries, addiction taps this vital spiritual force and draws off its energies to objects and processes that drain the addict instead of filling him. Accordingly, the addict longs not for God but for transcendence, not for joy but only for pleasure — and sometimes for mere escape from pain.[6] Some therapists believe that addicts can get high even on the vapors of guilt or, less simply, that desire, pleasure, guilt feelings, and a Nietzschean will to power sometimes run together into a high-octane blend that fuels addiction.[7]

4. People in treatment centers often describe crack cocaine simply as "the Devil" (William J. Bennett, "Drugs and the Face of Evil," *First Things,* December 1990, p. 6).

5. See Gerald G. May, *Addiction and Grace* (San Francisco: Harper & Row, 1988), p. 3. In *The Song of the Lark* (Cambridge, Mass.: Riverside Press, 1915), Willa Cather tells of one of those Nebraska spring mornings that are filled with the "sudden, treacherous softness which makes the Poles who work in the packing-houses get drunk. At such times beauty is necessary, and in Packingtown there is no place to get it except at the saloons, where one can buy for a few hours the illusion of comfort, hope, love — whatever one most longs for" (p. 249).

6. Even then the addict may have to settle for far less. Roger E. Meyer observes that although a "hedonistic rationale" lies behind a lot of alcohol and other drug abuse, "most chronic intoxications are marked by increasing depression, anxiety, and belligerence." Of course, given that alcohol is a central nervous system depressant, alcoholic dysphoria is partly predictable (*Psychopathology and Addictive Disorders,* ed. Roger E. Meyer [New York: Guilford Press, 1986], p. 10).

7. See William Lenters, *The Freedom We Crave — Addiction: The Human Condition* (Grand Rapids: William B. Eerdmans, 1985), pp. 15-17.

In any case, addiction taps into longing the way a blackmailer might garnish your wages. Every time you meet a demand, it escalates. Every time you recover self-respect, the will to love, or any other vital resource, it gets sapped away by this parasite.

Of course, people who are attached to cigarettes or to one cocktail at the end of every workday may not recognize themselves as players in such a drama. Some persons use, or even abuse, such substances as alcohol without becoming dependent on them. Some persons develop mild dependencies but not full-blown addictions. In some cases, genuine addictions can remain, at least for a time, at a minor-league level.

But to a big-league addict, addiction feels not only parasitical but also wily and perverse. It feels demonically alive, as if not just something but some*one* were trying to lure, hook, and land him — someone who first successfully tempts him and then accuses him of weakness for having succumbed. As the "Big Book" of Alcoholics Anonymous says, addiction is "cunning, baffling, powerful, and patient,"[8] a victor over every ordinary attempt to conquer it, a demon that rushes to fill vacuums, a dismissed shadow that keeps threatening to return. Thus, an addict who repeatedly makes and then breaks contracts with himself; who finds his longings narrowing and hardening into an obsession with things he knows will devastate his work, self-respect, relationships, and bank account and who yet seeks compulsively to satisfy those longings; who thus finds his will split between wanting to banish an addictive substance from the earth and wanting to protect his private cache of it; whose addiction, as it moves through mild and moderate stages, first enthralls him in one sense of the word and then in the other — an addict like this often comes to believe that his "struggle is not against enemies of blood and flesh, but against . . . spiritual forces of evil" (Eph. 6:12).

What follows is that treatments, like areas of addiction research, must typically be multilevel. Accordingly, a psychiatrist might ini-

---

8. Anne Wilson Schaef's characterization of the message of *Alcoholics Anonymous: The Story of How Many Thousands of Men and Women Have Recovered from Alcoholism* (New York: Works Publishing, 1950) in her *Escape from Intimacy,* pp. 25-26.

tially take a medical approach to an alcoholic addiction, then a psychological approach, and then a family-systems approach. Following Alcoholics Anonymous, she may all along attempt as well to help her patient regain a measure of spiritual hygiene. If she is a Christian, she may also undertake or propose ministries of prayer, healing, or, in extraordinary cases, even of exorcism.[9]

The Deadly Spiral

In 1983, Patrick Carnes published a pioneering book about sexual addiction that tells us as much about addiction in general as it does about sexual addiction in particular.[10] In his book, Carnes describes people caught in a cycle of delusion ("Sex is my most important need"), obsession (hours-long waits in a voyeur's blind for a seconds-long glimpse of nudity), and ritual behavior ("special routines" favored by voyeurs, molesters, and flashers). These pleasure-seeking behaviors, once indulged, leave the addict with a residue of despair. Predictably, what traps him, what converts him from a mere delinquent into an addict, is that he tries to relieve the despair by indulging his obsession all over again, thereby initiating a new round of addiction.

Carnes notes that sexual addicts often experience a tolerance effect. Whatever comforts they find in pornography, for instance, eventually pale. So the addict graduates to the hands-on experience of nontherapeutic massage and perhaps then to surreptitious, and clearly illegal, groping of strangers on crowded buses or subway trains. The escalating risk of these adventures enhances the addict's mood change, the "high" he seeks, and thus compensates for the tolerance effect.

9. See M. Scott Peck, *People of the Lie: The Hope for Healing Human Evil* (New York: Simon & Schuster, 1983), pp. 182-211.

10. Carnes, *Out of the Shadows: Understanding Sexual Addiction* (Minneapolis: Compcare, 1983). For introducing me to this and other addiction literature and for general instruction in the area, I owe a debt to my colleague and friend Melvin D. Hugen.

Of course, addicts try, often desperately, to manage their problem. They reproach themselves, confess their sins to God, make and break resolutions, set ever new dates for one last fling. They struggle to deal with the depressing accompaniments of their secret life — lies, deceptions, scapegoating, alternating rage and self-pity, isolation, fear of discovery, the loss of real intimacy with loved ones. But all this is uphill work, in part because the spiritual forces arrayed against an addict include various temptations that society approves and displays. A heavy gambler, for instance, may discover that his state government and even his local church have a game they would like him to play. An alcoholic who turns a magazine page may face a gin advertisement that has been crafted by an excellent mind. Similarly, a sex addict who views a TV newscast may meet a segment that seemingly has been shaped and shot as much to titillate as to inform. Typically, nobody in these settings protects or disabuses the vulnerable. Nobody plays the role of country priest, warning the addict that pleasure often masks anguish.[11] The result is that under such circumstances the addict, who desperately needs to deny himself in order to survive, may feel surrounded. How can he prevail against all these foes who pop up everywhere and who seemingly share scouting reports of his weaknesses?

In general, the addict must make his way in a culture that presumes everybody's fundamental right to gratify at least five of his senses and that discourages self-denial as foolish or even impious. For the self is a sacred object.[12]

Yet, the same culture that encourages self-indulgence also punishes the indulgent with scorn fit for a failed god. This is another demonic dimension of addiction. As Gerald May has observed, the addict's repeated failures of self-mastery devastate his self-esteem in part because he lives in a culture that teaches him that we are our

11. "The mask of pleasure, stripped of all hypocrisy, is that of anguish," writes Georges Bernanos (*The Diary of a Country Priest*, trans. Pamela Morris [London: John Lane, 1937], p. 136).

12. Cf. Robert C. Roberts: in a therapeutic culture, "we have been led to feel that the self is sacrosanct: just as in an earlier time it was thought never fitting to deny God, so now it seems never right to deny oneself" (*Taking the Word to Heart* [Grand Rapids: William B. Eerdmans, 1993], p. 304).

own creators.[13] A person who has succumbed to an addiction thus imagines a derisive question coming at him from his culture: What kind of moron creates but cannot control himself? (What kind of carmaker cannot drive his own product?)

When her attempts at self-management fail, as they usually do, and when her self-esteem plummets, as it always does, the addict feels compelled to seek solace in her obsessive behavior, and thus cycles down one more level. In this way, addictions flourish by feeding on human attempts to master them.[14]

According to Carnes, the sex addict's secret life may eventually get exposed in a way that is dramatic enough to nudge him forcefully toward full disclosure. The exposure event is thus a severe mercy, a potent bearer of shame and grace. "A moment comes for every addict," says Carnes, when

- The squad car pulls into your driveway and you know why they've come.
- Your teenage son finds your pornography.
- You have a car accident while exposing yourself.
- The money you spent on the last prostitute equals the amount for the new shoes your child needs.[15]

What now? An addict stands a chance of recovery only if he is finally willing to tell himself the truth. The only way out of the addict's plight is *through* it. He has to face it, deal with it, confess it. With the firm and caring support of people important to him, he has to rip his way through all the tissues of denial and self-deception that have "protected his supply." The addict has to take a hard step, the first of the famous twelve steps. Paradoxically, he must help himself by admitting that he is helpless. He must perform the courageous, difficult, and highly responsible act of acknowledging the hopelessness and wholesale unmanageability of his life. The addict must abandon "the uncanny game of hide-and-seek in the

13. May, *Addiction and Grace*, p. 42.
14. May, *Addiction and Grace*, p. 42.
15. Carnes, *Out of the Shadows*, pp. v-vi.

obscurity of the soul in which it, the single human soul, evades itself, avoids itself, hides from itself."[16] Only then is the way open for his return to a tolerably healthy life — a return that is likely to take time, vigilance, and the support of a number of other human beings, some of them professionals.

Carnes has much else of interest to say, including observations about the role of family systems in dependency and codependency, about the addict's awareness that his behavior pattern is perverse (a three-hour wait for twenty seconds of nudity is "insane even to the voyeur"), and about multiple and typically paired addictions (sex and food, gambling and alcohol).[17] But Carnes is clear from the outset that the behaviors of addicts are not chosen: "For the addict there is no choice. . . . The addiction is in charge." Sex addicts "have no control over their sexual behavior."[18]

Sin or Symptom?

Here the inevitable question arises. In his accounts of peepings, flashings, and uninvited fondlings, isn't Carnes actually describing *sin* — and, as a matter of fact, some pretty sleazy examples of it? When people habitually pay prostitutes to talk dirty to them on the telephone and then, once a month, guard their telephone bill from prying eyes; when they prowl public rest rooms, hunting for anonymous sex; when they sacrifice the happiness of their children in order to indulge private sexual preoccupations that are increasingly dangerous, time-consuming, and expensive — when they do these things, why not simply call the whole works sin? Why import the language of addiction, the kind of language that makes a john look like a victim?

These questions bring us to the main issue: What really is the relationship between sin and addiction?

16. Martin Buber, *Images of Good and Evil*, trans. Michael Bullock (London: Routledge & Kegan Paul, 1952), p. 54.
17. Carnes, *Out of the Shadows*, pp. 63-85, 87-113, 40, 59-61.
18. Carnes, *Out of the Shadows*, p. ix.

In trying to define it, we may begin by simply noting that addictions often do include morally wrong thoughts, words, and deeds. No serious person, Christian or otherwise, wants to defend self-destructive drug abuse, for instance, or incestuous fantasizing, or habitual lying to oneself and others. These acts wreck shalom, at least for the addict and usually for a number of others who get entangled in the addict's web. These acts are plainly wrong whether or not they fit into an addictive process, and people therefore ought not to do them.

But the question before us is whether these things, when they *do* fit into a pattern of addiction, are sin — that is, whether the persons who do them are culpable, whether they deserve blame and reproach, whether the solution to the problems their behavior raises is repentance or therapy or both.

Carnes says that sexual addicts lack choice, that "the addiction is in charge." But this is by no means a settled conclusion of expert observers (Gerald May, e.g., appears to demur) and would, in any case, be an extraordinarily hard conclusion to back with evidence. How does Carnes know that addicts can't help it? Given self-deception as ingredient in the addictive process, addicts themselves may not be the best witnesses on this topic. And who else *could* be an authoritative witness? Few of us, after all, can gauge the potent and subtle workings of will and choice even in ourselves, let alone in others. What we can see in addicts is a pattern of destructive delusion, obsession, and behavior. What we cannot see is the extent to which a person has control, the extent to which a person chooses her poison, and the degree to which her poisonous choices have been determined by various outside factors.[19]

Is an addict a person who has a bad habit of making sinful choices? Or is an addict the victim of biological and social forces she

---

19. *Pharmikon*, the Greek word from which we get "pharmacy," "pharmaceuticals," etc., means both "remedy" and "poison." When distressed, people choose remedies that are also poisons. It is in this sense that James G. Williams suggests that *pharmikon* is an appropriate metaphor for our whole drug-dispensing and drug-abusing culture (*The Bible, Violence, and the Sacred: Liberation from the Myth of Sanctioned Violence* [San Francisco: Harper, 1991], p. 248).

may resist but is ultimately powerless to overcome? Or is an addict a person who habitually makes bad choices because of such forces or who awakens such forces by making bad choices? Are some addictions, like some neuroses, in effect the addict's self-condemnation and self-sentence for bad behavior?[20] Are certain alcoholics, for example, busy with the undeclared project of drowning not just their sorrows but also their guilt? Or are addicts shortcut artists — people who want gratification "without effort, pain, or labor"?[21]

Of course, even if an addict does ultimately lack the power to choose and to act contrary to the tug of his addiction, he may still bear responsibility for the moral evil he does, and this evil might therefore count as sin. Perhaps he addicted himself. Perhaps he misbehaved at a time when he *did* have the power to choose and act well. If he is like other human beings, his habit has a prehistory of choices and acts. The habit that binds him is a part of the chain of his own acts. Perhaps he made himself an alcoholic, for example, by self-indulgently drinking too much for too many years. In short, to be physically and psychologically hooked on some substance or behavior pattern is not necessarily to be let off the hook morally. (Being high on crack cocaine is typically no excuse for running down pedestrians with your motorcycle.) Involuntary sin, as we saw in Chapter 1, may still be sin.

We are further and maybe more significantly responsible for what we do with our addictions once we have them — whether we seek help for them, for example, whether we wear them as merit badges (certain subcultures admire men who can hold a lot of liquor), or whether we use one addiction as an excuse for another. In any case, addicts who are serious about recovery must at some point take responsibility for the wreckage that surrounds their addiction and for the salvage work that now needs to start.

20. On neurosis as a self-imposed affliction, see O. Hobart Mowrer, "Psychopathology and the Problem of Guilt, Confession, and Expiation," in *Counseling and the Human Predicament: A Study of Sin, Guilt, and Forgiveness,* ed. LeRoy Aden and David G. Benner (Grand Rapids: Baker Book House, 1989), p. 82.

21. Adrian Van Kaam, "Addiction: Counterfeit of Religious Presence," *Studies in Formative Spirituality* 8 (1987): 251.

Suppose we assume that sinful behavior sometimes triggers the addictive process, or emerges from it, or both.[22] Addictions do typically include patterns of moral evil, after all. No doubt these moral evils are sometimes sin. Lying, gluttonous eating and drinking, beating up one's spouse while blaming her for provoking the beating, and engaging in the sexual rituals Carnes describes are prima facie sins. They are immoral acts that are, for all we know, chargeable to those who do them.

Still, none of us knows the degree to which other human beings bear responsibility for their behavior, the degree to which they "could have helped it." That is one important difference between us and God. So even if, for the purposes of discussion, we call an addict's immoral acts sin, we do so only provisionally. Perhaps, if we had all the facts, we might downgrade some of these acts to the more general status of moral evils. Indeed, when one observes the rifts and scars of children whose parents took turns slapping, deriding, ignoring, bullying, or, sometimes worse, simply abandoning them; when one observes the wholesale life mismanagement of grown-ups who have lived for years in the shadow of their bereft childhood and who have attempted with one addictor after another to relieve their distress and to fill those empty places where love should have settled, only to discover that their addictor keeps enlarging the very void it was meant to fill[23] — when one knows people of this kind and observes their largely predictable character pathology, one hesitates to call all this chaos sin. The label sounds smug and impertinent.

In such cases, we want to appeal to some broader category, perhaps the category of tragedy. Like the fallenness of the human race, the chaos of addiction comes out of particular human character and sin but also out of the temptations and disorganizing

22. Lawrence J. Hatterer asserts something similar in psychological terms: "Character defects (dishonesty, manipulation, blaming others, insatiability, irresponsibility, grandiosity, etc.) can provoke the [addictive] process or emerge from it" (*Encyclopedia of Psychology*, ed. Raymond J. Corsini [New York: John Wiley, 1984], s.v. "Addictive Process").

23. See Dan Wakefield, *Returning* (Garden City, N.Y.: Doubleday, 1988), p. 200.

forces resident in an addict's home and neighborhood and maybe even in her genes. The serpent is both within and without.[24] Family habits, cultural expectations (e.g., *machismo*), the behavior patterns of parents, the spiritual forces generated by television advertising and rock videos, and a host of other factors combine to exert pressure on candidates for addiction. If the pressure is strong enough, a person may surrender to it and enter the deadly spiral of dependency.

To think of addiction as tragic is to focus not simply on an addict's patterns of behavior but also on the person who behaves this way. Tragedy implies the weight and worth of its central figures. Tragedy is never the fall of simple victims or villains: these falls are dramatically uninteresting and untragic. Tragedy implies the fall of someone who is responsible and significant — a person of substance, not just of substance abuse. In fact, tragedy implies the fall of someone who is naturally great but whose greatness has been compromised and finally crushed by a mix of forces, including personal agency, that work together for evil in a way that seems simultaneously surprising and predictable, preventable and inevitable. A tragic figure is, in some intricate combination, both weak and willful, both foolish and guilty. We therefore want to accuse him and also to sympathize with him. (Think, for instance, of Shakespeare's King Lear and his featherheaded demand that his daughters declare their love for him.) In tragedy, sin is surely one of the forces at work, but it is by no means the only force and sometimes not even the most obvious one.

So it is in the phenomenon of addiction. Addicts are sinners like everybody else, but they are also tragic figures whose fall is often owed to a combination of factors so numerous, complex, and elusive that only a proud and foolish therapist would propose a neat taxonomy of them. In any case, we must reject both the typically judgmental and typically permissive accounts of the relation between sin and addiction: we must say neither that all addiction is simple sin nor that it is inculpable disease. These simplicities have histori-

---

24. See Stephen J. Duffy, "Our Hearts of Darkness: Original Sin Revisited," *Theological Studies* 49 (1988): 615.

cally been attached by turns to alcoholism, for example, but neither seems at all adequate.[25]

Remarkably enough, at the end of the day it might not matter very much how we classify the damaging behaviors of addicts. Whether these behaviors amount to sin or symptom, the prescription for dealing with them may turn out to be just about the same. Nobody is more insistent than A.A. that alcoholism is a disease; nobody is more insistent than A.A. on the need for the alcoholic to take full responsibility for his disease and to deal with it in brutal candor.[26] Moreover, nobody is more insistent that the addict must admit helplessness and therefore surrender his life to God or a "higher power." The idea is that those who surrender shall be free — or, at least, free for today.

People often notice that the twelve steps look like phases in the Christian program of renewal. You admit powerlessness, give yourself over to God, confess wrongdoing, make amends, seek growth in grace, and then witness to others. Through every phase, you consciously depend on the will and power of God.[27]

But nowadays new voices — proponents of Rational Recovery, for instance, and certain feminists — are asking the old questions about the paradoxical character of this program. How can a new surrender help the old one? If dependency was the problem, how can it also be the solution?

Charlotte Davis Kasl speaks for those feminists who suggest that the twelve steps of recovery programs have traditionally been stated in

25. See Herbert Fingarette, *Heavy Drinking: The Myth of Alcoholism as a Disease* (Berkeley and Los Angeles: University of California Press, 1988), p. 111; and Peele, *The Meaning of Addiction*, pp. 28-45.

26. I am indebted to Duane Kelderman for making this point clear to me.

27. The resemblance of the Twelve Steps to a basic Christian program of renewal is no coincidence. At its inception, Alcoholics Anonymous was much influenced by the "Oxford Group" of Frank Buchman, a Lutheran minister and college chaplain who identified himself consciously with the evangelism of Dwight L. Moody and who talked of "stages" in moving to a changed life. Toning down "Jesus saves" to, in effect, "Something saves," substituting "a Power greater than ourselves" and "God as we understand him" for God *simpliciter*, and changing the accent from guilt to failure, A.A. broadened and secularized Buchman's stages into twelve steps of common grace. For details of the linkage between the Oxford Group and A.A., see Ernest Kurtz, *A.A.: The Story* (San Francisco: Harper & Row, 1988), pp. 48-52.

a way that misses the special needs of women. In particular, the twelve steps assume that recovery begins with the admission of powerlessness over an addictor and then with surrender of will and lives to the care of God. But this recipe will not work for many contemporary women, says Kasl. "The steps were formulated by a white, middle-class male in the 1930s," she says; "not surprisingly, they work to break down an overinflated ego, and put reliance on an all-powerful male God. But most women suffer from the *lack* of a healthy, aware ego, and need to strengthen their sense of self by affirming their own inner wisdom."[28]

Kasl goes on to make the general claim that if they are to find health, women must stop depending on other things and persons altogether, including God. Instead, women must "awaken the wisdom that is within" by asserting and exercising their own power to take charge of their own lives. For help in this program, women may appeal to what Kasl calls "the universe/Goddess/Great Spirit," but this is apparently a skinny being whose slight status invites little by way of trust or worship.

The feminist recoil from the twelve-step program suggests a cluster of interesting questions that deserve more attention than we can pay them at this stage of our discussion. For now, let's suppose that sin sometimes takes the complementary forms of macho pride and passive subservience, of self-idolatry and other-idolatry, of self-exaltation and self-abnegation.[29] To what degree do traditional male

28. Kasl, "The Twelve-Step Controversy," *Ms.*, November-December 1990, p. 30. See also Kasl's *Women, Sex, and Addiction: A Search for Love and Power* (San Francisco: Harper & Row, 1990) and *Many Roads, One Journey: Moving Beyond the Twelve Steps* (San Francisco: Harper & Row, 1992).

29. See Daniel L. Migliore, *Faith Seeking Understanding* (Grand Rapids: William B. Eerdmans, 1991), pp. 131-33. For an intelligent discussion of the mysterious curse of Gen. 3:16 (God says to the woman, "Your desire shall be for your husband, and he shall rule over you"), see Mary Stewart Van Leeuwen, *Gender and Grace: Love, Work and Parenting in a Changing World* (Downers Grove, Ill.: InterVarsity Press, 1990), pp. 42-48. Van Leeuwen proposes an intriguing interpretive possibility: perhaps the fall subverted main dimensions of the image of God in gender-relevant ways. Perhaps men tend to convert proper dominion to sinful domination, while women tend to convert proper sociability to social enmeshment. In short, men tend to dominate, and women tend to let them do it. Both therefore need the full and glad mutuality that Jesus Christ came to champion and to model.

and female gender roles express these forms? Accordingly, to what degree must Christians take their audience into consideration when preaching humility? Who needs to hear this sermon? Big people or little people? Those who strut or those who slouch? Men or women? And how about the empowerment message of Scripture — the "I can do all things" and "You are more than conquerors" message. Who needs to hear *this* sermon? Flourishing chief executive officers? Or those harassed folk whose tenderest hopes keep getting shredded and tossed back at them like confetti?

Unhappily, though Kasl raises a vital question — namely, whether over- and underinflated egos may need prescriptions that are properly adjusted for inflation — her own analysis of the predicament of addicted women and her advice to them based on this analysis seem hardly less peculiar than the tradition she rejects. One peculiarity is that although Kasl thinks women tend to suffer from powerlessness, she does not want them to say so. She does not want them to begin their recovery by admitting bondage to some addictor. Why not? Apparently because such an admission would simply reinforce the general feeling of powerlessness from which women suffer. So Kasl recommends self-assertion instead — the "I can" as substitute for the "I can't." What women need is self-help and self-affirmation, she says, with no reliance on "something external" to lift or restore them.

And here we have a second peculiarity. How realistic is this revised program? After all, as Kasl readily observes, independent and overinflated males are just as likely to get addicted as women. Hence an obvious question: If independence has not worked for men, why is it likely to work for women?

Perhaps Kasl would reply that men suffer from a surplus of independence and women from a deficit so that, in the interests of a balance of trade, men need to lose independence and women to gain it. Fair enough. Still, if the goal of women's therapy is something in between male aloofness and female enmeshment — a nicely balanced ego that is neither macho nor minnow — the move toward restoration of this balance is going to take strength. The assertion of sound and sacred personhood will take courage. Where are these blessings to come from? To tap the self as their source is to write a check on the same account that Kasl says has been overdrawn.

Kasl and other feminists may have hold of a significant difference in the way that traditional gender roles play out with reference to addiction and other human troubles. But, if so — if males tend toward self-idolatry and females toward other-idolatry — then, as Mary Stewart Van Leeuwen proposes, surely the right move for both is to quit their idolatries and turn to God. But this is the move Kasl rejects in favor of total self-reliance, the very flaw A.A. was set up to combat.

In any case, for women to exchange their form of idolatry for the masculine form looks less like an improvement than like an infection caught from sleeping with the enemy.

Overlapping Circles

Given the relevant qualifications, let us say that addictions often include sin — or, putting matters the other way around, that some sin displays the addictive syndrome. Suppose we imagine sin and addiction as significantly overlapping circles. On the ends, in the quarter moons where the circles do not overlap, we have examples of addiction that include little or no actual sin by the addict himself and examples of sin that betray little of the addictive process. Cases of intrauterine addiction, for example, belong in the former category, as do any other chemical or process addictions innocently contracted — as when a clinically schizophrenic or depressed person slides into substance addiction while seeking relief from sickness. (Perhaps some addictions in these cases qualify as *physical* evils rather than as moral evils.)

In the latter category belong sins that hang around on the listless side of human life, particularly those that include little by way of mood change or a yearning for it. A person, for instance, who wholly neglects her aged parents because she finds them boring may present symptoms of sloth and filial ingratitude but not of addiction.

Sin and addiction overlap wherever sin displays the addictive syndrome, wherever sin shares with addiction certain typical dynamics.[30]

30. Generally speaking, minor-league addictions display at least a few of these dynamics, while major-league addictions display many more, or more intense forms, of them.

Dynamics of Addiction

1. Repetition of pleasurable and therefore habit-forming behavior, plus escalating tolerance and desire
2. Unpleasant aftereffects of such behavior, including withdrawal symptoms and self-reproach
3. Vows to moderate or quit, followed by relapses and attendant feelings of guilt, shame, and general distress
4. Attempts to ease this distress with new rounds of the addictive behavior (or with the first rounds of a companion addiction)
5. Deterioration of work and relationships, with accompanying cognitive disturbances, including denial, delusions, and self-deceptions, especially about the effects of the addiction, and the degree to which one is enthralled by it
6. Gradually increasing preoccupation, then obsession, with the addictor
7. Compulsivity in addictive behavior: evidence that one's will has become at least partly split, enfeebled, and enslaved
8. A tendency to draw others into the web of addiction, people who support and enable the primary addiction. These "codependents" present certain addictive patterns of their own — in particular, the simultaneous need to be needed by the addict and to control him. The codependent relationship is thus one in which primary and parasitic addictions join.

Where in the family of sins do we find displays of this syndrome? Not surprisingly, we typically find them among such appetitive sins as avarice, gluttony, and lust — the sins that exhibit some combination of exaggerated and misplaced longing. Healthy people keep a rein on their longings. Healthy people enjoy the freedom that is born of contentment (a "freedom from want"), which is, in turn, owed to a sturdy and persistent discipline of desire. Healthy people deliberately note, for instance, how many material goods they can do without and then take extra pleasure in the simple and enduring ones they possess. They make it their goal, most of the time, to eat and drink only enough to relieve hunger and thirst, not to sate themselves. They integrate their sexual desire into a committed relationship, bonded by vows and trust.

These disciplines are, of course, by no means easy to acquire or to preserve, and failures in this regard are drearily familiar to all of us. (In these respects, the discipline of desire resembles mastery of a foreign language or of a musical instrument.) But a disciplined person cuts losses and tries to contain failure. She knows the traps that lie in the shadows of failure and purposely tries to skirt them (e.g., the all-or-nothing trap, in which a dieter who has just fallen off the wagon by consuming a handful of peanuts concludes that she might as well now eat the whole can). Everybody fails. But for whatever reason, the candidate for addiction gives in to failure, seeks deadly comfort from the same kind of thing that caused the failure, and thus begins a war against herself that is likely to take a lot of skilled, compassionate, and expensive help to stop.

Unsurprisingly, given the overlap between sin and addiction, theologians report such wars just as often as therapists do. At the center of his *Confessions*, St. Augustine ponders the bondage of the will, "the violence of habit by which even the unwilling mind is dragged down and held." Scripturally, Augustine is moving among those Pauline passages (Gal. 5:17; Rom. 7:22-25) that speak of the war between flesh and spirit, the inner war we lose whenever we will what is right but do what is wrong. Experientially, Augustine is talking his long battle with lust. The fearful, inexplicable, and, finally, eerie dynamic of moral evil, he says, is that we enslave ourselves to it. As in all tragedy, the enemy is within as well as without. We know we are doing wrong, we want not to do it, and still we do it. The reason is that at some other level of our being we *do* want to do it. Giving in to that want at that level leaves a bondage we both create and resent. Each wrong choice forges a link in the chain that binds us:

> I . . . was bound not by an iron imposed by anyone else but by the iron of my own choice. The enemy had a grip on my will and so made a chain for me to hold me a prisoner. The consequence of a distorted will is passion. By servitude to passion, habit is formed, and habit to which there is no resistance becomes neces-

sity. By these links . . . connected one to another . . . a harsh bondage held me under restraint.[31]

Passages like this one from a father of the Christian church might be just as likely to appear in the confessions of a contemporary alcoholic or food addict, for Augustine's chain runs right through the dynamics of addiction. These are the dynamics of appetitive sin in particular, the kind of sin likeliest to display the classic addictive syndrome, likeliest to chain its subjects to their own sin so that they become at once its agents and victims.

But all sin shares with addiction at least a few of the dynamics on the list, as well as certain other common characteristics. For example, even when they do not display the full addictive syndrome, many forms of sin include patterns of self-seeking, childish impatience with delayed gratification, and refusal to accept reasonable limits on behavior. In addition, sin, like addiction, tends to split and bind the will, to work itself into a habit of the heart, and to hide itself under layers of self-deception. Moreover, people often commit sins in order to relieve distress caused by other sins. Hence the familiar spiral shape of certain patterns of sin.

In these and many other ways, addiction extends a tradition familiar to all of us, including all of us who would never dream of calling ourselves addicts. In important respects, "the addiction experience is the human experience,"[32] since we all "have a habit" where sin is concerned. Addiction shows us how the habit works, where it goes, and why it persists. In fact, we might think of addiction as a lab demonstration of the great law of returns, the law of longing and acting and the forming of habits that lead to renewed longing.

Addiction is a dramatic portrait of some main dynamics of sin, a stage show of warped longings, split wills, encumbered liberties, and perverse attacks on one's own well-being — some of the same dramatic machinery that moves the general tragedy of sin forward. Addiction shows us, once more, the progressive and lethal character

31. Augustine, *Confessions* 8.5.10-11.
32. Lenters, *The Freedom We Crave*, p. 4.

of moral evil, the movement of corruption that Patrick McCormick calls "a conversion unto death."[33]

For addicts this conversion begins and ends in an act of surrender — first to appetitive failure and then, in recovery, to God. The "theology of addiction," as Richard Mouw observes, is all about giving in, about "giving oneself over."[34] Addiction is about our hungers and thirsts, about our ultimate concern, about the clinging and longing of our hearts, and about giving ourselves over to these things. When it is in full cry, addiction is finally about idolatry. At last, the addict will do anything for his idol, including dying for it. According to Mouw, there comes a point in the life of every alcoholic in which he sings his own version of Martin Luther's hymn: "Let goods and kindred go; this mortal life also; I'm going to get loaded."[35]

The mix of willfulness and despair, defiance and futility in the texture of addiction rules out simple ways of addressing it. Indeed, redemption from addiction must eventually be as multifaceted and protracted as redemption from sin and its miseries. But the first question for addicts and for all sinners is plain and urgent: In whose name is your help? Who or what is your only comfort in life and in death? To whom or to what do you ultimately belong?

The addict who turns to God has made the big and right decision. That is because "the hardness of God is kinder than the softness of man, and His compulsion is our liberation."[36] But no mere decision is enough. Like all sinners, the addict also needs painfully to unlearn old habits, to dismantle old scenarios, to pay old debts, and then to move steadfastly along the road to recovery one

33. McCormick, *Sin as Addiction* (New York: Paulist Press, 1989), p. 152. McCormick lists a number of important advantages of "an addiction model" for sin (pp. 171-74) and, in general, writes knowingly of addiction but fails to distinguish sin from addiction.

34. Mouw, in an interview with David Neff entitled "The Life of Bondage in the Light of Grace," *Christianity Today*, 9 December 1988, p. 41. Adrian Van Kaam notes that the Latin *addicere* means "to give over," or "to give up" ("Addiction," p. 243).

35. Mouw, "The Life of Bondage in the Light of Grace," p. 42.

36. C. S. Lewis, *Surprised by Joy: The Shape of My Early Life* (New York: Harcourt, Brace & World, 1955), p. 229.

small, secure step at a time, always aware that the self we want to recover is never wholly at our disposal. "Evil," says Diogenes Allen, "is one of the ways we learn that we ourselves are a mystery; for we are not in full control of ourselves and cannot find any method of gaining control."[37] The addict therefore needs not just the God who forgives but also the God who heals, not just the good Pardoner but also the Great Physician. Like all sinners, the addict needs spiritual hygiene. For just as sin, addiction, and misery typically go together, so do confession, healing, and the long process of redemption. We need redemption not just from our sins and addictions but also from their miseries — particularly those miseries that occasion more sin and deeper addiction. As all recovering sinners know, this process of healing and liberation, this "conversion unto life," this set of lessons to teach us how to dance again will prove to be as cunning, baffling, powerful, and patient as addiction itself.

37. Allen, *Temptation* (Cambridge: Cowley, 1986), p. 135.

CHAPTER 9

Attack

By forbidding murder God teaches us that he hates the
root of murder: envy, hatred, anger, vindictiveness. In
God's sight all such are murder.

The Heidelberg Catechism,
Answer 106

He hath a daily beauty in his life
That makes me ugly.

Iago (of Cassio) in *Othello*

Lyndon Baines Johnson took the presidential oath of office aboard
Air Force One in Dallas hours after President Kennedy's assassination, collected the largest popular vote majority in U.S. history
while defeating Barry Goldwater in 1964, and then, only four years
later, amid the ruins of his executive prestige and credibility, announced that he would not seek a second term. In his last year in
office, the only places LBJ could appear without seeing pickets and
hearing protests were military bases. One protest chant, in particular,
gave expression to a mounting hatred of the war in Vietnam, distrust
of Johnson's public statements about it, and the fragments of the
president's shattered image: "Hey! Hey! LBJ! How many kids did
you kill today?"

Like most subjects of multivolume biographies, Lyndon Johnson was a complicated man — "a character out of a Russian novel," as Russell Baker once put it, "a storm of warring human instincts." He was "sinner and saint, buffoon and statesman, cynic and sentimentalist, a man torn between hungers for immortality and self-destruction."[1] This was a man who in 1949 joined a bloc of senators from the Old South to oppose President Truman's national civil rights legislation ("almost sadistic," Johnson called it) but who, twenty-five years later, motivated in part by large-hearted compassion, pushed forward the greatest movement of civil rights and voting reform the nation had ever seen.[2] As architect, engineer, and advocate of this new program of racial justice, as well as of other major reforms, LBJ distinguished himself as one of our most accomplished presidents.

He was also an accomplished liar who knew, at least as early as 1948, how to use his lies to pierce and bleed his political opponents. According to one of his major biographers, Johnson eventually ruined his own presidency by a pattern of "lies and duplicity that went beyond permissible political license," beyond a "credibility gap" (the euphemism that appeared during his administration), and that sometimes approached the level of hallucination.[3] Johnson had trouble telling the truth — not just saying it but *telling* it, recognizing it, seeing it. He was like a man who could not tell time. Under pressure, he simply said what he thought was necessary in order to prevail, and he seemed wholly unembarrassed when caught in a lie.[4]

1. Baker, *The Good Times* (New York: William Morrow, 1989), p. 282.
2. Robert Dallek, *Lone Star Rising: Lyndon Johnson and His Times, 1908-1960* (New York: Oxford University Press, 1991), pp. 8, 368.
3. Robert A. Caro, *Means of Ascent*, vol. 2 of *The Years of Lyndon Johnson* (New York: Alfred A. Knopf, 1990), p. xxvi. See also Lance Morrow, "The Long Shadow of Vietnam," *Time*, 24 February 1992, p. 21.
4. Robert Caro, *The Path to Power*, vol. 1 of *The Years of Lyndon Johnson* (New York: Alfred A. Knopf, 1984), pp. xviii, xx, 156. Caro states that a strong tendency, perhaps a compulsion, to lie was part of LBJ's very character. For decades he made up the truth as he went along (e.g., he would offer conflicting accounts of the same event to different audiences), and Caro gives multiple instances through two volumes. Robert Dallek presents a much more sympathetic portrait of Johnson in

In 1948, in the most notorious U.S. Senate race in the history of Texas, amid widespread charges and suspicions of election fraud, Congressman Lyndon Johnson defeated Governor Coke Stevenson by just eighty-seven votes out of nearly a million cast in the senatorial primary — "the eighty-seven votes that changed history." Stevenson was "Mr. Texas," a plain, self-educated, straight-talking, conservative attorney and rancher who enjoyed statewide admiration for his probity. Stevenson's great superiority in the race was his sterling reputation.

So Johnson attacked it. At first he was content to call Stevenson "an old man" and a "do-nothinger," but knowing that Stevenson's sense of honor would not permit him to reply to personal attacks, Johnson eventually made his attacks as personal as possible. He ridiculed Stevenson's quiet ways, impugned his honesty, and demanded that Stevenson "tell the truth" about his "secret deal" with "labor bosses." According to Johnson, Stevenson had agreed with the bosses that, if elected, he would vote to repeal the Taft-Hartley Act, which limited the power of labor unions.[5]

A strong conservative, Stevenson had made no such deal with labor and would not dignify Johnson's charge by replying to it; he actually supported Taft-Hartley and had said so.[6] He invited citizens to judge him on his record. But where Johnson's explicit charge was concerned, Stevenson's silence eventually began to disturb voters, particularly after Johnson encouraged them to interpret it as guilt. By way of speeches, radio advertisements, interviews, pamphlets, direct mail circulars, special election "newspapers," and paid gossips or "missionaries" who fanned out into unsophisticated precincts to

---

Lone Star Rising, deliberately writing to counterbalance Caro and other "vilifiers," as he calls them (unjustly, in the case of Caro). Dallek concedes that Johnson told a number of significant and public untruths but prefers to characterize them as "exaggerations" or "just rhetoric" or "political claptrap" (pp. 241, 276, 325).

5. Caro, *Means of Ascent,* pp. 210-11, 224-26. Dallek says only, and demurely, that Johnson "warned that Stevenson may have promised to support repeal of Taft-Hartley in return for AFL backing" (*Lone Star Rising,* p. 314).

6. One of Johnson's speechwriters later admitted that he felt terrible about writing up Johnson's charge against Stevenson: "We knew it wasn't true, and I felt almost ashamed of what I was writing sometimes. Coke was so honest you know" (Caro, *Means of Ascent,* p. 225).

spread rumors among the semi-literate, Lyndon Johnson kept repeating his claim that Coke Stevenson had cut a labor deal and kept hammering away at Stevenson's reputation. Stevenson meanwhile kept his peace even while his aides advised him that Johnson was badly denting him.[7]

Then, as election day approached, sensing that Stevenson had finally had enough and would answer him, Johnson conceived a stroke of evil political genius: he closed Stevenson's last window of opportunity by publicly *predicting* that "at this late date" and with desperate motives Stevenson would now come out in favor of Taft-Hartley. Stevenson would do this, Johnson said, only because he knew his "true feelings" were costing him votes.[8]

The Johnson coup was wickedly clever: he first pinned a phony charge on his opponent and then accused him of wanting to deny it. Johnson had boxed Stevenson in. He had him both ways.

Attack and Flight

Johnson's attack on Stevenson shows us the aggressive half of a famous pattern in sin. Christians have long noticed that human sin appears in characteristic "postures" or "movements." Among the most basic of these is a pattern of alternating attack and flight. Sinners assault other human beings or else they ignore them. They invade somebody else's life or they flee their responsibility for it. Since these other human beings belong to their Creator, sinful movements against them or away from them offend God as well. Thus, in these movements, as well as in direct blasphemy and irreligion, sinners rebel against God and turn away from him. They transgress God's prohibitions and avoid God's requirements. They may even treat themselves similarly, either by self-abuse or by self-neglect. Relative to others, God, or themselves, sinful people encroach or evade or do both in turn.

That's the pattern, and it's as old as sin itself. In Genesis 3 the

7. Caro, *Means of Ascent*, pp. 275-77.
8. Caro, *Means of Ascent*, p. 278.

Bible's primal pair of humans transgress the single prohibition of God ("You may freely eat of every tree of the garden; but of the tree of the knowledge of good and evil you shall not eat" — Gen 2:16-17) and then flee from God's presence. They attack God's uniqueness, God's exclusive prerogative to "know" or legislate good and evil. They rebel against their Creator and then, guilty and ashamed, they hide from him. What's more, they learn the fine art of simultaneous accusing and evading:

> The LORD God called to the man, and said to him, . . . "Have you eaten from the tree of which I commanded you not to eat?" The man said, "The woman whom you gave to be with me, she gave me fruit from the tree, and I ate." Then the LORD God said to the woman, "What is this that you have done?" The woman said, "The serpent tricked me, and I ate." (Gen. 3:9, 11-13)

Cain, the firstborn of Adam and Eve, follows suit. He attacks his brother Abel and then shrugs off God's question "Where is your brother Abel?" "I do not know," Cain replies; "am I my brother's keeper?" (Gen. 4:9).

Henry Stob has pointed out that this approach/avoidance pattern lies so deep in Scripture that it shows up even in the biblical images of hell. Alluding to the statements of Jesus that picture hell as "the outer darkness" and then, a few verses later, as "the eternal fire" (Matt. 25:30, 41), Stob suggests that these images reflect the natural outcome of the sinner's posture toward God:

> Hell in the Bible . . . is either very hot or very cold, depending on whether the sinner is perceived as a rebel or an alien. In either case hell is not a divine creation. Hell is made by those who climb the holy mountain and try to unseat the Holy One who, ablaze with glory, dwells in the light unapproachable. Those who mount an attack on God and cross the barrier of his exclusive divinity die like moths in the flame of him who will not and cannot be displaced. And hell is made by those who, turning their backs on God, flee the light and move toward the eternal blackness that marks God's absence. Hell, then, is unarrested sin's natural and programmatic end. Sin is either rebellion or flight, and, when

persisted in, leads either to the fiery furnace or to the cold and desolate night.[9]

Of course, the movements of attack and flight may express good as well as evil. Everything depends on whom or what we attack and from whom or what we flee. A person who attacks election fraud, for example, has served the cause of shalom. So has a person who, like Joseph in Potiphar's household, flees from the allure and embrace of adultery (Gen. 39:6b-12). But when parents assassinate their children's character or neglect their development, when husbands beat up wives or abandon them, when savings and loan entrepreneurs rip off investors and taxpayers and then move abroad to avoid prosecution, when human beings blaspheme God or ignore him — when, in short, people violate or defect from goodness, they involve themselves in moral and spiritual evil and, if culpable for doing so, in sin.

Suppose we consider each of these movements or postures in turn — the movement of attack in this chapter and the movement of flight in Chapter 10. And suppose that, for the sake of interest and variety, we try a new strategy in this chapter: instead of making general observations about the nature of sin and then giving brief illustrations (as in the previous paragraph), suppose we select a particular sin or sin-cluster, examine it in some detail, and let it stand for sins of its kind.

What we need is a representative sin of attack, of violation — one in which we can see the posture of *againstness* in its essence and at its base. Such high-profile crimes as murder, rape, and felonious assault spring naturally to mind, but only a relatively few members of the population commit these dramatic sins, and, anyway, deep motives and common states of mind lie behind them. It's in this deeper and more common area that we shall want to explore.

How about lying, the sin against the ninth commandment? According to the expert commentary of the Heidelberg Catechism, "You shall not bear false witness against your neighbor" rules out

---

9. Stob, "Sin, Salvation, Service" (Grand Rapids: Board of Publications of the Christian Reformed Church, 1984), p. 16. This paragraph gives the reader a sense of the theological imagination and verbal elegance that marked Henry Stob's teaching — virtues his students still treasure.

"lying and deceit of every kind," but particularly lies that slander others, twist their words, and unjustly accuse them.[10]

Of course, people often use lies to slip the noose of accountability ("Officer, I have no idea how that man's wallet got into my sport coat"), but they also use them as weapons. People use lies to assault other human beings, to squelch, mock, slander, or accuse them: "You've never amounted to anything, and you never will." "He's dumber than a post." "Martin Luther King Jr. was nothing but a Communist!" "Ronald Reagan thinks that Hawaii is one of the nation's most important allies." "Coke Stevenson made a secret deal with the labor bosses."

Sticks and stones can break our bones, but lies can break our hearts and our careers. They can ruin reputations, wreck marriages, and start riots. Even in the relatively urbane settings of great universities, calumnies cause faculty rivalries, tenure wars, and administrative feuds that make life hazardous for students and unpleasant for all but the callous.

And those are merely civilian lies. In wartime, as the saying goes, truth is the first casualty. Wartime propaganda characteristically involves a demonizing of the enemy, which is all the easier if he belongs to some other racial group. Thus, during the Second World War the U.S. Department of the Treasury discovered by market research that it could sell more war bonds if it concentrated its demonizing on the Japanese — depicting them as squinting, yellow, toothy, and alien — rather than on the whiter and more Lutheran-looking Germans. The government also rounded up and forcibly interned 110,000 Americans of Japanese ancestry, including 60,000 who were American citizens by birth, even though it had never found a single case of Japanese-American espionage. The government did this despite the fact that the Germans were both more dangerous to the U.S. and, as the liberating of the German work and slaughter camps revealed, more systematically evil.[11]

---

10. Answer 112: "God's will is that I never give false testimony against anyone, twist no one's words, not gossip or slander, nor join in condemning anyone without a just cause. Rather, in court and everywhere else, I should avoid lying and deceit of every kind. . . . I should love the truth, speak it candidly . . . and I should do what I can to guard and advance my neighbor's good name."

11. Neil Sheehan, *A Bright Shining Lie: John Paul Vann and America in Viet Nam* (New York: Random House, 1988), pp. 153-54.

But what *motivates* attacks by lie? Lots of things. People assault others with lies out of a competitive urge to defeat them, out of a relish for the controversy stirred up by slander, out of racism or sexism. Some people want the notoriety that comes with making public accusations, true or false. A few seem to hate almost everybody and speak ill of humanity in general. But one of the big, perennial motives for lying appears along the whole length of the fault line that runs through our humanity. This is a motive as old as Cain and Abel and as new as the barely concealed twist of displeasure on the face of a runner-up for the crown of high school homecoming queen. This is a motive that prompts people to slice up other people's reputations, to disparage their achievements, to minimize their virtues, to question their motives, to challenge their integrity (*"Nobody's that good!"*), and, failing other ways of bringing them down, to kill them.

I mean envy — an ugly sin and a motive for ugly sins.

A Select History of Envy

In 1989, newspapers in Iowa published a sequence of stories that centered on a classic love triangle.[12] Two striking young women found themselves grappling for the same boyfriend. Cindy and Sonya had grown up together, had gone to school together, and had competed in local beauty contests. Sometimes one would win, sometimes the other. For instance, Cindy won the county title of Miss Harvest Queen, while at the local high school Sonya was named Miss Homecoming.

But the main competition between these two women flared in the area of romance. It happened that both of them were in love with Jim, widely regarded in the area as strapping, promising, and eligible. Newspaper accounts do not say what Jim thought of the spectacle of two beautiful women fighting over him. Maybe he found this spectacle embarrassing or maybe he reveled in it, but in any case

12. Though my account of this triangle is based on an actual incident and largely follows newspaper accounts of it, I have changed names and details.

Jim had to choose. Which he did. He left Cindy for Sonya, and Jim and Sonya announced their plan to marry.

When Cindy heard the news, she must have felt as if she had been stabbed, as if Jim and Sonya were trying to twist a knife between her ribs. Cindy wasn't used to disappointment in romance, and she had no idea where to find an antidote for it. It was bad enough to have lost Jim, but what really poisoned Cindy was the thought that her rival had walked off with the prize, that her rival was pleased and satisfied, that her hated rival was filled to the brim with bliss. So Cindy rose up against Sonya and slew her. One autumn night in Iowa, Miss Harvest Queen strangled Miss Homecoming with a leather belt and left the whole community choking with grief.

This is a story we have heard before. It's a crime story so old and deep in our race that its first episode occurs almost as soon as human beings go wrong. Near the opening edge of Scripture, in the first biblical passage to use the word *sin*, two brothers come to grief over an offering.

> In the course of time Cain brought to the LORD an offering of the fruit of the ground, and Abel for his part brought of the firstlings of his flock, their fat portions. And the LORD had regard for Abel and his offering, but for Cain and his offering he had no regard. So Cain was very angry. . . . The LORD said to Cain, "Why are you angry, and why has your countenance fallen? If you do well, will you not be accepted? And if you do not do well, sin is lurking at the door; its desire is for you, but you must master it."
>
> Cain said to his brother Abel, "Let us go out to the field." And when they were in the field, Cain rose up against his brother Abel, and killed him. (Gen. 4:3-8)

In this terse and cryptic story, the crime is murder and the motive is envy. Something had gone wrong with Cain's worship of God. It hadn't worked. It didn't take. And Cain had gotten angry, not puzzled; he had gotten angry, not humbled. Cain had set himself against a mysterious God — an inscrutable God who was such a finicky eater that he wouldn't even touch his vegetables. But then, somewhere between the lines of the story, so quietly and subtly we can hardly see it happen, Cain's anger pivots. He had hated the God who was so hard to satisfy. But then, in his anger, Cain slowly swivels around till he has Abel in his sights.

After all, who turned God against him? Who seems to win at everything? Who keeps putting him in the shade? Cain looks over at Abel and no longer sees his brother. All he sees now is a rival — not somebody to love and lift up but somebody who needs to be cut down to size. Who does Abel think he is? Where does he get off? Why does he always make people feel like losers?

A poisonous little fire is eating Cain's innards. And his terrible conclusion is that only his brother's blood can put it out.

Was Abel's offering more costly and generous? Or was Abel preferred by the same mysterious providence that for centuries has been parceling out gifts so unequally? (As we all know, beauty, intelligence, and the gift of sleeping well come only to some.)

The text leads us toward a difference in offering and a difference in character between these two brothers. The writer wants us to find self-sacrifice and integrity in Abel's worship. Abel is not just blessed out of the blue; there is some reason why he's preferred.[13]

But what we have to see is that to Cain it doesn't make a bit of difference. An envier doesn't care whether you have earned part of your success or whether some golden parachute from heaven has dropped straight into your lap. To an envier, your advantage is totally unfair either way. In this respect, enviers are theological switch-hitters: sometimes they are Pelagians and sometimes they are Augustinians. But always they are potential killers.

From the dawn of the human race, says Genesis 4, human beings have clashed over their differences — not just their differences of opinion but, much more profoundly, their differences of wealth, status, race, gender, social acceptance, intelligence, physical attractiveness, achievement, and general flourishing. Down the ages, the haves and the have-nots keep glaring at each other and grappling over their differences. Using short, terrible strokes, the biblical narrator hammers out the first piece of this bloody history, a tale of blessing and cursing and envy and killing and the banishing of a

13. Abel offers what really costs him — the choicest cuts from his most valuable stock. Cain brings ordinary produce.

marked man — all of it because one brother was blessed and one was not.[14]

In telling us this tale, the writer starts a lot more business than he finishes. But of one thing we may be sure: the story of Cain and Abel is not just a snapshot of an isolated incident. This story is rather a kind of paradigm, the first case in Scripture of a pattern that will appear again and again. In this pattern, God surprisingly prefers one person over another — typically the younger over the older — and then has to deal with the loser and his lethal envy. So when we read of Cain and Abel, other names should be lining up along the horizon of our memory — names like Jacob and Esau, Leah and Rachel, Isaac and Ishmael, Joseph and his brothers, even Herod and Jesus.[15]

In this biblical history of blessing and envy, we find an especially revealing episode in the Saul and David narratives (1 Sam. 16–31). David, a teenage shepherd with beautiful eyes, slays Goliath the Philistine and thereby transforms himself not only into a giant killer but also into the public rival of his own sovereign, the stormy King Saul.[16] For years Saul had been Israel's undisputed war hero. But now a talented freshman is coming up — David, who has the touch of God on him; David, who is clearly a more gifted killer than Saul. And Saul, the old warrior, feels the demons beginning to stir within him. How appalling to be one-upped by some rural whippersnapper who has gotten lucky with his slingshot! How ominous to see this young hotshot lining himself up to take aim at your job! How mortifying to hear the crowds roar for him and women sing about him! One song, in particular, sticks in Saul like a blunt syringe: "Saul has killed his thousands, and David his ten thousands" (1 Sam. 18:7).

With discreet understatement the narrator notes that "Saul was very angry, for this saying displeased him. He said, 'They have ascribed to David ten thousands, and to me they have ascribed

14. For a splendid contemporary version of the Cain and Abel story, see Miguel de Unamuno, "Abel Sanchez," in *Abel Sanchez and Other Stories*, trans. Anthony Kerrigan (Washington: Regnery, Gateway, 1956).

15. My colleague Arie Leder alerted me to the pertinence of this pattern.

16. 1 Samuel 16:1-13 relates that in a private ceremony David had already been anointed as Israel's next king by God's prophet Samuel.

thousands; what more can he have but the kingdom?' So Saul eyed David from that day on" (1 Sam. 18:8-9).

Saul "eyed" David. Saul casts the evil eye of envy on David. And the next day, as David tries to calm the storms in Saul by playing his lyre for him (besides everything else, David is an accomplished musician), Saul tries to pin him to a wall with his spear.

In the life of King Saul, pride leads to anger, which leads to envy, which leads to attempted murder. In this classic case of a star eclipsed by a superstar, Saul sees, fears, and murderously resents the changing of the guard.

The story of Cain and Abel anticipates the story of Saul and David. In fact, the original story of envy anticipates a pattern woven into all of humanity, into a whole race that has been banished from Paradise.

We can see the pattern in the film *Amadeus*, in which Wolfgang Amadeus Mozart appears as a superlatively gifted jerk. He preens himself, chases girls around rooms, and giggles absurdly. He uses his wonderful mind for such inventive crudities as talking dirty backward. Scorning the dullness of other people's compositions, he praises the brilliance of his own. And day after day he creates music of such soaring, yearning, seamless beauty that it splits his rival Antonio Salieri into two persons, one of them wanting to worship and one wanting to kill.

For Salieri is the prince of mediocrity, the prototype of every also-ran who must live with the knowledge that by comparison with genius he is remarkably so-so. Salieri knows that Mozart is a sun to his candle, a torrent to his trickle. By an especially galling irony, Salieri is in fact just gifted enough to understand how much greater Mozart's music is than his own. Salieri had begged God to allow him to serve as the voice of God. God's response was to place the divine treasure in an obscene brat. While the musical incarnation of the glory of God (*Amadeus* means "beloved of God") prances from one musical triumph to another, sporting a coprophagous grin, his envious rival must wear what Angus Wilson calls "the painful grimace of sour good loserliness."[17]

17. Wilson, "Envy," in *The Seven Deadly Sins,* ed. Angus Wilson (New York: Morrow, 1962), p. 4.

The fault line of envy runs from Cain and Abel through Saul and David and on through Salieri and Mozart and on through Miss Harvest Queen — who one night begins to wind each end of a leather belt around her fists. Not surprisingly, the ancient fault line runs through all of us. For we are people, as Henry Fairlie says, who must struggle to rejoice "at someone else's good fortune, or even someone else's good joke,"[18] people in whom innocent Abel and guilty Cain are still fighting for supremacy.

If we trace the fault line, we find that envy is a nastier sin than mere covetousness. What an envier wants is not, first of all, what another has; what an envier wants is for another not to have it. Hence an eighteen-year-old will lobby against a liberal curfew for his sixteen-year-old brother even though the eighteen-year-old can gain nothing positive by winning his campaign. (All he gains is his brother's animosity.) The older boy simply doesn't want his brother to enjoy an advantage he had once lacked. He's like a fraternity member or a medical resident who once endured a hazing or an insane work schedule and who for that reason alone doesn't want standards relaxed for newcomers.

When an envier offers a backward intercessory prayer for his rival[19] ("Drain his swimming pool, O God, but fill his basement"), he doesn't do it out of some motiveless malignity or out of simple covetousness. To covet is to want somebody else's good so strongly ("inordinately," as the Christian tradition says) that one is tempted to steal it. To envy is to resent somebody else's good so much that one is tempted to destroy it. The coveter has empty hands and wants to fill them with somebody else's goods. The envier has empty hands and therefore wants to empty the hands of the envied. Envy, moreover, carries overtones of personal resentment: an envier resents not only somebody else's blessing but also the one who has been blessed. Coveting focuses much more on objects than on persons:

18. Fairlie, *The Seven Deadly Sins Today* (Notre Dame, Ind.: University of Notre Dame Press, 1978), p. 61.

19. See William F. May, *A Catalogue of Sins: A Contemporary Examination of Christian Conscience* (New York: Holt, Rinehart & Winston, 1967), p. 80. May adds that "when the envious person takes to invoking the powers that be to do their worst, it is not too long before he gives them a little assistance."

even when it focuses on persons, it tends to see them as objects. Thus, in 1 Samuel the envious eye of Saul falls on David, while in 2 Samuel the roving, covetous eye of David falls on Bathsheba, wife of the honorable Uriah.[20] An envier resents; a coveter desires. Of course, an envier may begin his career as a coveter. He may begin by hankering for somebody else's goods, just as Cain may have originally wanted the blessing God gave to Abel. But failed covetousness is likely to curdle into envy: the envier is often a disgruntled coveter.

If the envier can come away with another's goods, so much the better, but that is an incidental advantage. What the envier really wants is to spoil something — or someone. Thus, according to Genesis, Cain spurned God's blessing even when he was offered a second chance at it.[21] By that time Cain no longer wanted God's blessing; what he wanted was Abel's death.

In the land of Nod that lies east of Eden — the land of wandering, the land for envious exiles — the sons and daughters of Cain have multiplied and spread across the world. Now everywhere is east of Eden, and everywhere the green faces of envy keep glowing:

- A high school yearbook editor in Indiana takes vengeance on her rivals by defacing their yearbook photos. After the yearbook has been proofread, and just before it goes to the printer, the editor blacks out teeth and pencils in underarm hair on the photos of girls who have dated her boyfriends.
- A bright, studious fourteen-year-old African-American girl from a tough part of Oakland dreams of parlaying her intelligence and hard work into a medical degree. But her enthusiasm for this project runs into heavy weather from her less accomplished and more alienated peers, who resent her dream,

20. Christoph Barth remarks that David "acted as a king who has property rights to the bodies and souls of his people" (*God with Us: A Theological Introduction to the Old Testament*, ed. Geoffrey W. Bromiley [Grand Rapids: William B. Eerdmans, 1991], p. 214).

21. "The LORD said to Cain, 'Why are you angry . . . ? If you do well, will you not be accepted?'" (Gen. 4:6-7).

mock her determined attempts to achieve it, and revile her for being "uppity" and trying to "act white."

- Subordinates of a Chicago publishing executive ruin his reputation by lying about his work. They spread false tales of his poor judgment and dithering. The executive doesn't know he has been stabbed in the back until the day his superiors ask him to resign.
- The mother of an aspiring thirteen-year-old cheerleader in Texas contracts with a hit man to kill the mother of a rival cheerleader. The idea is to upset the bereaved daughter and thus disrupt her preparation for cheerleading tryouts.

When he acts on his resentment, the envier typically assumes the role of a vandal. He's out to mar, to deface, to despoil, to destroy. His target may be a reputation, a dream, a piece of property, a peaceful state of mind, or even a human life. To do his work he may use political lies or insults or conventional military weaponry. In August 1990, the army of Iraqi strongman Saddam Hussein invaded its more prosperous neighbor Kuwait and murdered a number of rich Kuwaitis in the invasion. Under strong international pressure, and then under fierce assault from U.S. armed forces, Saddam withdrew from Kuwait in the last week of February 1991. Before he left, he torched the oil wells he now could not harvest and polluted beaches he had to abandon.

The envious vandal cannot let beauty, riches, or wholeness be. At his worst, he resents anything that is really healthy or flourishing. He'd veto heaven itself if he could. Confronted by beauty or blessing, what an envier wants to do is to raise Cain. The envier is a child of the evil one: if he cannot have heaven, he can at least raise hell in the lives of others.

Resentment, Pride, and Destruction

From the time of Cain and Abel to the time of Miss Harvest Queen, from burning oilfields in Kuwait to junior high cheerleading wars in Texas, the goal of envy is always to strip someone of a particular good. The target for stripping may be radiant with moral beauty or may be simply smart or rich or handsome or funny or accomplished. The target may be a particular person — Abel or Mozart — or it may be a whole class or race or nation of persons — the rich, the educated, the wellborn; Asians, Japanese, royal Japanese — whose advantages the envier resents. What the envier wants is to remove such advantages and, if necessary, the persons who have them.

Why? What's the point?

The point is anger. The advantages of others make the envious angry. Alert readers will have noticed that in the Bible stories of envy, the writers talk explicitly not of envy but of anger. Thus, when God blessed Abel, "Cain was very angry." When the Israelite women sang to one another "Saul has killed his thousands, and David his ten thousands" the writer adds tersely that "Saul was very angry, for this saying displeased him." And, of course, Saul has his successors. Salieri was very angry, for both Mozart and God displeased him. Miss Harvest Queen was very angry too: according to newspaper accounts, her jury concluded she had murdered her rival "in a rage of jealousy."[22]

At its base, envy is a corrupted form of resentment and therefore of anger. Let's say that anger is a strong feeling of displeasure combined with a posture of antagonism: the angry person emotionally *opposes* something or someone. Anger rarely floats free. It flares against this person or that, against these states of affairs or those. Or, if anger settles into chronic irritability, it sets up against anything and everything. Whether it burns hot or just smokes and stinks, anger always sets itself against what causes its displeasure. Anger is passionate againstness.

Resentment is a special, and usually protracted, form of anger: resentment is anger aimed at what the angry person regards as

22. Though *envy* and *jealousy* are nowadays often used as synonyms, the words have traditionally meant different things. Envy wants to remove somebody's good; jealousy wants to protect the good it already has (sometimes justly). Hence Miss Harvest Queen's "fit of jealousy" is, strictly speaking, her determined passion to keep Jim, not her determined passion to prevent her rival from having him. The right description of this last passion is envy. But, as in this case, jealousy and envy often dovetail — which contributes to the popular confusion.

unjust, insulting, or demeaning, especially to her personally. She may resent her immigrant status, for example, together with its clothing, manners, and accent. She may resent her race or the arrogant ignorance of her relatives. She may resent her poverty, even if she caused it. She may resent her exam grade or traffic ticket, even if she deserves it.

Some resentments are wholly justified. In Montgomery, Alabama, in the forties, city fathers wrote municipal bus regulations to minimize proximity of black and white passengers. One of the regulations prohibited blacks from walking through the bus to their own seats since, to do so, they would have to pass through the white section and might accidentally make body contact with white passengers. Thus, in a demeaning alternative, blacks would pay their fare at the front, exit the bus, walk its length outdoors, and then reenter the vehicle at the rear. Inevitably, certain white bus drivers amused themselves by driving away before their black passengers could reboard.[23] Of course, the trouble here was not that blacks got angry at such humiliation but rather that whites did not.

Good people oppose evil emotionally as well as every other way. Good people have the capacity, in a word, for indignation — for justified anger. Sometimes they get righteously angry at the oppression or diminishment of others: they feel indignant at injustices halfway across the world. At other times they get hot over an insult or injustice to themselves. They feel indignant at a malicious injury that has hit terribly close to home, and they justifiably resent it.

Anger lies at the base of both the virtue of indignation and the sin of envy. Consider those who get indignant at being mocked, humiliated, or cheated. Both they and envious people feel injured. But the difference between them is crucial: while the indignant resent what is evil, the envious resent what is good. An envious person feels *disgraced* by somebody else's skill or integrity. She feels injured by somebody else's natural attractiveness. Politically, she feels oppressed by ordinary law and order and diminished by the economic and

---

23. Taylor Branch, *Parting the Waters: America in the King Years, 1954-1963* (New York: Simon & Schuster, 1988), p. 14.

political power of others.[24] She feels that even the hard-won achievement of another is actually unjust ("Why should *she* win all the time? It's so *unfair!*"). To a truly envious human being, the success or blessing of another — particularly a rival, and most particularly a close rival — is an affront, a kind of insult.

But why think of someone else's good as an injury to oneself? Again, what's the point?

The point is pride. The point is personal preeminence. The envier resents another's good because it scuffs his pride. To the envier, every good in a rival is a diminishment of himself — maybe even an *intended* diminishment. As Miguel de Unamuno observes, because of the envier's self-centeredness and cynicism, he may begin to imagine that his rival succeeds just in order to torment him![25]

Envy, like the pride that spawns it, is inevitably comparative. The envier wants to tear down a competitor because "he hath a daily beauty in his life/That makes me ugly."[26] The core of envy is the desire to cut somebody down to size, to change the basis of comparison with oneself, to hamstring rivals so that they have to drop out of the race in whatever competition the envier cares about.

Predictably, the good an envier resents is usually one that is slightly superior to his own. In the classic pattern, the prosperous resent the rich, the 3:58 miler resents the 3:54 miler, the pretty resent the beautiful, and the hardworking B+ student resents the straight A student, especially the happy-go-lucky one who never seems to study.

24. Solomon Schimmel points out that in political settings it is easy to detect resentment but often hard to tell whether it amounts to indignation or envy, in part because "deprived social groups sometimes mask their envy of more privileged groups as righteous indignation, and some privileged groups falsely accuse oppressed groups of envy when the oppressed are justifiably indignant" (*The Seven Deadly Sins: Jewish, Christian, and Classical Reflections on Human Nature* [New York: Free Press, 1992], p. 81). For a fine brief history of modern social and political envy, of *ressentiment* in its relation to jealousy, ostentation, and revolution, see Stanford M. Lyman, *The Seven Deadly Sins: Society and Evil* (New York: St. Martin's Press, 1978), especially pp. 185-98; and Max Scheler, *Ressentiment*, ed. Lewis A. Coser, trans. William W. Holdheim (New York: Schocken Books, 1972).

25. Unamuno, "Abel Sanchez," pp. 28-29.

26. Iago of Cassio in *Othello*, act 5, sc. 1, ll. 18-19.

That's the classic scenario. But, as Henry Fairlie notes, in an egalitarian culture envious losers have an option: instead of attacking winners directly, they can attack the rules of the game. They can take revenge for their failure by leveling the playing field.[27] If they feel diminished by someone's superiority measured by conventional standards, why not abolish the standards? Once the standards are gone, everybody's a poet, everybody's a painter, anybody with a microphone and an amplifier is a singer. If you cannot play ordinary tennis very well, take down the net. Fairlie ponders this move:

> What we are unable to achieve we will bring low. What requires talent and training and hard work, we will show can be accomplished without them. W. H. Auden once said that he could not understand the point of writing poetry if one did not obey at least the basic rules of prosody. It was like doing a crossword puzzle and, on being unable to find the correct word of seven letters, writing in one of nine letters that spills over the margin. Where is the point and satisfaction in that?[28]

If he is very proud, an envious person will resent not only a superior good in somebody else but also an equal one. Thus, if he gets an A on an examination in school he'd like to be the only one. If he wins first place in a piano competition, the envier wants to win it alone. Having to share first place makes him feel like a loser. If he wins the Nobel Prize, thereafter each year's announcement of it makes him melancholy, for now others are prizewinners too, and their prizes are newer than his.[29] To the truly envious person, other persons and their goods are so much underbrush that needs to be trimmed away so that one's own tall tree can stand unobscured. We might say that the proud envier keeps running for the office of God — not the biblical God who creates and cherishes good in others but the pantheist God who swallows all good into himself.

27. Fairlie, *The Seven Deadly Sins Today*, pp. 63, 65.

28. Fairlie, *The Seven Deadly Sins Today*, pp. 63-64.

29. Joseph Epstein, "A Few Kind Words for Envy," *The American Scholar* 58 (1989): 492. In the three cases just mentioned, the envier is, of course, also jealous — in these cases of his preeminence.

Envy is resentment of someone else's good, plus the itch to despoil her of it. Its natural corollary is what the Germans call *Schadenfreude,* the enjoyment of someone else's despoilment. The envier not only sorrows over another's good fortune and wants it to change; he also rejoices in another's misfortune and wants it to persist. Hence an envious conservatory student may feel privately delighted at the memory lapse of a rival during her recital performance. A Christian minister may act sad but feel pleased that a more admired minister has been arrested for drunk driving. A professional baseball player may take secret satisfaction from the fact that his own son, also a player, has struggled through just enough off years so as to assure that he will never surpass his father's lifetime records. Clive James once wrote a poem entitled "The Book of My Enemy Has Been Remaindered."[30]

In general, why is it, Walker Percy wants to know,

that the self — though it professes to be loving, caring, to prefer peace to war, concord to discord, life to death; to wish other selves well, not ill — in fact secretly relishes wars and rumors of war, news of plane crashes, assassinations, mass murders, obituaries, to say nothing of local news about acquaintances dropping dead in the streets, gossip about neighbors getting in fights or being detected in sexual scandals, embezzlements and other disgraces?[31]

30. Sample lines:

The book of my enemy has been remaindered
And I rejoice. . . .
What avail him now his awards and prizes,
The praise expended upon his meticulous technique,
His individual new voice?
Knocked into the middle of next week
His brainchild now consorts with the bad guys,
The sinkers, clinkers, dogs and dregs,
The Edsels of the world of movable type, . . .
And I am glad.

James, "The Book of My Enemy Has Been Remaindered," *New York Times Book Review,* 6 June 1993, p. 12.

31. Percy, *Lost in the Cosmos: The Last Self-Help Book* (New York: Farrar, Straus & Giroux, 1983), p. 57.

Envy (and its gloating subsidiary, *Schadenfreude*) shows us human antagonism in one of its basest and most unheroic forms. Envy is pure evil, as toxic and sickening to the envier as to everybody else. For, as Edmund Spenser says in nine of the most famous lines in the English language on this topic, what eats away at the envier is his own sin:

> And next to him malicious Envy rode,
> Upon a ravenous wolf, and still did chaw
> Between his canker'd teeth a venomous toad,
> That all the poison ran about his jaw.
> But inwardly he chewed his own maw,
> And neighbor's wealth, that made him ever sad;
> For death it was when any good he saw,
> And wept that no cause of weeping more he had,
> But when he heard of harm, he waxed wondrous glad.[32]

Envy poisons the envier, introducing gangrene into his own soul. (Indeed, knowing this, the really wicked envier will try to sow in a rival an envy of some third party.) But *being* envied is, at least for a person of character, no delight either. Of course, some "would rather be envied than respected," but only because they are themselves infected with pride and *Schadenfreude*. These are people who live life the way trash-talkers play basketball: what makes them happy is not only to crush their rivals but also to taunt them into an impotent rage.

Enviers want to be envied: they want to turn the tables on the people whose success makes them so miserable. Not so for persons of good character. For them, being envied is an awkward sorrow. Why so? To be envied is to have something venomous aimed at you for which it's surprisingly hard to find the right anti-venom. If you do well, you will be resented. If you ignore the envier, you nick his pride. If you try to be nice to the envier, you may be thought patronizing. Even a whiff of pity in your attitude is natural gas to the fires of envy. In their study of the Cinderella story, Ann Belford Ulanov and Barry Ulanov point out that Cinderella is helpless before

32. Spenser, *The Faerie Queene*, 1.4.30.

her sisters' envy. She can do nothing to turn it. They reduce her life to ashes, and, in return, she treats them with natural beauty and grace — an excellence they find galling.[33]

Envy, says Chaucer's parson, is sin "flatly against the Holy Ghost." It's "a foul sin . . . the worst sin there is, for . . . envy is against all virtues and against all goodnesses."[34] In his tale, the parson adds up the damage. Wherever we find envy, he says, we find the wreckage of human and Christian community. Envious people backbite. They deliver congratulations with a smile that, in another light, might be taken for a sneer. They acknowledge someone's praise of a rival but then push their rival into the shadow of a master (Yes, he's a pretty fair cellist, but have you ever heard Rostropovitch?). The envier gossips. He saves up bad news of others and passes it around like an appetizer at happy hour. The envier grumbles. He murmurs. He complains that all the wrong people are getting ahead. Spite, bitterness, "discord which undoes all friendship," accusation, malignity — all these things flow from envy and together turn friendship and good fellowship into a rancorous shambles.

What Chaucer's parson does is to run his eye down the New Testament vice lists and notice the shabby company that envy keeps. Envy appears in the lists along with debauchery and dissension (Rom. 13:13); with quarreling, factions, anger, and slander (2 Cor. 12:20); with friction, suspicion, and malice (1 Tim. 6:4). These are devastating anti-community sins, the sins of attack on communal peace. These are the sins that show Cain and Abel still struggling down the ages, struggling in us and in our society and in our churches.

But we have reason to think the struggle will one day cease. The reason is, as Oliver O'Donovan puts it, that Jesus Christ "represented both innocent Abel and guilty Cain, and reconciled them to each other and to God."[35] Jesus Christ, the naturally innocent

33. Ulanov and Ulanov, *Cinderella and Her Sisters: The Envied and the Envying* (Philadelphia: Westminster Press, 1983), pp. 19-24.

34. Chaucer, *Canterbury Tales*, ed. and trans. J. U. Nicolson (Garden City, N.Y.: Garden City Publishing, 1934), pp. 573-74.

35. Oliver O'Donovan, *Resurrection and Moral Order: An Outline for Evangelical Ethics* (Grand Rapids: William B. Eerdmans, 1986), p. 74.

one, the natural Abel, "became sin" for us (2 Cor. 5:21). He took Cain's place as well as Abel's. And when the terrible struggle between these old foes was over, on resurrection morning God raised the victim of envy, the one who had been slain, the one whose blood had been crying out from the ground for so many centuries.

On this event, all Christians center their hope for shalom.

CHAPTER 10

Flight

The West has finally achieved the rights of man . . . but
man's sense of responsibility to God and society has grown
dimmer and dimmer.

Aleksandr Solzhenitsyn

At Yale University in the early sixties, Stanley Milgram conducted
a controversial set of psychological experiments to test human
willingness to act harshly on command. Milgram wanted to know
whether ordinary people would do as they were told, even if they
were told to inflict pain on an innocent stranger. What he discovered
tells us much — much more than is comfortable to know — about
our readiness to attack others and to evade responsibility and to do
both at once.

Milgram placed an ad in the New Haven daily newspaper solic-
iting volunteers at a generous hourly rate for help in completing "a
scientific study of memory and learning." By this means and a later
random mailing, he gathered a pool of subjects including laborers,
clerks, salespeople, teachers, engineers, and others. By appointment,
these people appeared singly at Yale's Interaction Laboratory, where
they met the experimenter, a youngish man in a gray laboratory coat,
and also a portly, middle-aged man they supposed to be another subject
like themselves but who was actually an actor trained by Milgram.

By casting rigged lots, the experimenter arranged in each case for the genuinely naive subject to be the "teacher" in the study and for the actor to be the "learner." The subject was told that the idea of the experiment was to test the effect of punishment on learning and that, as teacher, his task would be to administer penalty shocks to the learner each time the learner returned an incorrect answer to one of the test questions.

The actor-learner was then strapped into a kind of electric chair and assured in the subject's presence that though the shocks could be "extremely painful," they would cause "no permanent tissue damage." The subject, in turn, was placed before an imposing shock generator said to be connected to the learner. This generator featured a long horizontal row of switches labeled in voltages ranging from "15 VOLTS" to "450 VOLTS," with groups of the switches additionally designated as "SLIGHT SHOCK," "MODERATE SHOCK," "STRONG SHOCK," "INTENSE SHOCK," up to "DANGER — SEVERE SHOCK," and, finally, to a simple, ominous "XXX." Milgram's technicians arranged as well for an authentic-sounding buzzer to buzz, a voltage meter needle to swing to and fro, and relay clicks to accompany the pressing of switches.

During the tests, the actor (who, of course, was actually receiving no shocks at all) proved to be a most unpromising student. Out of every four questions, he got about three wrong. After each miss, the experimenter instructed the subject to shock the learner with the next highest jolt — beginning at 15 volts and moving up through 30 levels to the maximum 450 volts — and to announce before each shock the present level of voltage.

The actor-learner responded convincingly to this steadily intensifying punishment: he grunted at 75 volts, protested at 120 volts, and demanded at 150 volts to be released from the experiment. At 180 volts the learner cried out "I can't stand the pain," and, at 270 volts, he emitted what "can only be described as an agonizing scream." At 300 volts the learner shouted desperately that he would no longer cooperate by trying to answer questions, and after 330 volts he lapsed into dead silence.[1]

---

1. Milgram, *Obedience to Authority: An Experimental View* (New York: Harper & Row, 1974), pp. 4, 23.

Naturally, many subjects found their role in this drama progressively upsetting.[2] Thus, when they turned questioningly to the experimenter, he prodded them, as necessary, with a sequence of increasingly authoritative commands: "Please continue," then "The experiment requires that you continue," then "It is absolutely essential that you continue," and finally, "You have no other choice, you *must* go on."

Under such pressure, most subjects began to show signs of strain. Some merely blipped the victim for a millisecond instead of really zapping him. Some tried to reduce the strain by such subterfuges as signaling the answer to the victim. Many also dissented verbally from the unexpectedly painful course the experiment was taking — while still continuing to press the switches. At every stage a number of disobedient subjects quit.[3] But obedient subjects reduced their distress by some ploy, maintained loyalty to the experimenter, and kept on buzzing the learner right through his protests.

How many obeyed? Much depended on the proximity of subject and victim. When the learner was in another room and could not be heard except for his urgent pounding on the wall late in the

2. A number of critics have found the whole set of experiments upsetting. In an appendix to *Obedience to Authority* entitled "Problems of Ethics in Research," Milgram defends his experiments against charges that they were deceptive, violent, and traumatizing to subjects by pointing out that many psychological experiments have, and need to have, an element of deception; that the procedure only seemed to be violent but wasn't; and that subjects were carefully and thoroughly debriefed (e.g., they met and were reconciled to the actor). Milgram adds that if subjects — and observers, for that matter — were to suffer distress over the knowledge that we human beings are capable of cruelty on demand, that might not be such a bad thing.

3. One, Jan Rensaleer, a 32-year-old engineer and "a member of the Dutch Reformed Church," responded to the experimenter's final prod ("You have no choice") by saying indignantly, "I *do* have a choice . . . I can't continue . . . I've gone too far already, probably." Another, an Old Testament professor at a major divinity school, balked at 150 volts, claiming that God's authority superseded and trivialized that of the experimenter. With astonishing ungratefulness, Milgram remarks that the professor had merely substituted divine for human authority instead of altogether repudiating authority in this situation (*Obedience to Authority*, pp. 47-52).

test, 65 percent of the subjects inflicted the harshest punishment. When subjects could hear the victim's cries but not see him very well, their compliance dipped slightly to 62 percent. When the victim moved into the same room with the subject — who now had to hear the victim's protests and see his looks of panic and reproach — compliance dropped to a still substantial 40 percent. (Some of the compliant subjects reduced their strain by trying to twist their heads around so that they would not have to see the victim.) Even when subjects were ordered to force their dull student's hand down onto a shock plate in order to stimulate him to do better, an alarming 30 percent still shocked their victim clear up to 450 volts.[4]

Why? Why would any ordinary person punish an innocent, protesting, screaming, and finally silent stranger in this way? None of the obedient shockers looked like scrofulous monsters. Most gave little outward indication that they were even particularly aggressive, let alone hostile. A number identified themselves as members in good standing of Christian churches. Virtually all of them, when interviewed, stated their opposition, in principle, to hurting innocent people. Yet, what they rejected in principle they did in practice, however distressed they felt about it. They did it because somebody in a laboratory coat told them that they had no choice.

Living Tools

As suggested in Chapter 9, sinners make moves or assume postures. In a classic pattern, human beings attack and then they flee. They assault or evade or do both simultaneously, as in passive forms of aggression. A person who is covering a lot of his anger, for example, might express it not by cursing the powers that be or by busting up some furniture but by habitual lateness for appointments or by smiling in a way that reminds you of a skull.

What the Milgram experiments show is that the same pattern of obedience to authority that binds children to parents, pupils to teachers, citizens to police officers, and even airline passengers to

4. Milgram, *Obedience to Authority*, pp. 34-36.

flight attendants — the same pattern on which society depends for order and stability — can also transform people into tools of evil. The sobering truth is that, given their readiness to obey, given enough pressure to reinforce this readiness, decent people will assault innocent strangers on demand and thus evade one of their most basic moral and spiritual responsibilities.

What is this responsibility? In its interpretation of the sixth commandment ("You shall not kill"), the Heidelberg Catechism, following a fine old Reformed custom, states not only what the commandment prohibits but also what it requires:

107 Q. Is it enough . . . that we do not kill our neighbor?

A. No. . . . God tells us to love our neighbors as ourselves, to be patient, peace-loving, gentle, merciful, and friendly to them, to protect them from harm as much as we can. . . .

Of course, the subjects in the Milgram experiments were caught in a bind. They knew as well as anybody that we ought to be friendly to others and protect them from harm as much as we can. In interviews they *said* they knew this. But they were also in the habit of obeying authority. Moreover, by signing up for the experiment and accepting payment for their role in it, they had implicitly promised to comply with its provisions. And, initially at least, what reason did they have for distrusting these provisions? Weren't the subjects entitled to assume that a social scientist within the walls of a prestigious university knew what he was doing?

They were. But as their auditory space began to fill with the learner's protests, pleas, and agonizing screams, the subjects also had to face the realization — almost unthinkable — that they had blundered into the laboratory of a madman and had made themselves his agents. Some quit. Others resolved the conflict by obediently electrifying their neighbor — a number of them continuing to defend their compliance even in the post-experiment dehoaxing sessions.

Again, why? In his analysis, Milgram describes what he calls "the agentic state."[5] A person is likely to shift into this state, says

5. Milgram, *Obedience to Authority,* p. 133.

Milgram, every time he enters a hierarchical structure held together by various levels of authority. Once inside the structure, he no longer thinks of himself as a responsible moral subject but only as an agent of others. He comes to see himself not as a person but as an instrument, not as a center of moral responsibility but as a tool.

Moreover, once shifted into an agentic state, he finds it remarkably hard to shift back. He is in too deep. He has too much momentum built up. Shifting into disobedience is at that point like trying to shift a car into reverse at thirty miles per hour. He finds himself bound to a morally deteriorating situation that he wants to abandon, but he cannot find a good, clean place to break off. It seems so bumptious to say to a person with a laboratory smock, a clipboard, and the aura of science about him that his experiment is obviously out of control and that it is time to quit. Who can say that? Who dares to disrupt a well-defined social situation in this way?

Not enough of us. The recent record of wrongful subservience to authority — from Nazi Germany to My Lai to Watergate to everyday life in business and industry — is notorious and discouraging. Somebody commands a soldier to shoot civilians through the back of the neck, or a plant foreman to fire a whistle-blower, or an attorney to suborn perjury, or a secretary to destroy evidence, and people obey. They may not like to do it or want to do it, but they do it. Then they defend themselves with the standard rationalization: "I was only following orders." "If it were up to me, I wouldn't do it, but I have to do as I'm told."[6]

In her penetrating account of the career of Franz Stangl, the commandant of Treblinka, Gitta Sereny tells of Stangl's enmeshment in the Nazi command structure. By his efficiency in relatively benign assignments, Stangl caught the attention of powerful Nazis, who then began to reward him by giving him more "difficult" assignments,

6. Humanists and Christians characterize these statements as rationalizations — humanists because the statements reflect an abandonment of the autonomy of the individual conscience, and Christians because the statements represent a form of idolatry, a reversal of the biblical axiom that, whenever faced with a conflict between divine and human orders, "We must obey God rather than any human authority" (Acts 5:29). Other sorts of thinkers find the humanist and Christian position anarchic. See Milgram, *Obedience to Authority*, p. 2.

including an assignment to supervise and assist in the mercy killings of nursing home residents. Each time Stangl balked, commanders reminded him of what he had already done and said, in effect, "The experiment requires that you continue." Finally, Nazi hierarchs appointed Stangl to the post at Treblinka — a position he could refuse or abandon only if he were willing to pay the same price as his prisoners.

In his new position, Stangl appears to have struggled with his conscience over supervising the slaughter of five thousand Jews every day. But his culture had taught him to obey his superiors, and his experience had taught him to fear them. For questions or doubts about his assignment brought not only reminders of his past complicity but also warnings ("You have no choice; you must go on") that raised the stakes on his obedience. Fearing the penalty for challenging his orders, Stangl complied. Obedience got him his job, and cowardice pinned him to it.

At one point, Stangl's wife, who was tortured by the knowledge of her husband's work, consulted their priest. He comforted her. "We are living through terrible times, my child," said Father Mario. "Before God and my conscience, if I had been in [Franz's] place I would have done the same. I absolve him from all guilt."[7]

By obedience to authority, Franz Stangl abandoned his duty to his neighbor and turned himself into a tool of evil — a move familiar to his colleagues in the killing business. Rudolf Höss, ordered to carry out mass exterminations at Auschwitz, later stated, "I had been given an order, and I had to carry it out. Whether this mass extermination of the Jews was necessary or not was something on which I could not allow myself to form an opinion, for I lacked the necessary breadth of view."[8] Of course, those with a broader view also had *their* orders, as had their superiors, all the way up the command chain to the Führer, whose view was so broad as to encompass all of Europe. James Burtchaell sums up the strange

7. Gitta Sereny, *Into That Darkness: From Mercy Killing to Mass Murder* (New York: McGraw-Hill, 1974), p. 235.
8. Höss, *Commandant of Auschwitz*, trans. Constantine FitzGibbon (Cleveland: World Publishing, 1959), p. 160.

world of Nazi accountability, a world in which everybody received orders but nobody gave them:

> By universal testimony, the Nazi extermination programs were accomplished under the cloak of firm authority. Equally universal was the testimony that it was always by someone else's authority. . . . The medical people claimed to be working at the behest of the law people; the government stated that the doctors were making their own professional decisions. Lower officials invoked directives from their superiors; higher officials claimed that their subordinates were always exceeding their warrants. All things were done in the name of the Führer; yet the Führer's signature never appeared on any death orders.[9]

Part of Stanley Milgram's agenda in conducting and writing up his experiments was to test whether the same obedience that put ordinary Germans in service of the Holocaust would also show up in New Haven, Connecticut, years later among ordinary Americans. As we have seen, the results of his test are disquieting.

Multiple Evasions

But shifting into the agentic state is only one way we shirk responsibility. Let's look at eight other ways, and then consider the most significant of our evasions.

1. Conforming

In the spring of 1993, Lakewood, California, a middle-class suburb of Los Angeles, made national news with a scandal involving teenage

---

9. Burtchaell, *Rachel Weeping: The Case against Abortion* (San Francisco: Harper & Row, 1984), p. 160. Burtchaell states, documents, and reflects on seven moves made both by the agents of holocaust and the agents of convenience abortion: they depersonalize their victims, euphemize the vocabulary of death, discharge responsibility onto others, disavow vicious intent, kill with progressively less discrimination, make money from their killing, and quash timid opposition.

peer pressure and conformity. News sources revealed that a number of Lakewood's most popular high school boys had formed a sexual conquest group (the "Spur Posse") in which members scored a point every time they achieved orgasm with a girl. What disgusted observers was not merely that these young studs competed with each other in this way or that their scores ranged into the fifties and sixties or that some of their victims were as young as ten but also that the members of the Posse were proud of their exploits, that a number of their fathers defended them ("Nothing my boy did was anything any red-blooded American boy wouldn't do at his age"), and that several of their mothers blamed the victims ("Those girls are trash") or threw up their hands in resignation ("What can you do? It's a testosterone thing"). Some Lakewood girls felt pressured into having sex with twenty or twenty-five members of the Posse (especially naive ninth graders who thought that sex with the Posse was de rigueur for social acceptance in Lakewood). Other social climbing girls actually sought the notoriety of having "done" the whole Posse. After several of the boys had been arrested on various felony charges and then released, they returned to their high school classes, where class members cheered them.[10]

The story of the Spur Posse is a story of subcultural conformity. We should note that conforming and obeying are distinct phenomena. People obey superiors but conform to peers. Conformity typically includes imitation; obedience does not. To obey is to comply with an explicit requirement; to conform, with an implicit one. Finally, when accounting for our actions (especially questionable ones), we readily acknowledge our obedience but minimize our conformity.[11] The reason is that we tend to see obedience as a social strength and conformity as an individual weakness.

But however we view conformity, we do conform, and sometimes to fine effect, as when small-town businesspeople conform to each other's high standards of honesty or when, according to community precedent, almost every able-bodied person assists in a local disaster relief effort. But suppose our peer group is a mob or a gang. Suppose

10. Jill Smolowe, "Sex with a Scorecard," *Time*, 5 April 1993, p. 41.
11. Milgram, *Obedience to Authority*, pp. 114-15.

our peer group is the Spur Posse — or their parents, whose casual "boys will be boys" attitude perfectly exemplifies the flight from adult responsibility. Suppose our peer group is Charlie Company at My Lai on 16 March 1968. Suppose it is merely a standard congregation of people occupying "some local pocket of human society," as C. S. Lewis puts it, "inside which minimum decency passes for heroic virtue and utter corruption for pardonable imperfection."[12] All too few of us dare to be a Daniel under such circumstances. Peer habits and expectations are too strong: they pressure us not only into acting but also into failing to act. Hence the existence of "happy families" in which nobody challenges incest or mentions alcoholism, and "groupthink" — an eerie phenomenon in which cozy groups of decision makers "tacitly conspire to ignore crucial information" on the ground that it doesn't fit what the group already assumes.[13]

2. Conniving

To shut one's eyes to an injustice, to look the other way, to pretend ignorance of evil — to do these things is to connive. We generally think of connivance as a case of active conspiracy, but it needn't be and often isn't.

At about 3:20 A.M. on 13 March 1964, Kitty Genovese, a twenty-eight-year-old manager of a bar in Queens, New York, returned to her quiet residential neighborhood, parked her car in a lot adjacent to her apartment building, and began to walk the thirty yards through the lot to her door. Noticing a man at the far end of the lot, she paused. When he started toward her, she turned the

---

12. Lewis, *The Problem of Pain* (New York: Macmillan, 1962), p. 62.

13. Groupthink lay behind the failure to plan the Bay of Pigs invasion in Cuba, behind American military unreadiness for the bombing of Pearl Harbor, and behind numerous smaller disasters that derive from a failure to face the facts. See Daniel Goleman, *Vital Lies, Simple Truths: The Psychology of Self-Deception* (New York: Simon & Schuster, 1985), pp. 174-89; Martin Bolt and David G. Myers, *The Human Connection: How People Change People* (Downers Grove, Ill.: InterVarsity, 1984), pp. 95-107; and Irving L. Janis, *Victims of Groupthink*, rev. ed. (Boston: Houghton-Mifflin, 1983).

other way and tried to reach a police call box half a block away. The man caught and stabbed her. She screamed "Oh, my God, he stabbed me! Please help me! Please help me!" Lights went on in the apartment building across the street, windows opened, and a man called out, "Let that girl alone!"[14]

The assailant shrugged and walked away. Windows closed and lights went out. The assailant returned and stabbed Genovese again. This time she screamed, "I'm dying! I'm dying." Windows opened and lights went on — many more of them than before. The assailant walked to his car and drove away. After he left, Kitty Genovese crawled along the street, bleeding from her wounds, reached the outside door to her apartment building, and dragged herself inside. The assailant returned once more, walked to the apartment building, tried one door and then another, found Genovese on the floor at the foot of her stairs, and stabbed her again. This time he succeeded in killing her.

During three separate attacks spanning thirty-five minutes, none of Kitty Genovese's neighbors tried to intervene. No burly neighbor grabbed a baseball bat and dashed outside to save her life. Worse, while more than thirty respectable people saw at least one of the knife attacks and heard Genovese's screams and her pleas for help, not one of them picked up a telephone to call for help. After much deliberation, one man did call a friend to ask for advice about what he should do; he ended up urging *another* neighbor to call authorities, which she did. Police arrived in two minutes, but Kitty Genovese was already dead.

Interviewed afterward, conniving residents admitted, sometimes sheepishly, "I didn't want to get involved," or "I didn't want my husband to get involved." One mumbled that he had been too tired to call police and had gone back to bed. Several didn't know why they hadn't helped. Many residents stated that they had been afraid to call. When asked why within the safety of their own homes or apartments they should be afraid to make a (perhaps anonymous) call to police, they gave meaningless answers.

14. New York *Times*, 27 March 1964, pp. 1, 38. My account paraphrases that of the *Times*.

The Kitty Genovese incident — so dramatic, appalling, and public — has become notorious, a defining moment, perhaps *the* defining moment, in American consciousness of urban apathy in the latter half of the twentieth century. At the time it occurred, many thought the incident shocking, bizarre, and atypical. In some ways it was.

But the connivance it revealed is certainly not unique — not unique where urban street crime is concerned and not unique in general. People connive everywhere. Family members avert their eyes from domestic abuse that is obvious to outsiders. Church councils connive at humiliation of members by power-hungry pastors who discourage questions and rebuke dissent.[15] These councils show elaborate mercy to their pastor and offer his victims little justice — sometimes listening hospitably to the pastor's "explanations, disavowals, and reinterpretations" while ostracizing plaintiffs as troublemakers.[16] Advisers, board members, and chief executive officers of major investment houses overlook runaway greed, check-kiting, entertainment receipts issued by brothels, and links with Mafia laundering schemes. When these signs of trouble do come home to them, they respond by raising the corporate advertising budget (an image of health is healthy) and by trying to pick "a few choice bits off the company's skeleton" before it collapses.[17] Officers of manufacturing corporations reject the addition of a relatively minor safety feature to the vehicle they make, weighing the cost of the addition against paying legal settlements to the victims of crashes which that safety feature would have prevented. Board members and other officers know of this gamble, approve it, and try to ignore the plight of the maimed with whom they have to settle.[18]

15. See Ronald M. Enroth, *Churches That Abuse* (Grand Rapids: Zondervan, 1992), especially pp. 147-65.

16. See Melvin D. Hugen, "Who's Minding the Preacher?" a review of *Is Nothing Sacred? When Sex Invades the Pastoral Relationship,* by Marie M. Fortune, *Reformed Journal,* November 1990, p. 28.

17. James Sterngold, *Burning Down the House: How Greed, Deceit, and Bitter Revenge Destroyed E. F. Hutton* (New York: Summit, 1990), p. 154.

18. See Russell Banks, *The Sweet Hereafter* (New York: HarperCollins, 1991), p. 91; and Stephen Greenleaf, *Impact* (New York: William Morrow, 1991).

3. Leaving Town

Human beings follow fashions not only in clothing, automobiles, and worship but also in going AWOL. Take two examples of dereliction from opposite ends of the social spectrum. In the summer of 1939, Winston Churchill kept trying to warn his colleagues in the British government that the great nation of Germany had fallen into the hands of a band of criminals, that shadows were lengthening, and that emergency decisions needed to be made. The trouble was that the upper-class men who had the power to make such decisions — the ones who ran Parliament and the government — kept leaving town each weekend, putting themselves out of the reach of telephones and government business. William Manchester comments:

> To Churchill's exasperation, Britain's ruling class continued "to take its weekends in the country," as he put it, while Hitler "takes his countries in the weekends." . . . Suggestions that country weekends be shortened, or that provisions be made for emergencies, were met with icy stares. Britain's leaders detested being pushed. . . . Haste was somehow regarded as un-British. The ruling class was not called the leisured class for nothing.[19]

In *Streetwise,* a book about life in the Northton section of Philadelphia, Elijah Anderson tackles one of the most serious, sensitive, divisive, and expanding social problems in contemporary America — the soaring unwed pregnancy rate in the black underclass (nearly two-thirds nationally). As elsewhere, teenagers and young adults in Northton make more babies than they take care of, and this is especially true of males. In Northton's inner-city culture, young black males show little relish for raising a family or caring for one that they have begun. They deride "playing house" (their term for accepting responsibility for one's family), mock those who attempt it, and, in any case, mistrust females to identify accurately the fathers of the children they have borne. (Street-corner jokes sometimes center on whom babies look like and on the uncertainty of their

19. Manchester, *The Last Lion: William Spencer Churchill — Alone, 1932-1940* (Boston: Little, Brown, 1988), p. 483.

parentage.) For Northton's young males, to "get over" on a woman (i.e., to lure her into sex with vague promises of love and marriage), to impregnate one (or three or five), and to "get away without being held legally accountable for out-of-wedlock children" is to prove strength, virility, and status.[20] To a number of underclass youths, love is just another hustle.

4. Specializing

While conducting his experiments at Yale, Stanley Milgram noticed that certain subjects would ease the strain of what they were doing to the shrieking victim in the other room by taking an exaggerated interest in the merely technical features of the experiment. They began to articulate the test words exquisitely. They began to press the generator switches officiously and with extra care. They began to *perform*.[21] By specializing in this way, people shrank the event ("I'm just trying to do my job well") so as to get it past their conscience.

Similarly, navigator-bombardiers focus their educated minds not on the human beings they will kill but on a skillful operation of the high-tech weaponry that does the killing. Attorneys make themselves expert in manipulating technicalities of the law while avoiding questions about the cause their expertise serves. Jesus indicted Pharisees and other respectable believers for specializing in certain details of religious observance while neglecting the weightier matters of justice, mercy, and faith (Matt. 23:23).

5. Minimizing

People try to settle moral debts by paying just a part of them. They offer an apology, for example, when what they owe is repentance.[22]

---

20. Anderson, *Streetwise: Race, Class, and Change in an Urban Community* (Chicago: University of Chicago, 1990), pp. 103, 112, 114, 132.

21. Milgram, *Obedience to Authority*, p. 7.

22. See Lewis B. Smedes, "Forgiving People Who Do Not Care," *Reformed Journal*, April 1983, p. 15.

They offer kindness in place of the much tougher virtue of love. Thus, instead of struggling to open in her children a space for long-term joy, a mother settles for short-term happiness. Instead of being a father to his children, a man sends a child-support check. Instead of a child-support check, a birthday card. Instead of a birthday card, the thought of sending one. Some husbands, in lieu of loving their wives, sit on a bar stool and *talk* about how much they love them.

6. Going Limp

One way to evade responsibility is to play dead, to do absolutely nothing and to do it repeatedly. Hence lazy employees who accept a day's pay for much less than a day's work. Hence idlers who think it hypocritical to get out of bed when they don't feel like it. Hence middle-aged professors who, once tenured, sink into boring repetitions of old courses and into dull, uninquiring habits of mind. Hence flat-souled college students whose main judgment of life's sacred acts is that they are "no big deal."[23] Hence lazy speakers of English who cannot be bothered even to state their indifference accurately: "I could care less."

In what really amounts to a cartoon, Proverbs 19:24 describes a sluggard's approach to his meal: he "buries his hand in the dish, and will not even bring it back to his mouth" (RSV). As a former student of mine once put it, the sluggard's body tells him he needs food, but his wasted will can manage only a straight hand drop into the pot. That's it. The sluggard will not attempt the return trip because it includes an uphill battle against the massed forces of

---

23. Allan Bloom writes, "I once asked a class how it could be that not too long ago parents would have said, 'Never darken our door again,' to wayward daughters, whereas now they rarely protest when boyfriends sleep over in their homes. A very nice, very normal, young woman responded, 'Because it's no big deal.' That says it all. This passionlessness is the most striking effect, or revelation, of the sexual revolution, and it makes the younger generation more or less incomprehensible to older folks" (*The Closing of the American Mind: Education and the Crisis of Reason* [New York: Simon & Schuster, 1987], p. 99).

gravity. He cannot think of a good enough reason to test those forces. In fact, he cannot think of a good enough reason to think.[24]

Making a career of Nothing — wandering through malls, killing time, making small talk, watching television programs until we know their characters better than our own children — robs the community of our gifts and energies and shapes life into a yawn at the God and savior of the world. The person who will not bestir herself, the person who hands herself over to Nothing, in effect says to God: you have made nothing of interest and redeemed no one of consequence, including me.

C. S. Lewis has the devil Screwtape explain to the junior devil Wormwood that the man he is after can be drawn from God by Nothing:

> Nothing is very strong: strong enough to steal away a man's best years not in sweet sins but in a dreary flickering of the mind over it knows not what and knows not why, in the gratification of curiosities so feeble that the man is only half aware of them, in drumming of fingers and kicking of heels, in whistling tunes that he does not like, or in the long, dim labyrinth of reveries that have not even lust or ambition to give them a relish, but which, once chance association has started them, the creature is too weak and fuddled to shake off.
>
> . . . The only thing that matters is the extent to which you separate the man from the Enemy. . . . Murder is no better than cards if cards can do the trick. Indeed, the safest road to Hell is the gradual one — the gentle slope, soft underfoot, without sudden turnings, without milestones, without signposts.[25]

7. Cocooning

Some of us retreat into the small world defined by our friends, work, church, and family and build a snuggery there. Inside it, we

---

24. Rolf Bouma, in an unpublished sermon on sloth written in 1986.
25. Lewis, *The Screwtape Letters and Screwtape Proposes a Toast*, rev. ed. (New York: Macmillan, 1982), p. 56.

may be busy enough, but with only local concerns. Perhaps on television we watch with disdain or amazement the passing show of misery, novelty, and grief in the larger world outside, but if our insulation is good enough we needn't be significantly disturbed by it, and, in any case, we do not wish to be inconvenienced by it. We do not welcome strangers into our lives or homes, and we do not go out to meet them. We do not inform ourselves of events abroad and cannot locate them on maps or in context. We dismiss the needs of future generations. We have never dealt seriously with a homeless person. We do not grieve over news stories of poverty or starvation, and we make only token efforts to relieve such suffering by our charity. Claiming allegiance to the Christ who speaks in active imperatives (Go! Tell! Witness! Declare! Proclaim!), we Christians nonetheless prefer to keep the bread of life in our own cupboard and to speak of it only to those who already have it. Do we subconsciously suppose that in such inbred silence we can keep our dignity, and unbelievers can go to hell where they belong?

Perhaps the last refuge of the self-protective soul is the web of its own feelings. This is true of the modern neurotic who, after the fashion of Woody Allen, rummages endlessly through the layerings of his obsessions and hang-ups, seeking the sources, contours, streams, and eddies of his own creativity and of his own consciousness of his own creativity.[26] It is true as well within the less neurotic world of etiquette. Judith Martin ("Miss Manners") remarks that in this age of the imperial self and its sovereign feelings, ill-mannered persons no longer feel embarrassed over their sins of omission; to the contrary, they expect credit for them:

> Such omissions as not visiting the dying or attending funerals, and not sending thank-you letters in return for hospitality, favors, or presents were once perceived as evidence of rudeness, presumably prompted by selfishness or sloth. Now the explanations ("I want to remember him as he was"; "Funerals give me the

26. For a fine example, try Philip Roth's Peter Tarnopol in Part II of Roth's *My Life as a Man* (New York: Holt, Rinehart, & Winston, 1974).

creeps"; "I hate to write letters"; "People should do things just because they want to, not because they expect to be thanked") imply that there is virtue in [these failures].[27]

8. *Amusing Ourselves to Death*

If we had no other barometer of American interest in amusement, we could measure it by the salaries of professional athletes and other entertainers. By this barometer, we value amusement more than good law, medicine, government, ministry, education, architecture, or scientific research. For these are all salary- or fee-compensated professions in which, very often, the financial rewards pale by comparison with those for baseball players, rock singers, and talk show hosts. In a capitalist culture, money is how you keep score, and in the professions, such as medicine and football, salaries and fees separate the winners from the also-rans. Thus, the orthopedic surgeon who examines the anterior cruciate ligament of a bench-sitting guard for a professional basketball team is looking, and likely looking up, at his cultural superior.

And, of course, jocks and clowns *are* important people. We need them and what they do. Who doesn't need and relish amusement now and then? Who doesn't need a partly playful attitude toward her own work? Isn't it the sin of pride that turns so much of human life gray with earnestness? Isn't grace, not achievement, the light of the gospel and the center of the Reformation? Still, the value we place on entertainment suggests that it has become a diversion not only in the sense of a playful relief from the main business of life but also in the sense of a distraction from it, an evasion of it, a sometimes grim, big-business alternative to it.

By its nature, amusement should not be taken seriously. Nothing comes of it. The winner of the World Series makes front page news, but, objectively speaking, who wins doesn't matter at all. All that matters is that the contest be entertaining. Similarly, televised discussion of whether the celebrity du jour of a talk show will spend

27. Martin, "The World's Oldest Virtue," *First Things*, May 1993, p. 22.

January by the sea at Malibu or on golf courses in Palm Springs amounts, in the greater ball game of life, to little more than a whiffer.

So when people begin to focus their lives more on amusement than on doing their work well, raising their children securely, gaining an education, and helping those in need, they begin to evade responsibility. The problem is that the evasions are lots of fun and therefore very tempting to all of us. It takes strength to resist them. When we fail, when a whole society fails to resist, life turns around in such a way that consumerism and the hunger for unreality converge and spending our leisure time becomes our occupation. Being a deft and knowing *consumer* of clothes (clothes that make a statement), films, sports events, pro wrestling, concerts, tapes, compact discs, and video games — and especially of the entertainment products in which these things combine — becomes a main goal of one's life and a measure of its success.[28]

However far we take them, our flights of amusement cost us more than time and money. They may also cost us our grasp of the general distinction between reality and illusion. On a segment of National Public Radio's *Morning Edition* in late 1993, a National Parks ranger explained in an interview why the rate of accidental injury and death in Arizona's Grand Canyon has been rising in recent years. The main reason is that many tourists no longer obey ranger signs and warnings. They think of the Grand Canyon as an amusement park in which dangers, and warnings about them, have all been contrived for their entertainment.

Another cost of the national obsession with amusement is that such serious activities as education, the dissemination of news, political debate, and reasoned public life get shaped, shortened, lightened, and, in the worst cases, trivialized by the requirement that they entertain us. Thus colleges award credit for courses in leisure activities, networks package their news presentations with music and the smiling faces of celebrities who are at least as much actors as journalists, and politicians shape their messages to fit this package. "In

28. See Quentin J. Schultze et al., *Dancing in the Dark: Youth, Popular Culture, and the Electronic Media* (Grand Rapids: William B. Eerdmans, 1991), pp. 111-45.

America," as Neil Postman says in a prophetic book about these matters, "the fundamental metaphor for political discourse is the television commercial."[29]

Even Christian worship has been affected, perhaps in part because worshipers watch a lot of television, and some of them watch a lot of televised worship. But worship doesn't fit the television medium very well, just as the music of a string quartet doesn't fit well into the warm-up events of Saturday night auto races. The reason, as Postman observes, is that we cannot consecrate the space in which we experience TV religion — it's the same room and the same screen we associate with sitcoms, hockey games, and cartoons. Moreover we are able, and we know we are able, to change channels on anything, including a prayer, that lacks pizzazz. Everything about our experience of TV tells us that it is an entertainment medium; everything about our experience of TV religion tells us that its producers know this at least as well as we do. After watching many hours of TV evangelism, Neil Postman reports what every sober viewer can see with her own eyes: on TV, "everything that makes religion an historic, profound and sacred human activity is stripped away; there is no ritual, no dogma, no tradition, no theology, and, above all, no sense of spiritual transcendence. On these shows, the preacher is tops. God comes out as second banana."[30]

When television-saturated worshipers attend their local churches or wonder how to draw secular seekers there, it's therefore not the songs of Zion they want but the songs of Babylon and Hollywood — or something like them. People attend worship with expectations shaped by television, and evangelical preachers try to meet them. In such cases worship may degenerate into a religious variety show hosted by some gleaming evangelist in a sequined dinner jacket and patent leather dancing slippers who chats with celebrities and introduces for special music a trio of middle-aged women in pastel evening gowns with matching muffs for their microphones. He may also include, or even perform, certain eye-

29. See Postman, *Amusing Ourselves to Death: Public Discourse in the Age of Show Business* (New York: Penguin, 1986), p. 126.
30. Postman, *Amusing Ourselves to Death*, p. 117.

popping acrobatics or karate moves.[31] Each act in the show is pre-timed, including estimates of the length of audience applause. Imagine a High Five for Jesus replacing the Apostles' Creed; imagine praise time beginning when the evangelist shouts, "Gimme a G! Gimme an O! . . ."

Naturally, services of this kind give an impression of a religion somewhat different from historic Christianity. One could imagine a visitor walking away from such a service and saying to himself: "I had it all wrong. I had thought Christianity included a shadow side — confession, self-denial, rebuke of sin, concern with heresy, a willingness to lose one's life for the sake of Jesus Christ. Not so, apparently. The Christian religion isn't about lament or repentance or humbling oneself before God to receive God's favor. It's got nothing to do with doctrines and the struggle to preserve truth. It's not about the hard, disciplined work of mortifying our sinful self and learning to make God's purposes our own. It's not about the inevitable failures in this project and the persistent grace of Jesus Christ that comes so that we may begin again. Not at all! I had it wrong! The Christian faith is mainly about celebration and fun and personal growth and five ways to boost my self-esteem. And, especially, it's about entertainment."

These developments remind us that corruptions of true religion generally proceed in the same direction as corruptions of the general culture and that our contemporary religion, to borrow some words from Newman, would therefore benefit from becoming "vastly more superstitious, more bigoted, more gloomy, more fierce" — not because these qualities are desirable, but because they would serve as antidote to our superficial cheeriness, because they would shorten the grins on the happy faces of show-biz religion.[32]

---

31. For more, consult the testimony, rich in pathos and detail, of David Wells in *No Place for Truth; or, Whatever Happened to Evangelical Theology?* (Grand Rapids: William B. Eerdmans, 1993), especially pp. 173-75.

32. John Henry Cardinal Newman, "The Religion of the Day," in *Sermons and Discourses, 1825-39,* ed. Charles Frederick Harrold (New York: Longmans, Green, 1949), p. 136.

The Flight from Shalom

We evade responsibility in lots of ways, including some we have discussed in earlier chapters. Several of these (compartmentalizing, self-deception, the adoption of moral subjectivism or relativism) amount to mental shifts by which we evade the *knowledge* of our responsibility and of our failure to meet it.[33] Dimensions of this shiftiness may be found as well in specializing, minimizing, and conniving, as we have just seen. Other evasions — conforming, co-cooning, going limp, leaving town, amusing ourselves to death — involve a more straightforward dereliction of duty to our neighbor. Of course, these two kinds of evasions usually appear together (as in connivance) because they are linked: the same laziness and coward-ice that keep us from doing our duty also keep us from knowing it and from facing the fact that we have shirked it.

But at the heart of all such evasions lies another — or, perhaps, two others. The sinner who abandons his children or who goes on permanent safari within his own psyche or who shuffles back to bed instead of going outside to help someone being stabbed in the street has turned his back not only on his neighbor but also on God, and even, in some way, on himself. By refusing his calling, he extracts his own core, hollowing himself out to a shell of a human being, without weight or substance. Spiritually, he begins to move out into that "cold and desolate night" of which Henry Stob speaks. He has made himself an alien to the gospel and a stranger to Jesus Christ.

How so? Our neighbor is God's child just as we are: to sell a neighbor short is therefore to sell God short and to fail a brother or sister.[34] We ourselves are God's children: to fail God and our brothers

33. Mary Midgley says of Sartre, Nietzsche, and other "immoralists" who deny objective right and wrong that their denials finally amount to little more than an evasion of traditional morality. They do not and cannot step outside the moral sphere altogether (which is like trying to step outside the universe), as evidenced by their strong moral recommendations of their own positions. "Beyond good and evil" is mere hyperbole for "beyond conventional morality" (*Wickedness: A Philo-sophical Essay* [London: Routledge & Kegan Paul, 1984], pp. 36, 40-44).

34. In hell, as C. S. Lewis pictures it, the distances between houses are very great: people keep moving farther and farther away from each other (*The Great*

and sisters is to shrink our own role in the great drama of redemption and to cut some of the lines that attach us to its center. The gospel, after all, is a portrait of the courage of Jesus Christ — the one who "set his face like flint" to go to Jerusalem and meet its terrors, the one who gathered himself to undertake there the one piece of work by which he might protect his neighbors from harm as much as he could.

The gifts of God — vitality, love, forgiveness, courage against evil, joy at our depths, and everything else that flows from the terrible work of Christ — may be found only in the company of God. And we keep company with God only by adopting God's purposes for us and following through on them even when it is difficult or initially painful to do so. To place ourselves in range of God's choicest gifts, we have to walk with God, lean on God, cling to God, come to have the sense and feel of God, refer all things to God. Contrary to our self-interested impulses, we have to worship God with a disciplined spirit and an expectant heart.

But just here lies our main evasion, the one we have all practiced a thousand times: like the Israelites indicted by Jeremiah, we "forget God" (Jer. 2:32; 13:25; 18:15). For weeks at a time we go through the motions, never seriously attending to God, never focusing on God, never — with all the weight of mind and heart — turning ourselves over to God. The thought that by such negligence we keep on wounding the only being who loves us with a perfect and expensive love, the thought that we are deeply entangled not only in our sin but also in the bloody remedy for it — these thoughts become bearable and then routine. At last we put them away and sink into functional godlessness. When we are in that state, God does not seem very real to us. So we do not pray. The less we pray, the less real God seems to us. And the less real God seems to us, the duller our sense of responsibility becomes, and thus the duller our sense of ignoring God becomes.

It's important to emphasize that the loss is ours. The loss is God's, but it is also ours. It's not just that we owe God our respects

---

Divorce [New York: Macmillan, 1946], pp. 18-22). For them, as Sartre famously put it, hell is other people.

and fail to pay them. Despite certain modern assumptions, life with God isn't mainly a matter of knuckling under to our superior — the image modernity so much detests. We do have to trust and obey God, we do have to express our devotion to God, but not merely because God is stronger than we are, and surely not because God wants to bully us into submission. We must trust and obey because these responses are *fitting*. After all, we know something of God's goodness and greatness. We know that we have been made and rescued by God. We know that we have been *graced* by God — forgiven, accepted, renewed as slowly and arduously as addicts. Indeed, only inside the cradle of grace can we even see the true depth and stubbornness of our sin.

This knowledge of God and ourselves opens us up to a whole range of opportunities and duties — to worship God, to try to please him, to beg his pardon when we fail, to receive God's renewing grace, and, out of gratitude, to use our lives to weave a whole pattern of friendship, service, and moral beauty.[35]

We could describe our situation like this: we must trust and obey in order to rise to the full stature of sons and daughters, to mature into the image of God, to grow into adult roles in the drama of redeeming the world. God has in mind not just what we should be but also what, one day, we *could* be.[36] God wants not slaves but intelligent children. God wants from us not numb obedience but devoted freedom, creativity, and energy. That's what the grace of God is for — not simply to balance a ledger but to stimulate the spurts of growth in zeal, in enthusiasm for shalom, in good hard work, in sheer delicious gratitude for the gift of life in all its pain and all its wonder.

In short, we are to become *responsible* beings: people to whom God can entrust deep and worthy assignments, expecting us to make something significant of them — expecting us to make something

35. See Richard Swinburne, "Original Sinfulness," *Neue Zeitschrift für systematische Theologie und Religionsphilosophie* 27 (1985): 238-39.

36. See Richard C. Erickson, "Reconciling Christian Views of Sin and Human Growth with Humanistic Psychology," *Christian Scholar's Review* 8 (1978): 124.

significant of our lives. None of us simply finds herself here in the world. None of our lives is an accident. We have been called into existence, expected, awaited, equipped, and assigned. We have been called to undertake the stewardship of a good creation, to create sturdy and buoyant families that pulse with the glad give-and-take of the generations. We are expected to show hospitality to strangers and to express gratitude to friends and teachers. We have been assigned to seek justice for our neighbors and, wherever we can, to relieve them from the tyranny of their suffering. Some of us have been called, in imitation of Christ, to bear unusual suffering of our own.

But we have also been called, and graced, to delight in our lives, to feel their irony and angularity, to make something sturdy and even lovely of them. For such undertakings, we have to find emotional and spiritual funding from the very God who assigns them, turning our faces toward God's light so that we may be drawn to it, warmed by it, bathed in it, revitalized by it. Then we have to find our role within God's big project, the one that stretches across the border from this life into the next. To be a responsible person is to find one's role in the building of shalom, the re-webbing of God, humanity, and all creation in justice, harmony, fulfillment, and delight. To be a responsible person is to find one's own role and then, funded by the grace of God, to fill this role and to delight in it.

In the first chapter of this book I said that shalom is God's design for creation and re-creation and that sin is a blamable vandalism of shalom. Here at the end, let's expand the image: by the sins of attack we vandalize shalom; by the sins of flight we abandon it. When we flee responsibility, we turn our backs on God's presence and blessing, we walk out on the one work project that will outlast every recession, and we begin the slow process of converting ourselves into derelicts. We "hate the light and do not come to the light" (John 3:20). Instead, we gather all we have and make our way toward a far country, toward the outer darkness, toward a place of self-deprivation, a place of our own making.

Epilogue

In a book about Ronald Reagan and his times, Garry Wills pauses, oddly enough, to comment on the Christian doctrine of original sin. In referring to the "linked sequences of disaster, the *series calamitatis* of history," Wills states that

> we are hostages to each other in a deadly interrelatedness. There is no "clean slate" of nature unscribbled on by all one's forebears. . . . At one time a woman of unsavory enough experience was delicately but cruelly referred to as "having a past." The doctrine of original sin states that humankind, in exactly that sense, "has a past."[1]

But, of course, our past also includes saints, civilizations, generous laws for gleaners, hospices, relief agencies, virtuoso peacemakers, and rural traditions of pitching in at a neighbor's barn raising. Our experience today includes wonderful bursts of hospitality by strangers for confused Alzheimer's patients who wander into their homes. It includes exultant worship, fifty-year wedding anniversaries, and, on some May mornings, a sense of life's sweetness and of God's goodness so sharp that we want to cry out from the sheer promise of it.

1. Wills, *Reagan's America: Innocents at Home* (Garden City, N.Y.: Doubleday, 1987), p. 384. Ronald Reagan, says Wills, never believed in original sin, finding it uncheery.

Evil rolls across the ages, but so does good. Good has its own momentum. Corruption never wholly succeeds. (Even blasphemers acknowledge God.) Creation is stronger than sin and grace stronger still. Creation and grace are anvils that have worn out a lot of our hammers.

To speak of sin by itself, to speak of it apart from the realities of creation and grace, is to forget the resolve of God. God wants shalom and will pay any price to get it back. Human sin is stubborn, but not as stubborn as the grace of God and not half so persistent, not half so ready to suffer to win its way. Moreover, to speak of sin by itself is to misunderstand its nature: sin is only a parasite, a vandal, a spoiler. Sinful life is a partly depressing, partly ludicrous *caricature* of genuine human life. To concentrate on our rebellion, defection, and folly — to say to the world "I have some bad news and I have some bad news" — is to forget that the center of the Christian religion is not our sin but our Savior. To speak of sin without grace is to minimize the resurrection of Jesus Christ, the fruit of the Spirit, and the hope of shalom.

But to speak of grace without sin is surely no better. To do this is to trivialize the cross of Jesus Christ, to skate past all the struggling by good people down the ages to forgive, accept, and rehabilitate sinners, including themselves, and therefore to cheapen the grace of God that always comes to us with blood on it. What had we thought the ripping and writhing on Golgotha were all about? To speak of grace without looking squarely at these realities, without painfully honest acknowledgment of our own sin and its effects, is to shrink grace to a mere embellishment of the music of creation, to shrink it down to a mere grace note. In short, for the Christian church (even in its recently popular seeker services) to ignore, euphemize, or otherwise mute the lethal reality of sin is to cut the nerve of the gospel. For the sober truth is that without full disclosure on sin, the gospel of grace becomes impertinent, unnecessary, and finally uninteresting.

Index

Accountability, 67-68, 103, 196-97. *See
also* Culpability; Evasion, sins of
Adams, Robert M., 22, 23n.26, 24n.29
Addiction, 130-49; and Alcoholics
Anonymous, 132-33, 141, 141n.27;
definition of, 130; dynamics of, 145-
49; and feminism, 141-44; sexual,
133-37; and sin, 136-49; as tragedy,
139-41
Akst, Daniel, 97
Anger, 165-67
Alexander, John, 83
Allen, Diogenes, 149
Alton, Bruce S., 105n.13, 106n.14
Anderson, Elijah, 185
Athanasius, 48
Augustine, 23n.27, 33, 48n.15, 54, 62,
82, 146-47

Baker, Russell, 151
Beatty, Jack, 64
Begin, Menachem, 57-58
Berkouwer, G. C., 74n.32, 74n.33
Bernanos, Georges, 123
Boszormenyi-Nagy, Ivan, 55
Bloom, Allan, 187n.23
Bouma, Henry, 40n.1

Branch, Taylor, 78-79
Bromiley, Geoffrey W., 89, 111
Buber, Martin, 107, 135-36
Buechner, Frederick, 116
Burtchaell, James T., 58-60, 63, 179-
80, 180n.9
Butler, Joseph, 111

Cadwalader, George, 49
Carnes, Patrick, 133-37
Caro, Robert, 151n.4
Cellini, Benvenuto, 42-43
Chaucer, Geoffrey, 171
Childs, Brevard S., 74n.34
Churchill, Winston, 85, 185
Clines, David A. J., 30n.4
Concupiscence, 41n.2
Corruption, 28-30, 32-33, 54; and
death, 47-48, 54-55; and despoil-
ment, 31-32; and disintegration, 47-
51; and dividedness, 45-46; images
of, 33, 53; and perversion, 40-43; and
pollution, 43-45, 43n.6; in religion,
107-12, 192-93; spread of, 54-72
Creation, 29
Crites, Stephen, 107
Cowley, Geoffrey, 91n.28

Culpability, 25, 26n.31, 137-39; in defi-
    nition of sin, 13, 14, 23. *See also* Ac-
    countability

Dallek, Robert, 151n.4
Dean, John, 106
Dillman, John, 96

Envy, 157-72; and covetousness, 162-
    63; and jealousy, 165n.22; and
    anger, 165; and pride, 167-68; and
    Schadenfreude, 169-70
Evasion, sins of, 176-97; and amuse-
    ment, 190-93; and cocooning, 188-
    90; and conformity, 180-82; and
    connivance, 182-84; and flight, 185-
    86; and laziness, 187-88; and min-
    imizing, 187-88; and shalom, 194-
    97; and specializing, 186
Evil, 25-27; attractiveness of, 91-95,
    98-99; definition of, 14

Fairlie, Henry, 162, 168
Faithlessness, 12-13, 45, 195-96. *See
    also* Evasion, sins of
Fall of human race, 29-31, 31n.5
Fleming, Ian, 92
Folly, 119-21; and sin, 121-27
Fraser, Sylvia, 46-47
Friedman, Thomas, 57-58

Genovese, Kitty, 182-84
Goleman, Daniel, 106
Grace, 199

Heart: role of in sin, 62-63, 62n.21, 67

Idolatry, 44-45, 142-44; and folly, 122-
    23
Immorality, 18-19, 19n.18
Irenaeus, 9n.4
Ivy League Graduate, strikingly beauti-
    ful, 84

Johnson, Joyce, 49
Johnson, Lyndon Baines, 150-53

Kasl, Charlotte Davis, 141-44
Koestler, Arthur, 67-68

Lasch, Christopher, 124
Law of returns, 68-72
L'Engle, Madeleine, 83n.13
Lewis, C. S., 38, 48n.15, 79n.4, 89, 90,
    93, 120, 123, 125, 127, 188, 194n.34
Lincoln, Abraham, 99-100
Livy, 50-51
Lovelace, Richard, 79n.3, 123
Lying, 155-57

MacArthur, Douglas, 85-86
Manchester, William, 85, 86, 185
Martin, Judith ("Miss Manners"), 189
May, Gerald, 134-35
McCormick, Patrick, 148n.33
Midgley, Mary, 95, 101n.9, 194n.33
Milgram, Stanley, 173-77, 186
Mouw, Richard, 148
Muehl, William, 66

Newman, John Henry Cardinal,
    37n.14, 47, 127, 193
Niebuhr, Reinhold, 61

Obedience to authority, 173-80
Oden, Thomas C., 126
Original sin, 26, 26n.33, 31, 54, 198.
    See also Corruption
O'Donovan, Oliver, 171

Pattison, Robert, 93n.32
Peck, M. Scott, 73, 98-99
Percy, Walker, 169
Postman, Neil, 192
Powers and principalities, 75-76
Pride, 81-87; and envy, 167-68; and
    folly, 122-25

Psychopathy, 97-98

Relativism, 104n.12
Roberts, Robert C., 21n.21, 36n.12, 134n.12, 122

Satan, 74, 90, 93, 94, 95, 98
Schimmel, Solomon, 167n.24
Schuller, Robert, 102-3, 102n.11
Self-deception, 18, 105-12
Sereny, Gitta, 178
Shalom, 9-12, 16, 194-99. *See also* Spiritual hygiene
Sin: abnormality of, 5, 88; and addiction, 136-49; causes of, 62-67, 72-77; definition of, 13-14; dynamics of, 55-60, 68-72, 145-49; and evil, 14, 16, 18-19; in family systems, 55-57; and folly, 114, 121-27; images of, 5, 53; involuntary, 22-24; ironies in, 79-81, 89; minimizing of, 99-104; motives of, 61-63, 65; "movements" or "postures" in, 153-55 and chaps. 9 and 10 *passim;* parasitical quality of, 89-95; rejection of the concept of, 17; and religion, 107-12; seriousness of, 2-5, 76-77; and

shalom, 14, 16, 197; social and structural, 25-26, 64-65, 70-72, 75-76, 110, 134-35, 184-86; spread of, 52-72, 90-91
Smedes, Lewis B., 73n.29, 81, 107, 117
Solzhenitsyn, Aleksandr, 41
Spenser, Edmund, 170
Spiritual hygiene, 34-38, 145-46
Spur Posse, 181-82
Stangl, Franz, 178-79
Stegner, Wallace, 91
Steinbeck, John, 75n.37
Stevenson, Coke, 152-53
Stob, Henry, 154-55
Subjectivism, 104n.12

Van Leeuwen, Mary Stewart, 142n.29, 144
Van Reken, Calvin P., 106n.15
Vizinczey, Stephen, 89

Wells, David, 83
Westerholm, Stephen, 88n.21
Will, George F., 71n.27
Westphal, Merold, 108-11
Wills, Garry, 50
Wisdom, 69, 115-18